Dedication

I would like to dedicate this book to my amazing wife, Kimberly, and my children, Madison and Bryce. They have brought me more joy than I could ever have imagined. Thank you for understanding the countless hours away from you that it takes to write a book. I love you all.

Contents at a Glance

Table of Contents

What do you think of this book? We want to hear from you!

Microsoft is interested in hearing your feedback so we can continually improve our books and learning resources for you. To participate in a brief online survey, please visit:

www.microsoft.com/learning/booksurvey/

Part II   SharePoint Core Administration

Part IV   SharePoint Performance and Operations

What do you think of this book? We want to hear from you!

Acknowledgments

I knew when starting this project that it would be difficult and time consuming, but it was more challenging than I ever imagined. One of the challenges when writing a Pocket Consultant is that you don't have the space to fully explain every facet of a product. In addition, this Pocket Consultant actually covers two products: Windows Share-Point Services 3.0 and SharePoint Server 2007. Because they are intertwined so closely, there really is no way to discuss SharePoint Server without discussing SharePoint Services. In addition, many readers will use only SharePoint Services, and I wanted a guide for them as well. I have left out information unessential to administrative tasks and therefore provided a technically dense, daily reference guide. This narrow scope allowed the book to be very detailed in the areas that are poorly documented or poorly understood. I really wanted to provide an accurate reference guide that could also be read cover to cover, and I think it fills that bill.

I first want to thank Bill English, who gave me the opportunity to write part of the Microsoft Office SharePoint Server 2007 Administrator's Companion. Thank you, Bill. As part of that process, I was introduced to Martin DelRe at Microsoft Press and was presented with the opportunity to write the work in your hands. I want to thank Martin DelRe, acquisitions editor, because he believed in this book from the very beginning. Maureen Zimmerman was the project editor, and she kept me on track and on schedule throughout. She is a wonderful editor, and I learned a great deal from her. Although it is difficult to write original content, answering the technical edits is sometimes harder! Microsoft Press has the most thorough editing review processes in the business, and though they create more work for the author, they result in a better book for the reader. Mark Harrison was the technical reviewer for this book; his input and assistance were invaluable in creating a relevant and accurate book. He was top notch and made sure things worked as expected.

Because there were so many new features in the products, it was impossible for a single person to write this book. To assist me, I asked several SharePoint Products industry experts to contribute content to the book. First of all, I want to thank Jim Curry (yes, he's related, and I admit it here!). In addition to contributing content, Jim built and maintained the computer lab where the book was written; he also tested procedures and researched technical details when needed. In addition, I want to thank Bill English, Josh Meyer, John Holliday, Milan Gross, and William Jackson for their contributions to the book. They all wrote content in their areas of expertise, and that really helped make the book solid. Short biographies of the contributing authors appear in the back of the book.

Thank you to all of the staff at Microsoft who helped along the way; there are too many of you to count. I also want to thank Steve Daugherty; he helped start my career and served as a role model during my early years as a professional. If I forgot someone, it was truly an accident!

Introduction

From the beginning of the project, the *Microsoft SharePoint Products and Technologies Administrator's Pocket Consultant* was written to be a concise and accurate guide that you can use when you have questions about Windows SharePoint Services and SharePoint Server administration. The purpose of the *Administrator's Pocket Consultants* series is to give you valuable, real-world information in an easily referenced format. A thorough index has been provided to help you quickly find the information you need. This is a guide you will want close by when working with the new versions of SharePoint Products and Technologies.

Because Windows SharePoint Services and SharePoint Server are closely related, they are covered together, with their differences clearly demonstrated. This book provides administrative procedures, quick answers, tips, and tested design examples. In addition, it covers some of the most difficult tasks, such as scaling out to a server farm and implementing disaster recovery. It also covers the command-line options available with Windows SharePoint Services and SharePoint Server. The text contains illustrative examples of many advanced tasks required to implement a SharePoint Products solution for almost any size of organization.

For Whom Is This Book Designed?

Microsoft SharePoint Products and Technologies Administrator's Pocket Consultant covers Windows SharePoint Services 3.0, SharePoint Server 2007 Standard, and SharePoint Server 2007 Enterprise editions. This book is designed for the following:

- Administrators migrating from Windows SharePoint Services 2.0 and SharePoint Portal Server 2003
- Administrators who are experienced with Windows Server 2003 and Internet Information Services
- Current Windows SharePoint Services 3.0 and SharePoint Server 2007 administrators
- Administrators new to Microsoft SharePoint Technologies
- Technology specialists, such as site collection administrators, search administrators, and Web designers

Because this book is limited in size, and I wanted to give you the maximum value, I assumed a basic knowledge of Windows Server 2003, Active Directory, Internet Information Services (IIS), SQL Server, and Web browsers. These technologies are not presented directly, but this book contains material on all of these topics that relate to SharePoint Products' administrative tasks.

How Is This Book Organized?

Microsoft SharePoint Products and Technologies Administrator's Pocket Consultant is written to be a daily reference for administrative tasks. The ability to quickly find and use information is the hallmark of this book. For this reason, the book is organized into job-related tasks. It has an expanded table of contents and an extensive index for locating relevant answers. In addition, there is a cross-reference in the back of the book to many of the Stsadm.exe command-line options. If you are looking for a comprehensive guide to implementing SharePoint Products, you should consider purchasing the *Microsoft Office SharePoint Server 2007 Administrator's Companion*, since the books in the *Administrator's Pocket Consultant* series are stripped to the bare essentials required to complete a task.

The book is organized into four parts and fifteen chapters: Part I, "SharePoint Products and Technologies Fundamentals," introduces you to the new features, functionality, and installation options of Windows SharePoint Services 3.0 and SharePoint Server 2007. Chapter 1 provides an overview of the products and the minimum hardware requirements, as well as an introduction to the applications, services, and administrative interfaces. Chapter 2 includes instructions for preparing for and installing SharePoint Products and Technologies, implementing database best practices, and upgrading from Windows SharePoint Services to SharePoint Server.

Part II, "SharePoint Core Administration," covers the core technologies required by every Windows SharePoint Services and SharePoint Server implementation. Chapter 3 covers the Central Administration interface, including farm operations and Web application management. Chapter 4 provides a detailed guide to creating and managing site collections. Chapter 5 is a site customization tutorial, including scripts and examples. Chapter 6 shows you how to build and use workflows and Information Management Policies. Chapter 7 walks you through the basic requirements of implementing security for Windows SharePoint Services and SharePoint Server.

Part III, "Working with SharePoint Server 2007," focuses on tasks exclusively available with SharePoint Server 2007. Chapter 8 shows you how to create and manage a Shared Services Provider. Chapter 9 discusses portals and the best practices when creating Corporate, Internet, and Personal portals. Chapter 10 is a guide to the new functionality provided by Enterprise Content Management. Chapter 11 shows you how to install and configure Excel Calculation Services. Chapter 12 simplifies the configuration and administration of Search and Indexing.

Part IV, "SharePoint Performance and Operations," explains the best practices and procedures when increasing performance and monitoring your implementation. In addition, backup and restore tools are discussed in detail. Chapter 13 provides examples and instructions for scaling out to a Windows SharePoint Services and SharePoint Server farm. Chapter 14 explains and details the native backup and restore tools. Chapter 15 is an introduction to monitoring and reporting on your new or existing installation.

Conventions Used in This Book

A variety of elements are used in this book to help you understand what you need to know and to keep it easy to read. When you see text with the > symbol in it, it defines a navigation path. For example, "Central Administration > Operations > Backup And Restore" directs you to open Central Administration, go to the Operations tab, and open Backup And Restore. In addition, terms that are new are in *italics*.

- **Note**   A Note points out an easily overlooked detail or design issue.

- **Tip**   Tips provide helpful information or spotlight the command-line option available for an administrative task.

- **Caution**   When you see a Caution, you should look out for potential problems. Many Cautions were learned through real-world experience.

- **Real World**   These occasional features explain what has been learned the hard way, through constant research and customer implementations.

I really hope you find the *Microsoft SharePoint Products and Technologies Administrator's Pocket Consultant* useful and accurate. I have an open door policy for e-mail at *bcurry@mindsharp.com*. Because my inbox stays quite full, please be patient; replies sometimes take a week or longer. You may also visit *http://pocketconsultant.mind-sharp.com* for updates and discussion boards concerning the latest in SharePoint Products and Technologies news.

Questions and Support

Every effort has been made to ensure the accuracy of this book. Microsoft Press provides corrections for books at *http://mspress.microsoft.com/support/*. If you have questions or comments regarding this book, please send them to Microsoft Press using one of the following methods:

Postal mail:

> *Microsoft Press*
> *Attn: Editor, Microsoft SharePoint Products and*
> *   Technologies Administrator's Pocket Consultant*
> *One Microsoft Way*
> *Redmond, WA 98052-6399*
> *E-mail:*
> *msinput@microsoft.com*

Please note that product support is not offered through these addresses. For support information, visit Microsoft's Web site at *http://support.microsoft.com*.

Part I

SharePoint Products and Technologies Fundamentals

Chapter 1
Overview of SharePoint Products and Technologies Administration

Microsoft Windows SharePoint Services 3.0 and Microsoft Office SharePoint Server 2007 begin a new age in content aggregation, business process management, business intelligence, enterprise collaboration, and the content management lifecycle, as shown in Figure 1-1.

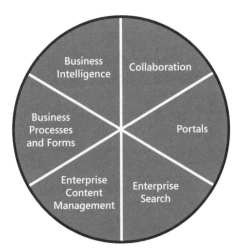

Figure 1-1   SharePoint Server provides a full suite of functionality for business.

Those familiar with the previous versions of Windows SharePoint Services and SharePoint Portal Server will be pleasantly surprised with the complete rework of the product functionality and its robust ability to scale to any organizational requirement. The administration user interface (UI) has been completely redesigned to make it easier and quicker to navigate and perform administrative tasks. To understand the role that each of these products plays in the overall SharePoint Technologies suite, descriptions of Windows SharePoint Services and SharePoint Server follow.

- **Windows SharePoint Services**   Provides the core functionality for SharePoint technologies, including storage, security, search, management, deployment, site model, application programming interfaces (APIs), and collaboration. A much-appreciated improvement in Windows SharePoint Services is the addition of a common Central Administration Web interface that expands as products are installed onto the platform. Windows SharePoint Services requires Windows Server 2003 SP1 or later, Microsoft SQL Server 2000 Service Pack 3a or Microsoft SQL Server 2005, or Microsoft SQL Server Express 2005.

- **Microsoft Office SharePoint Server 2007**   Delivers further functionality beyond what is provided with Windows SharePoint Services, including InfoPath forms services, expanded search and indexing capabilities, Business Data Catalog (BDC) to connect line-of-business (LOB) products, business intelligence, user profiles, records management, Web content management, and more. In addition, SharePoint Server provides rich Shared Services Providers and the ability to scale using IntraFarm or Inter Farm Shared Services. Figure 1-2 shows the logical architecture when implementing the entire product suite.

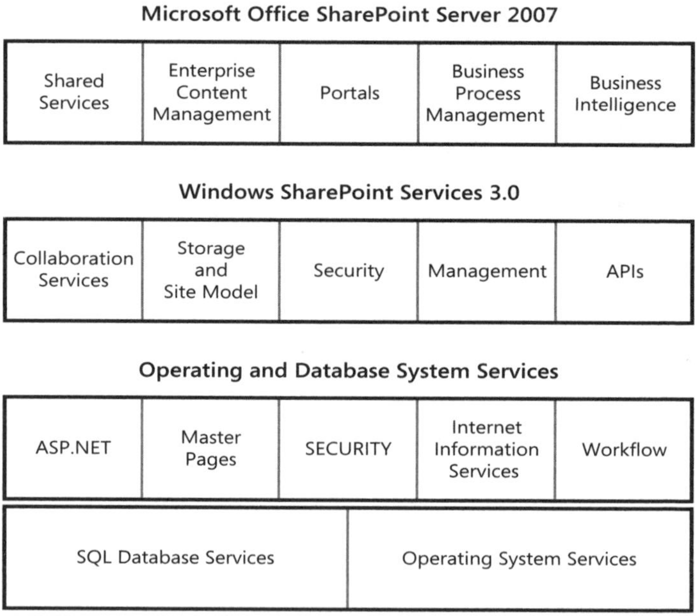

Microsoft Office SharePoint Server 2007

Shared Services	Enterprise Content Management	Portals	Business Process Management	Business Intelligence

Windows SharePoint Services 3.0

Collaboration Services	Storage and Site Model	Security	Management	APIs

Operating and Database System Services

ASP.NET	Master Pages	SECURITY	Internet Information Services	Workflow

SQL Database Services	Operating System Services

Figure 1-2   Microsoft Office SharePoint Server 2007 builds on and depends on the foundation laid by Windows SharePoint Services.

Although Windows Server 2003 and SQL Server are required components for any Windows SharePoint Services or SharePoint Server implementation, they are not covered in great detail here except where a specific configuration for Windows SharePoint Services is required. There are many resources detailing the installation and configuration of both products, most notably the *Administrator's Companions* and *Administrator's Pocket Consultants* series from Microsoft Press.

SharePoint Products and Your Hardware

When choosing hardware for installing your SharePoint product, it is wise to start with at least the minimum hardware required for that product. The SharePoint Server products have many new features, which require an investment in hardware to realize their full potential. With the majority of new servers being 64-bit systems, the SharePoint product team has made it possible to include 32-bit and 64-bit systems in the same farm. This design allows organizations to tailor their usage of new and existing hardware to meet their individual needs.

The following guidelines should be considered the bare necessity when installing Windows SharePoint Services. These guidelines are not sufficient for heavily used or highly customized SharePoint installations.

Memory

Implementing a different application pool and username for each Web application strengthens your overall security stance, but every additional application pool requires more memory. Every Web application consumes 150 to 200 MB of memory in addition to the already existing application pools. As a general rule, 2 gigabytes (GB) of RAM is recommended for serving any SharePoint technology beyond a test environment. Installations requiring more than 2 GB of RAM benefit from the more efficient memory management of a 64-bit server platform. Individual service memory requirements, like those of Excel Calculation Services, are presented in their corresponding chapters. The following list details the memory requirements for each server role:

- **Windows SharePoint Services single box installation**   The minimum memory capacity for a single box installation is 1 GB of RAM, with 3 GB being recommended. A single farm box installation must be able to support all components of a SharePoint farm, including SQL Server Express 2005. If your databases will grow quite large, you should begin with 3 GB or consider using a dedicated SQL Server for database storage.

- **Windows SharePoint Services farm deployment**   When Windows SharePoint Services is deployed across multiple servers, the maximum overhead is likely reduced because the workload is distributed. That being the case, the minimum capacity is 1 GB, but the recommended is at least 2 GB. Refer to performance monitoring information in Chapter 15, "Logging and Processing Analysis," to find out when to add RAM.

- **Office SharePoint Server single box installation**   The minimum memory capacity is 1 GB, but this amount is likely to be insufficient if any of the SharePoint Server added services are enabled. If using Document Conversions or Excel Calculation Services, 2 GB is the minimum memory capacity, with 3 GB being recommended. Remember that large application servers, like Search or Excel Calculation Services, require a significant amount of dedicated resources. Refer to their individual chapters for hardware requirements. A single box SharePoint Server installation is primarily for workgroup or lab environments and is not sufficient for full-scale production deployments.

- **Office SharePoint Server farm deployment**   Despite the more efficient load distribution of a SharePoint Server farm environment, an absolute minimum of 2 GB of RAM is recommended to accommodate enterprise-class applications. Most enterprise-scale installations require a minimum of 3 GB of RAM for all application-tier servers.

- **SQL Server 2000 SP3a or SQL Server 2005**   The minimum memory requirement for a SQL Server when supporting SharePoint Server farms is 2 GB of RAM. Depending on your specific scenario, you may require more memory. For example, more than 2 GB is required when using fail-over farms for high availability or when several databases exceed 200 GB in size. It should also be noted that SQL Server 2005 will show markedly increased performance over SQL Server 2000, even when installed on equivalent hardware.

More information on configuring hardware for SQL Server can be found at http://www.microsoft.com/technet/prodtechnol/sql/default.mspx.

CPU

Although the installation of SharePoint products with slower CPUs than recommended will successfully complete, the outcome may be less than desired. When installing in test or development environments, you may install with legacy hardware and have adequate performance. However, be forewarned that Windows SharePoint Services developers may require *higher* CPU speeds than found in your production environment because of the heavy demands needed when developing custom code. Consult with your developers before deciding which hardware to use.

- **Windows SharePoint Services and SharePoint Server single box deployments**   When installing Windows SharePoint Services or SharePoint Server on a single box, a single 2.5-GHz processor is the absolute minimum. If your needs go beyond collaboration, creating Web pages, or another basic functionality, then you should give serious consideration to dual processors of 2.5 GHz or more.

- **Windows SharePoint Services and SharePoint Server Web front-end server (WFE)**   In many implementations it is necessary to split the processing duty among multiple tiers. When this situation arises, a single processor of 2.5 GHz for a WFE is the minimum and is often enough, unless you also have an application service, such as Excel Calculation Services (ECS), or process thousands of search queries as well. Chapter 13 covers in detail the scaling of WFEs.

- **Windows SharePoint Services and SharePoint Server application servers**   The new versions of both products allow for unrestricted scaling to almost any requirement. Application servers, such as Excel Calculation Services (ECS), Indexing, Query, and InfoPath forms services, can be very processor intensive. For this reason, dual 2-GHz processors are the recommended minimum CPU for dedicated application servers. Windows SharePoint Services and SharePoint Server use symmetric multiprocessing, which enables greatly increased performance of application-tier services. In addition, 64-bit hardware can noticeably improve the performance of Indexing and Excel Calculation Services.

- **SQL Server 2000 SP3a or SQL Server 2005**   You should consider upgrading your current SQL Server environment to 64-bit hardware if you have not already. The bottleneck of many busy Windows SharePoint Services and SharePoint Server installations is the SQL Server installation. Medium scale and larger implementations should consider a minimum of dual 2.5-GHz processors or data processing delays could occur.

Disk Drives

The many storage options available include integrated drive electronics (IDE), small computer system interface (SCSI), Fibre Channel, and Low-Cost Fibre Channel (LCFC). Serial Advanced Technology Attachment (SATA) drives should be considered the minimum for any serious implementation, with Fibre Channel providing the highest level of performance and longevity. A full discussion of storage technologies is beyond the scope of this book, but be aware that many organizations now use storage area networks (SANs) to facilitate provisioning and disaster recovery. Modern SANs can include SATA, LCFC, or Fibre Channel drives and enable error checking on the storage frame, instead of on the server system itself. Check with your SAN administrator for more information.

For information on data protection using technologies such as RAID (redundant array of independent disks), consult the Windows Server TechCenter at http://www.microsoft.com/technet/windowsserver/default.mspx.

Applications and Services

Windows SharePoint Services and SharePoint Server provide an integrated group of applications that can be managed from a central location. Understanding what each of these applications does, and in which product feature set it resides, is important to a successful installation and a positive administrative experience. Take the time to learn where product suite applications and services reside, before inserting the installation media and clicking *next*. Don't let the large feature set intimidate you; use only what you need in the beginning and add applications as your requirements mandate.

Operating System Services

The Windows Server operating system provides the foundation for all SharePoint products. The required operating system services are described here:

- **Microsoft .NET 1.0 (if supporting legacy 1.0 Web Parts)**   Although .NET 1.0 was required for the previous versions of SharePoint products, it is optional when installing Windows SharePoint Services and SharePoint Server. It is only required if you wish to support legacy Web Parts from Windows SharePoint Services 2.0 or SharePoint Portal Server 2003.

- **Microsoft .NET 2.0**   Windows SharePoint Services, and therefore SharePoint Server, was built on .NET 2.0 and is required to be installed prior to Windows SharePoint Services or SharePoint Server.

- **Microsoft .NET 3.0**   The newest version of the .NET framework provides many new features; the most notable for SharePoint technologies administrators is the ability to create customized workflows. With .NET 3.0 you can connect your business processes, such as content approval, to out-of-the-box (OOB) workflows in SharePoint Server. These OOB workflow patterns are only available with SharePoint Server. In addition, you can create and reuse custom workflows with SharePoint Designer 2007. For organizations desiring the richest business processes available, Visual Studio 2005 gives developers the ability to create highly customized workflows and corresponding Web pages.

- **Internet Information Services**   Internet Information Services (IIS) is the Web service that hosts all of the SharePoint Web applications on its secure and easily managed platform. IIS 6.0 or IIS 7.0 can successfully handle SharePoint Web traffic, but IIS 7.0 improves the manageability of Web applications and can reduce the surface attack area presented to hackers. This book refers to IIS generally, and versions are only pointed out where they make a difference in configuration.

- **Internet Explorer 6.0 or later**   Internet Explorer 6.0 or later is required to manage your standalone SharePoint server or server farm. If you have a customized Internet Explorer installation, you may need to add your Central Administration URL and other namespaces to the Intranet zone or Trusted Sites zone as shown in Figure 1-3.

Figure 1-3   Always add the Central Administration URL to the Intranet zone or Trusted Sites zone in your browser.

Windows SharePoint Services 3.0

Windows SharePoint Services 3.0 provides all of the core functionality, such as backup/restore and scalability. Windows SharePoint Services gives you the ability to collaborate with team workspaces, calendars, tasks lists, and alerting. It also offers a rich custom development environment to build Web-based applications. Windows SharePoint Services provides servers with the ability to communicate with Office clients, such as Excel, Word, PowerPoint, Outlook, InfoPath, Project Professional, and third-party applications. It is a free download for Windows Server 2003 license holders and should also be available to license holders of the newer Windows Server version codenamed "Longhorn." The investment areas of the Windows SharePoint Services are described here.

- **Core workspace platform**   Windows SharePoint Services provides the platform for users and developers to customize and extend SharePoint technologies. By providing the object model, Windows SharePoint Services allows for browser-based database manipulation including creating, reviewing, deleting, managing, alerting and schema management. It also allows rich customization, portability of code, and a single platform for development, collaboration, and deployment. Organizations with Internet and Intranet Web sites can save a significant amount of money because Intranet and Internet development can be performed in the same application programming environment, while still using all of the benefits of Windows SharePoint Services. In addition, Windows SharePoint Services installation creates the configuration database that provides the foundation for scaling to a Windows SharePoint Services or SharePoint Server *farm*.

Note   A *farm* consists of multiple servers that host or share the same configuration database: the *config DB*. This centralization of a configuration database allows for fast and easy deployment and repurposing of servers, giving you the ability to *right-size* your implementation as needed. As shown in Chapter 2, "Deploying SharePoint Products and Technologies," you can move services between farm servers without reinstalling software or provisioning additional servers. Think of the config DB as the farm's "Registry." This Registry is the heart and soul of a server farm and allows scaling of Web and application servers. A server is a member of a given farm when it shares a common config DB. If a server attaches to a different config DB, it is in a different farm. If the config DB is the server farm's heart and soul, then the *SPTimer* service is its heartbeat. The SPTimer service is installed with every server on which you install the binaries. It provides the communication between all services and servers in the farm for timed events, such as backups, workflow events, and alerts. The SharePoint Administration Service (WSSADMIN) propagates all changes in the config DB to farm servers as necessary.

- **Next generation collaboration**   Windows SharePoint Services also provides you with integrated collaboration and full Outlook 2007 integration, including two-way calendaring, tasks, offline document, and mail-enabled document libraries. Mail-enabled document libraries capture e-mail discussions by enabling indexing of critical institutional (tacit) knowledge. The user interface now includes full breadcrumb trails and tabs for easier navigation. These tabs and trails previously required extensive programming or third-party Web Parts.

Tip   From Site Actions > Site Settings, you must enable the *Portal Connection* for breadcrumb trails to lead back to the portal root (see Figure 1-4).

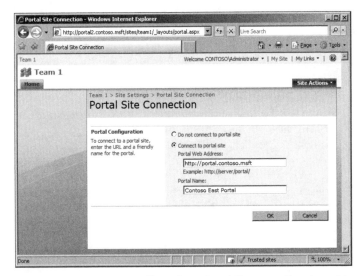

Figure 1-4   You must manually configure Portal Site connections to enable breadcrumb trails to the Portal URL.

■ **Easy extensibility for SharePoint Server application servers**   Windows Share-Point Services provides the necessary foundation for SharePoint Servers and allows them to be extended and customized.

For basic collaborative solutions, Windows SharePoint Services provides the core site model. For workgroups or small organizations, this product offers a free alternative to expensive third-party collaboration solutions if you already own Windows Server 2003 or later. In addition, you are guaranteed complete operating system compatibility with your Windows Server, which is a compelling reason to use Windows SharePoint Services as your Web-based collaboration solution. The following services are provided by Windows SharePoint Services:

■ **Application management**   Windows SharePoint Services provides the Central Administration Web interface that is used by all SharePoint 2007 Products and Technologies.

■ **Site model**   Site collections are at the root of the site model and are a collection of one or more *sites*. A site contains users, lists, document libraries, Web pages, content types, and more. All site item storage is via lists and document libraries. Every Web page, Web Part, document, task, or calendar item is a list item. This storage format allows for rich customization and content linking, as well as versioning of all content. In addition, Windows SharePoint Services 3.0 and SharePoint Server 2007 include the much-anticipated capability of a Recycle Bin. The Recycle Bin usually prevents the permanent deletion of objects; with this feature, it is no longer necessary to go to database backups for item-level deletion. Content types are also provided by the site model and allow for metadata tagging of almost any object type. Based on this metadata, you can manipulate objects via workflows or information management policies effecting extensive business process management.

> **Note**   Almost every object in Windows SharePoint Services and SharePoint Server 2007 is a *content type*. A content type is a collection of settings, such as metadata and a document template, that can have policies and workflow attached for use across multiple sites in a site collection. This allows management at the site collection level of list items, such as records or Web pages. Used in conjunction with document libraries, for example, you can now have multiple content types in a single document library or schedule Web content for deployment. Content types are covered in detail in Chapter 10, "Configuring Office SharePoint Server Enterprise Content Management."

■ **Customization**   SharePoint Server is designed to enable extensive, user-friendly customization. Users and administrators can add many customizations without the aid of developers through the native browser-based graphical user interface (GUI) or SharePoint Designer 2007. Virtually unlimited customization can be accomplished using ASP.NET. Custom code written as Web parts are reusable, allowing developers to create new functionality that can be used by administrators and users across multiple sites.

- **Web applications** At the root of Windows SharePoint Services and SharePoint Server is the *Web application.* In previous versions the Web application was also known as a *Virtual Server.* Since the release of Microsoft *Windows Virtual Server R2,* the name has been changed to eliminate confusion. A Web application is created from Central Administration and associates an IIS Virtual Server with a content database created on your SQL Server. Remember that this Web application is an empty shell and contains no site collections by default. You are prompted to create a site collection during initial installation, and you should complete it then. Figure 1-5 shows the relationship among site collections, Web applications, and content databases.

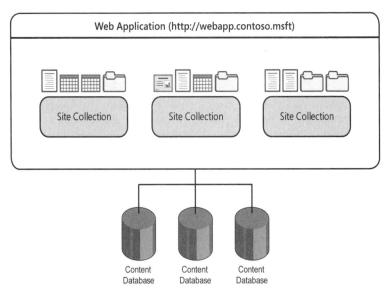

Figure 1-5 Site collections exist within Web applications. Web applications store their content in associated content databases.

- **Collaboration** The collaboration features provided by Windows SharePoint Services include Office 2007 integration, limited Office 2003 integration, calendaring, tasks, and e-mail integration. Both inbound and outbound e-mail are now integrated. This integration creates a seamless connectivity, decreasing the learning curve for new users and speeding the time to achieve effective collaboration.

- **Security** Windows SharePoint Services also leverages the operating system and database system security and continues through IIS, Web application, and site collection levels. This version now provides per-item security in site collection lists and document libraries. Subsites (sub-Webs) also can inherit permissions or use their own as in the previous version. Security at the site collection or item level is of little use if care isn't taken at the Web server. Because this version of Windows SharePoint Services is built on .NET 2.0 and .NET 3.0, you now can use .NET Pluggable authentication to authenticate users. This feature is extremely useful when Extranet and Internet users are not authorized for internal organizational Active Directory accounts. You may maintain a third-party database for usernames and password and authenticate with pluggable authentication. As you install and learn this product, be aware that the user interface (UI) is "security trimmed." Users (including you) only see the portions of the UI that permissions allow.

- **Windows SharePoint Services search**   Windows SharePoint Services provides a search engine similar in appearance to the SharePoint Server "Big Brother" search service. Windows SharePoint Services uses this service for all searching, but it is limited to the site collection from which you are searching. After installing Share-Point Server, the Windows SharePoint Services search service is used for indexing Help files only.

- **Scalability**   Because the config DB is a function of Windows SharePoint Services; all Office Servers rely on it to provide scalability. If you were familiar with the previous version, you know there were limitations with the configuration topology of your farm. This later version lifts the majority of restrictions. However, with this freedom of configuration also comes the possibility for mistakes. Take your time, do research, and make an educated decision about the correct topology to use. Figure 1-6 is a suggested example of a medium server farm.

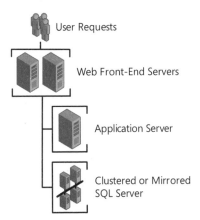

Figure 1-6   A medium server farm introduces SQL Clustering for database redundancy, dedicated Web front-end servers for user requests, and a middle tier of application servers for Excel Calculation Services, Query, and Indexing.

In Figure 1-6 there are two Web front-end servers (WFEs) serving Web content, search queries, and proxying Excel Calculation Services requests The middle tier is a single server providing high-value, CPU-intensive applications like indexing and Excel Calculation Services. You could have several middle-tier servers or WFEs if needed. In this example, the SQL Server third tier is a cluster providing high availability. Whatever size farm topology you begin with, remember it is easy to provision additional servers and grow as your requirements change. You can also detach servers from a config DB and attach to another farm when needed. This functionality is very useful to organizations looking to lower costs when transitioning custom code from development to test.

Microsoft Office SharePoint Server 2007

SharePoint Server 2007 builds on the core platform services provided by Windows SharePoint Services and adds rich functionality, such as Business Process Management, Content Management, Portals, Search, Business Intelligence, and Shared Services. In contrast to the previous version, SharePoint Server 2007 extends the existing familiar interfaces, easing the transition from Windows SharePoint Services. The following components are included in SharePoint Server 2007 Standard Edition:

- **Rich search and indexing functionality**   SharePoint Server search adds functionality far beyond what is provided by Windows SharePoint Services. Its ability to crawl external content, such as line-of-business systems, Exchange Public Folders, Lotus Notes, generic Web sites, remote SharePoint sites, and file shares, provides a solid reason to move to SharePoint Server 2007. This version also provides extensive customization capabilities using the native, in-browser editor to fine-tune your search results and experience.

- **My Sites (personal portals)**   My Sites functionality represents a noteworthy improvement in SharePoint Server 2007. Unlike SharePoint Portal Server 2003 where My Sites shared a common home page, My Sites are now truly a "personal portal" providing rich customization and one-to-many collaboration. With My Sites, users have the ability to create meeting workspaces from Outlook calendaring; store, collaborate, and version files; provide details of specialties for indexing; create blogs and wikis; and much more.

- **Corporate and Internet presence portals**   One of the most-asked questions about SharePoint Server 2007 is "Where did the portal go?" This question is a fair one. The product team wanted to make SharePoint Server 2007 more than just another portal product so it created a collaborative portal in this version. It is a site collection with a portal template (Publishing Collaboration Portal) applied. This can be customized by users so that the information is timely and relevant to them. Because portals are largely user specific, portal functionality is provided via Web parts. These Web parts, in addition to almost every portal feature, can be targeted to a specific audience.

There is also an Internet Publish portal template that enables you to easily create, modify, and maintain an Internet presence site. It includes a built-in editor and can be designed and deployed by the average SharePoint power user.

- **Business Data Catalog**   The Business Data Catalog (BDC) allows you to connect to third-party line-of-business (LOB) applications, such as SAP, Siebel, and PeopleSoft. The BDC enables you to amalgamate content from LOB systems without writing custom code. Although it presents a leap forward in LOB connectivity, it does require a custom application definition and expertise in its creation.

    For more information on the BDC, visit http://msdn2.microsoft.com/en-us/library/ms551230.aspx.

In addition to the services provided by the Standard Edition, SharePoint Server 2007 Premium Edition adds Excel Calculation Services and InfoPath Forms Server.

- **Excel Calculation Services**   With Excel Calculation Services you can render Excel workbooks in a browser. Excel Calculation Services offer in-browser input and an ability to hide formulas from the end user. The user also now can take a snapshot of the current view of the spreadsheet without gaining access to the entire workbook. Allowed clients are Microsoft Excel 2007, supported Web browsers, and custom applications. Although ECS offers functionality far beyond what was previously capable, it does not allow authoring of Excel workbooks in the browser.

- **Office Forms Server**   InfoPath Forms Server is not covered in any detail in this book. Office Forms Server is primarily a developer tool and its administration isn't difficult. The advantage of SharePoint Server 2007 is its single management interface used to manage Office Forms Server and perform disaster recovery. Forms created from the InfoPath Office client are automatically rendered via a friendly interface in the browser. For more information on InfoPath Forms Server visit *http:/www.microsoft.com/infopath.*

Administration Overview

The new SharePoint products introduce the concept of multi-tiered administration, thus allowing for isolation of processes and separation of duties. This separation of duties enables the better use of expertise within your organization and can prevent accidental mishaps.

Graphical Administration Tool

In a dramatic improvement over SharePoint Server 2003 and Windows SharePoint Services 2.0, SharePoint Server 2007 and Windows SharePoint Services 3.0 now have simple-to-navigate administration tools. All farm-specific tasks are located in Central

Administration, and SSP administrative tasks are broken out from portal administration and are a standalone entity. The product team has also drastically improved the site administration interface, making it easier for you to perform tasks quickly.

- **Central Administration**   Central Administration is a site collection with a "special" site collection template applied. Its easy-to-navigate interface readily presents all administrative tasks at a glance. There are three main areas on installation: Home, Operations, and Application Management. Figure 1-7 shows an example of the Central Administration Operations screen. Home provides a shared space for the administrator to track tasks, Operations is where all farm-related tasks reside, and Application Management is the interface to manage Web applications, site collections, and Shared Services, among others. Central Administration can be restricted to a group of users who may not have access to any site collections or Shared Services Administration.

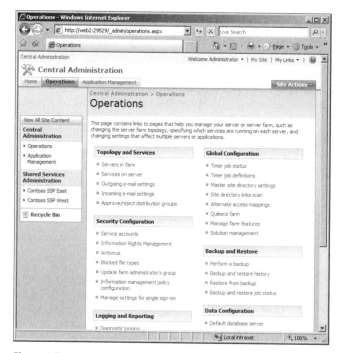

Figure 1-7   Central Administration provides a single location to perform both Windows SharePoint Services and SharePoint Server tasks.

- **Shared Services Provider administration (SharePoint Server 2007 Only)**   The high-value, CPU-intensive applications of Shared Services Providers (SSP) allow the sharing and reuse of these applications throughout the server farm or shared with another server farm through Inter Farm Shared Services. In many organizations dedicated SSP administrators have limited access to all other areas of the farm. This feature allows you to target skill sets, such as search and indexing, to a specific audience without granting unneeded access and preserving "need-to-know" access to content. Figure 1-8 shows the Shared Services Administration interface.

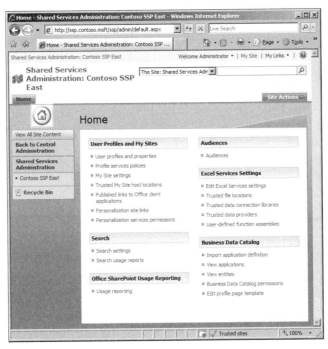

Figure 1-8   Shared Services is a separate and isolated administration interface.

- **Site collection administration**   In Windows SharePoint Services and SharePoint Server 2007 administrators do not have automatic access to site collections. To access a site that you are not a member of, you must take ownership and escalate your privileges from Central Administration. Although this requirement does not stop administrators from visiting unauthorized sites, it is a huge improvement to security because the action is logged and can be audited. Site collection administration represents the third tier in the administration of SharePoint technologies, which further enhances the ability to define and delegate tasks for administrators. Site collection administrators are often the data owners and can more reliably and quickly grant access for content requests. Properly training your site administrators and enabling them to manage their workspace will save you much time and energy.

Command-Line Tool

In addition to the user interface administration tools, there is also a very powerful command-line tool, Stsadm.exe. Although many products have tens or hundreds of individual command-line tools, Microsoft has provided you a single tool with over 100 options. It resides in the 12 Hive\Bin directory and is referred to often in this book. Stsadm.exe is located at C:\Program Files\Common Files\Microsoft Shared\ web server extensions\12\Bin\.

As a SharePoint administrator you should begin early on to learn the basics of this tool. Stsadm.exe is used for many advanced administrative tasks, such as site collection backups, migrations, and catastrophic disaster recovery. Many actions cannot be done in the UI and must be done at the command prompt, such as a configuration database restoration. Because you will be using this tool quite often, it is convenient to insert the C:\Program Files\Common Files\Microsoft Shared\web server extensions\12\Bin directory into your system path. Doing so prevents the need to change to this directory every time you need the tool. Some examples of using the Stsadm.exe tool follow.

```
stsadm.exe -o backup -url
http://portal.contoso.msft/sites/teamsite1
-filename c:\filename.bak
```

```
stsadm.exe -o renameweb
-url http://portal.contoso.msft/sites/web1 -newname web2
```

An appendix in the back of the book provides a complete cross-reference for Stsadm.exe command-line options. As a starting point, you can get help by executing *stsadm.exe -help <operation>*. You can also see the property of almost any SharePoint Products and Technologies configuration setting by using

```
stsadm.exe -o getproperty <property name> [-url <url>]
```

The *getproperty* options are:

```
SharePoint cluster properties:
avallowdownload
avcleaningenabled
avdownloadscanenabled
avnumberofthreads
avtimeout
avuploadscanenabled
command-line-upgrade-running
database-command-timeout
database-connection-timeout
data-retrieval-services-enabled
data-retrieval-services-oledb-providers
data-retrieval-services-response-size
data-retrieval-services-timeout
data-retrieval-services-update
```

```
data-source-controls-enabled
dead-site-auto-delete
dead-site-notify-after
dead-site-num-notifications
defaultcontentdb-password
defaultcontentdb-server
defaultcontentdb-user
delete-web-send-email
irmaddinsenabled
irmrmscertserver
irmrmsenabled
irmrmsusead
job-ceip-datacollection
job-config-refresh
job-database-statistics
job-dead-site-delete
job-usage-analysis
job-watson-trigger
large-file-chunk-size
token-timeout
workflow-cpu-throttle
workflow-eventdelivery-batchsize
workflow-eventdelivery-throttle
workflow-eventdelivery-timeout
workflow-timerjob-cpu-throttle
workitem-eventdelivery-batchsize
workitem-eventdelivery-throttle

SharePoint virtual server properties:
alerts-enabled
alerts-limited
alerts-maximum
change-log-expiration-enabled
change-log-retention-period
data-retrieval-services-enabled
data-retrieval-services-inherit
data-retrieval-services-oledb-providers
data-retrieval-services-response-size
data-retrieval-services-timeout
data-retrieval-services-update
data-source-controls-enabled
days-to-show-new-icon
dead-site-auto-delete
dead-site-notify-after
dead-site-num-notifications
defaultquotatemplate
defaulttimezone
delete-web-send-email
job-change-log-expiration
```

```
job-dead-site-delete
job-diskquota-warning
job-immediate-alerts
job-recycle-bin-cleanup
job-usage-analysis
job-workflow
job-workflow-autoclean
job-workflow-failover
max-file-post-size
peoplepicker-activedirectorysearchtimeout
peoplepicker-distributionlistsearchdomains
peoplepicker-nowindowsaccountsfornonwindowsauthenticationmode
peoplepicker-onlysearchwithinsitecollection
peoplepicker-searchadcustomquery
peoplepicker-searchadforests
presenceenabled
recycle-bin-cleanup-enabled
recycle-bin-enabled
recycle-bin-retention-period
second-stage-recycle-bin-quota
send-ad-email
```

Chapter 2

Deploying SharePoint Products and Technologies

Before inserting the installation media and choosing Next, take the time to understand the different options available to you in the setup wizard. If you make the wrong selection during setup, it could mean a complete uninstall and reinstall of the binaries. In addition, making good choices in the beginning will make it considerably easier to scale SharePoint products. The following decisions must be made before installing SharePoint products:

- **Choose a SQL Server type**   During installation you will have the option either to install all components (including SQL Server Express Edition) on a single computer or to choose a dedicated SQL Server installation for the databases. Choose the SQL Server Express Edition option only when you are sure that you will not scale to a server farm in the future. Although scaling to a server farm is technically possible, migrating SharePoint products from SQL Server 2005 Express Edition to SQL Server Enterprise or Standard is a tedious task.

- **Use either host headers or assigned IP addresses**   Host headers ease installation and reduce administrative overhead, but assigning IP addresses strengthens your overall security posture. Assigning an individual IP address for every Web application simplifies your logs and allows for separate firewall rules.

- **Process security isolation**   Depending on the level of security your organization requires, you may choose to install with one or several accounts for Internet Information Services (IIS) application pools and database access. It is much easier to install with separate accounts in the beginning than it is to change and isolate application pools later.

- **Assign administrators**   You must define the administrative roles and separation of duties. If you wish to granularly define administrative roles, pay close attention to the details of service accounts and groups. If you are in a small organization, consider using a dedicated farm account for all administrative tasks.

- **Create a site template for the Web application root**   When creating your first Web application (other than a Shared Services Provider or My Sites dedicated Web application), it is wise to create a site collection in the root. This site can be modified, but the site definition cannot be changed, so give careful consideration to the template type. Many SharePoint Server 2007 implementations use Portal templates when creating the root site collection.

This chapter covers Microsoft Windows SharePoint Services 3.0 and SharePoint Server 2007 deployments, whether using Internet Information Services (IIS) host headers or assigned IP addresses. When neither Windows SharePoint Services nor SharePoint Server is stated, the material applies to both software products.

Preparing for Installation

At a minimum, before installation, sketch out your design, including IIS configuration, SQL Server databases, accounts, administrators, and any other pertinent data you will need. Microsoft Office Visio is a very helpful tool when designing and maintaining server farms with multiple Web applications, IIS servers, and SQL Server databases. In addition, verify that you have met the minimum hardware requirements and have created all Active Directory accounts, if using Active Directory for authentication, before beginning the installation wizard.

Software Requirements

Before you can install SharePoint products and technologies, you need to install the following foundational components:

- Windows Server 2003 (any edition) SP1 or later
- Fresh install of IIS 6.0 or later (install *before* ASP.NET 2.0 or 3.0)
- SMTP Server (if implementing mail-integrated document libraries)
- ASP.NET 2.0
- ASP.NET 3.0

> **Note**   You cannot install Windows SharePoint Services or SharePoint Server in Basic or Standalone mode when using Windows Server 2003 Web Edition.

If possible, always install Windows SharePoint Services or SharePoint Server on a freshly installed Windows Server. Using servers that previously hosted other applications, or were imaged and had the SID changed, has proven to be a bad idea.

Security Accounts

Before starting the installation wizard for any SharePoint product, create all the accounts required for installation. If you require program isolation within Windows SharePoint Services or SharePoint Server, you must create an application pool identity account for every Web application created. If yours is a low-security implementation, you can create a single application pool identity to be shared by multiple Web applications. When planning for enhanced security, create IIS application pool process accounts that correspond with the SQL Server security accounts for their respective Web applications. The following list describes the basic accounts needed to install SharePoint products and gives suggested service account names:

- **Setup account**   The account used for installing SharePoint products should be a domain user account if using Active Directory for authentication, and a member of the local administrator's group on every farm server. It should also have the following rights in the SQL Server:

  - ❑ SQL Server Logins

  - ❑ SQL Security Admin

  - ❑ Database (DB) Creator

- **Server farm account (domain\SAfarm)**   Put the server farm account in Active Directory when possible, and do not use it for installation. The server farm account can be used for all application pools in an unsecured installation. This use makes account management and administration easier, but reduces the ability to isolate users and processes. The server farm account is granted server permissions automatically during setup, but the following permissions must pre-exist in SQL Server:

  - ❑ SQL Server Logins

  - ❑ SQL Server Admin

  - ❑ SQL Server DB Creator

  - ❑ DBO (Database Owner) for all databases

- **First Web application account (domain\SAwss1)**   If you don't want to create an account for every Web application, strongly consider creating *at least* one account for all Web applications to share.

  Best Practices   Always use a dedicated account for the Central Administration IIS application pool.

This account requires the following SQL Server permissions:

❑ Database Owner for content databases associated with the Web application

❑ Read/Write access to the associated Shared Services Provider (SSP) database (SharePoint Server only)

❑ Read access to the configuration database

■ **Additional Web application accounts (domain\SAwssn)** If security is important to your organization, create an additional account for each Web application. For example, create multiple accounts, such as domain\SAwss2, domain\SAwss3, or any naming convention you choose, as long as it is consistent.

■ **Shared Services Provider accounts (SharePoint Server only)** The SSP IIS application pool and SSP service should use the same authentication account, but it must be different from the server farm or other Web application accounts. This account requires the following SQL Server permissions:

❑ DBO for the SSP content database

❑ Read/Write to the SSP content database

❑ Read/Write to associated content databases (associated Web applications)

❑ Read from the configuration database

❑ Read from the Central Administration database

Although creating multiple application pools and corresponding accounts enhances your security posture, it is important to note that creating each additional application pool adds another W3wp.exe process, thereby consuming additional memory. If you have installed using the minimum recommended hardware, you must either configure with fewer application pools or increase the memory in your server.

Important   Each application pool process account must be a member of the *Local Administrators* group on every server in the farm.

■ **Windows SharePoint Services search service** This account can be a local account or domain account. If you are using SharePoint Server, you need only one server running Windows SharePoint Services search for indexing the Help files.

■ **Windows SharePoint Services content access** The account used for Windows SharePoint Services content access should have the ability to crawl all data in your environment. For ease of administration, it can be the same account that is used for the Windows SharePoint Services search service.

■ **SharePoint Server Search service account** This account can be the same account used for either Windows SharePoint Services search or your server farm account. Most installations use the server farm account.

■ **SharePoint Server Search content access**   The default content access account should have wide-reaching access to your content. Often, this account has only Read-Only privileges across much of an enterprise. For ease of administration, this account should not expire or at least should expire infrequently because you must reset the service password when the password changes.

■ **SharePoint Server user profile import account**   If you have multiple forests, isolated administrative access among domains, or a third-party Lightweight Directory Access Protocol (LDAP) provider, you must provide an account for importing accounts.

■ **SharePoint Server Excel Calculation Services unattended service account**   For default source access to Excel Calculation Services data, use the SSP account for IIS and database access. If security is of paramount concern in your organization, change this account to one that does not have database access.

SQL Server Security Accounts

Creating SQL Server security accounts is done very similarly to creating your other SharePoint accounts. In many circumstances these accounts are the same ones used for creating Web applications, thereby essentially isolating similar processes and providing enhanced security. You may modify these accounts to fit your situation, but be careful when restricting access between Web applications and their databases, as unexpected negative behavior is possible when modifying access. The following are recommended settings when installing SQL Server and creating security access accounts:

■ **SQL Server 2005 Express Edition (Basic, Stand-alone)**

❑ Verify that the default accounts created and used during setup are Local Administrators.

❑ The *Network Service* account must be a System Administrator in SQL Server.

■ **SQL Server Standard or Enterprise Editions**

❑ The SQL Server setup account (*setupadmin* in SQL Management Studio) should be a domain account if possible. However, when installing Windows SharePoint Services in a workgroup, the SQL Server setup account can be a local account.

Installing Windows SharePoint Services or SharePoint Server in a workgroup environment using local authentication accounts is beyond the scope of this book. For ease of installation and administration, use Active Directory for user and services authentication. For more information on the topic, browse: http://www.microsoft.com/technet/prodtechnol/office/sharepoint/ default.mspx.

❏   The SQL Server service account should be a domain account and should *not* be the same account used for the Central Administration application pool identity. This account does not need to be a domain administrator. Although it is possible to use SQL Security for authentication, only consider doing so in highly customized environments with experienced developers on staff.

Installing the First Windows SharePoint Services Server in the Farm

When installing your first Windows SharePoint Services Server, whether it is standalone or the first in a server farm, you have the option of changing the data location. However, changing this location is strongly discouraged and should only be attempted by an experienced administrator who has very specific requirements.

Note   When installing SharePoint Server, Windows SharePoint Services is installed automatically during the installation process. Although it is possible to install Windows SharePoint services manually before installing SharePoint Server, you are not required to do so.

When installing the first server in the farm you are presented with two choices:

■   **Basic**   The Basic option installs all components, including SQL Server 2005 Embedded Edition. If you choose this option, you cannot scale out your farm to multiple servers. However, if you do not have SQL Server 2000 SP3a or later (Standard or Enterprise editions), you must choose this option to install Windows SharePoint Services.

■   **Advanced**   The Advanced option allows you to install the binaries necessary to create a server farm. This option is the preferred installation mode for all Windows SharePoint Services implementations.

Active Directory Account Creation Mode

Windows SharePoint Services allows corresponding accounts to be created automatically in Active Directory (AD) when they are created in SharePoint site collections, in addition to using accounts created by administrators. This installation mode requires site collections to be created from the command-line interface (CLI). SMTP settings also must be configured correctly before you can create site collections. You must create an Organizational Unit (OU) in Active Directory to use during setup, which is where all accounts are automatically created. However, allowing users to create accounts in the Active Directory (AD) is a bad choice for most organizations as it decreases security and complicates user management. Only consider AD account creation mode for Intranet-only applications or perhaps an Internet Service Provider.

Using the Configuration Wizard

After selecting the Basic option you are not prompted to create a Web application or a team site collection, because these are created automatically. Your first site is created in the root of a Web application, with the server name as the Web address. You have little ability to extend or customize a basic install. For this reason, limit the use of Basic or Stand-alone installs to labs or very small groups.

When selecting the Advanced option, choose Web Front End to continue with a farm installation. Selecting the alternate option, Stand-alone, results in a similar installation as Basic, with the exception that you must create the Web application after completing the installation wizard. After the Advanced installation has completed copying the binaries to the machine, you are prompted to run the configuration wizard. You may choose to run it at a later time; doing so allows you to image the server for configuration later, primarily for disaster recovery. After you choose to continue, you are presented with the farm-level configuration wizard. You are then asked to reset IIS and related services and continue with the option of connecting to an existing farm. For the first server in the farm, select *No, I Want To Create A New Server Farm* as shown in Figure 2-1. The default is *Yes, I Want To Connect To An Existing Server Farm.*

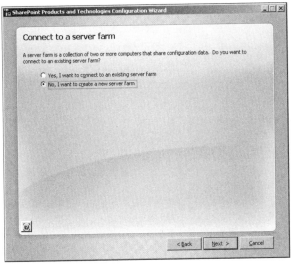

Figure 2-1   To create the first server in a farm, select No, I Want To Create A New Server Farm.

To continue, you must have the server farm username and password combination available. Remember that this account must be a local administrator on this machine. The database server name and database name are also required. If you plan to host multiple SharePoint configuration databases on this SQL Server instance, rename the configuration database to an easily identifiable name for this server farm. Figure 2-2 shows an example when creating a server farm for Human Resources (HR).

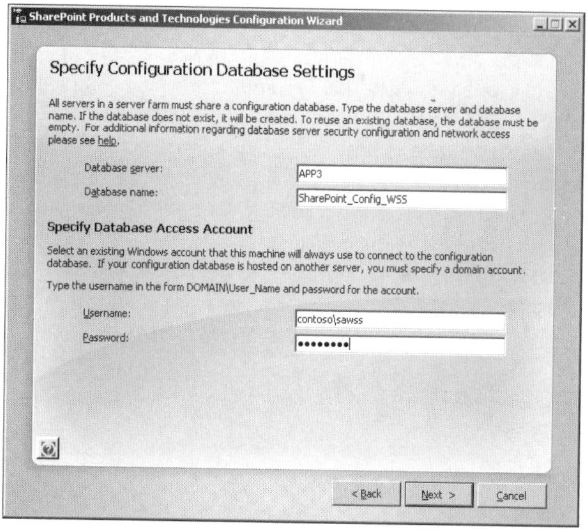

Figure 2-2   Specify unique configuration database settings.

Central Administration Setup

Configuring the SharePoint Central Administration Web application is the next step and must be planned for beforehand. If you are managing your SharePoint farm from remote locations, the TCP port used for administration must be allowed via firewall rules, or you must employ another mechanism such as Windows Remote Desktop for remote access. If you plan to use Kerberos for Central Administration authentication, you must create an Service Principal Name (SPN) before continuing past this point.

> **Tip**   An SPN is used by Kerberos as a unique identifier for the Web application, thus allowing the Kerberos ticket to be encrypted with a corresponding key. To set an SPN for a Web application, download the Setspn.exe tool from *http://downloads.microsoft.com* and execute the following from the CLI:
>
> ```
> setspn -A HTTP/ServerName Domain\UserName
> ```

Figure 2-3 gives an example of configuring an easy-to-remember port number and using NTLM (default) for authentication.

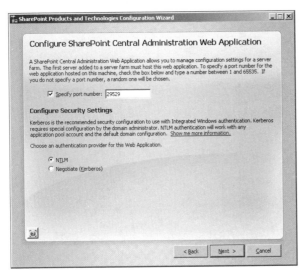

Figure 2-3   Select an easy-to-remember administration TCP port number when configuring the SharePoint Central Administration Web Application.

> **Tip**   After Installation, you can query the administration port number by running *sstadm.exe -o getadminport*. You can also get the full URL of Central Administration by using the obsolete command, *stsadm.exe -o createadminvs*.

After the installation wizard finishes, you are taken to Central Administration to continue configuring your server farm. Several administrative tasks are listed under the Home navigation tab along with a quick view of the farm topology. You can modify this list as needed, but the following tasks should always be completed after a new install:

Start the Windows SharePoint Services Search Service

From Central Administration > Operations > Topology and Services > Services on Server, select *Windows SharePoint Services Search*. You must specify an account and password for the service account and the account for default content access. Most implementations use the same account. The account should have a broad scope and have the ability to read all Windows SharePoint Services content. Best practice is using a Read-Only, nonadministrative account. You should create a search database that is easily recognizable, and select the Windows Authentication option in most circumstances. An example is shown in Figure 2-4.

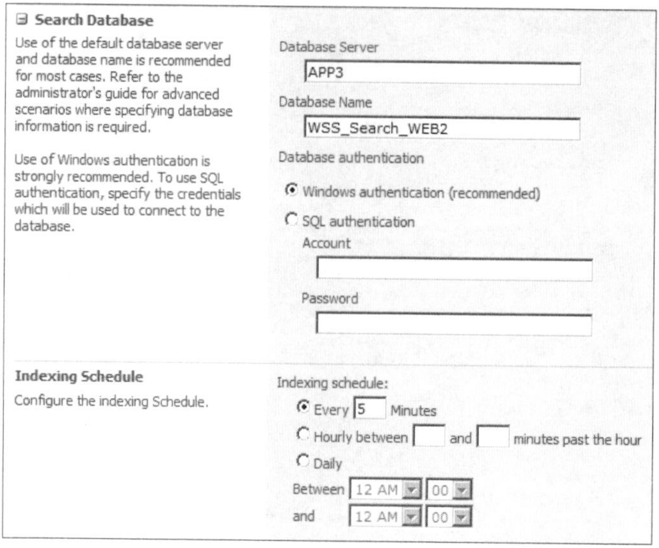

Search Database

Use of the default database server and database name is recommended for most cases. Refer to the administrator's guide for advanced scenarios where specifying database information is required.

Database Server

APP3

Database Name

WSS_Search_WEB2

Use of Windows authentication is strongly recommended. To use SQL authentication, specify the credentials which will be used to connect to the database.

Database authentication

⦿ Windows authentication (recommended)

◯ SQL authentication

Account

Password

Indexing Schedule

Configure the indexing Schedule.

Indexing schedule:

⦿ Every [5] Minutes

◯ Hourly between [ ] and [ ] minutes past the hour

◯ Daily

Between [12 AM ▾] [00 ▾]

and [12 AM ▾] [00 ▾]

Figure 2-4 Configure the Search Database, Database Authentication, and Indexing Schedule to match your specific requirements.

In the above example, a Windows SharePoint Services Search database was created with a correlating name as the server hosting the service. This practice eases backup, restore, and content recovery should they be necessary in the future. You can also change the Indexing Schedule if desired, but the defaults work quite well for most implementations.

Configure the Farm Administrators Group

From Central Administration > Operations > Security Configuration, select *Update Farm Administrator's Group*. This option gives you the ability to add or remove users and groups. By default, the account used to install Windows SharePoint Services is a farm administrator, along with local machine administrators and the server farm account that you specified in the installation wizard. Unlike in previous versions of SharePoint Products and Technologies, server farm administrators do not have access to all site collections; they only have access to the Central Administration site collection. You must deliberately specify site administrators or take ownership of a site to allow uninvited access to site collections.

Configure Outgoing E-mail Settings

At a minimum, you should select outgoing mail settings or alerting will not function. Incoming mail settings only need to be enabled when using mail-enabled document libraries. Mail-enabled document libraries allow the e-mailing of files to document libraries. To configure outgoing e-mail settings, select from Central Administration >

Operations > Topology and Services > Outgoing E-mail Settings. The SMTP Relay Server, From Address, and Reply To Address must be defined for outgoing e-mail to work.

Important   The SMTP Server specified in Windows SharePoint Services and SharePoint Server for outgoing e-mail *must* allow relaying by IP address. SharePoint products do not authenticate outbound e-mail. You must use another method for high-availability, as neither Windows SharePoint Services nor SharePoint Server allows for multiple SMTP server addresses.

Create a Web Application to Host Site Collections

Unless you chose a Basic/Stand-alone installation, you must create a Web application to host your content. Select Central Administration > Application Management > Create Or Extend Web Application to create your first Web application. Figure 2-5 shows the location and URL for creating a Web application.

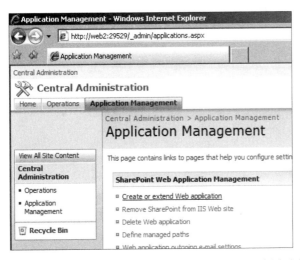

Figure 2-5   Create or extend Web applications in Central Administration > Application Management.

When creating a new Web application it is generally better to use most of the default settings for the URL and host headers, modifying IIS and Central Administration to suit your specific circumstances later. All settings entered in Central Administration are written to the configuration database and will be used whenever you add new servers to the farm. You must define the following items when creating a Web application.

- **Create a new IIS Web site or use an existing Web site**   You can create IIS Web sites before creating a Web application, but doing so increases the risk for errors. The Central Administration UI creates the IIS virtual servers automatically, and you can change the IP addresses or host headers later. Be aware that the TCP port used for HTTP traffic will be written to the configuration database and automatically assigned to all new servers added to the farm. If you choose this method, you will not need to use host headers, but you must always change the TCP port number in IIS Manager before the Web application will be available from that server.

    Tip   Whichever method you choose, use an easy-to-recognize IIS description that matches the name of the content database.

- **TCP port used for HTTP traffic**   If you are using host headers, you may set the TCP port when creating a Web application. If you plan to assign IP addresses, leave the TCP port to default and modify it later in IIS Manager with the correct IP address.

- **Host headers**   You should always input the Fully Qualified Domain Name (FQDN) of the server as the host header. Even if you assign IP addresses later, the host header will not interfere. The host header information is written to the configuration database and is used when adding a new server to the farm. This new server will then have a Web application created and corresponding host header. If you plan to access this server by more than one FQDN, you must enter additional host headers in the IIS Manager application. Verify that the DNS entry has been created for this entry or your Web application will fail. Pinging the DNS Fully Qualified Domain Name is one method for verifying that the IP address is active.

- **Web site path**   The path for the Web site should be consistent across your server farm. Creating a new Web site path, c:\WSS\Web1, c:\WSS\Web2, for example, makes managing the associated Web applications easier as your farm grows.

- **Authentication provider**   If you are creating an Intranet Web application, strongly consider using Kerberos for user authentication. Kerberos is more secure and offers better performance than NTLM. If you have multiple subnets, are separated by firewalls, or the Web application is Internet facing, you should use NTLM (default) for authentication. If users cannot see your KDC (Kerberos Distribution Center) or the time is out of synchronization, Kerberos will fail. It is possible to enable both types of authentication from the command line after installation. See *http://support.microsoft.com/kb/326089/en-us* for information on enabling Kerberos after the creation of a Web application.

Tip   You can change the authentication mechanism for a Web application from the command line by running:

```
stsadm -o authentication -url <Web application>
-type <windows/forms/Websso>
-usebasic (only when selecting windows authent)
-exclusivelyusentlm (only when selecting windows authent)
-allowanonymous
```

An example of a Web application name portal using Windows integrated authentication and basic authentication follows:

```
stsadm -o authentication -url http://portal.contoso.msft
-type windows -usebasic -usewindowsintegrated
```

- **Anonymous or non-anonymous access**   Unless you are serving content for public consumption, you should not allow anonymous access. Although enabling anonymous access is allowed for collaborative site collections via its Web application, it is generally a bad practice. Allowing anonymous access prevents user-level auditing.

- **Load-balanced URL**   Change the default entry if you are serving content via multiple Web front-end (WFEs) servers or if you plan to publish via a different URL than specified during setup. The load-balanced URL is the domain name (namespace) for all site collections users who have access in this SharePoint Web application. This URL is used in all links shown on pages within the Web application. By default, it is set to your servername and port. Remember to change the port if using SSL; the default TCP Port for SSL is 443. When changing the default load-balanced URL, you must also have a corresponding DNS entry before continuing.

- **Zone**   The 3.0 version of Windows SharePoint Services gives users the ability to differentiate incoming traffic based on *zones*. Zones can help "sort" incoming traffic to different extended Web applications with matching URLs. The URL entered in the user's browser is mapped to the correlating zone, allowing greater flexibility in isolating and directing incoming traffic.

  Tip   *stsadm -o* [*-addzoneurl* | *deletezoneurl*] can be used to modify and map zones and associated URLs.

- **Application pool creation or reuse**   If security is important to your organization, you must create an application pool for each Web application. Consider using an existing application pool if you are short on resources OR plan to use the same application pool identity (username) for all Web applications. Creating an application pool requires additional resources such as memory and administrative time, so creating one purely for performance is discouraged. In addition, use a domain account for the identity as doing so eases the pain of scaling to a farm later. *Verify that this account is in the local administrators group.*

- **Reset Internet Information Services**   After installation, IIS must be manually reset on this server, regardless of which option is selected. This option is for resetting *other* WFEs in a server farm. To manually reset IIS, run *IISReset /noforce* from the CLI on the WFE.

- **Database server**   For most installations, use the default SQL Server. This server is what was specified during setup for the configuration database. If you have several large Web applications, consider using dedicated SQL Servers for serving content.

- **Database name**   Always change the default database name to correlate to the Web application name. For example, if the Web application is *http://sales.contoso.msft,* then use WSS_Content_Sales for the database name. Intelligent naming of Web applications, application pools, and databases greatly eases the management of medium to large Windows SharePoint Services implementations.

- **Database authentication**   The recommended authentication type is always Windows Authentication. Only use SQL authentication when working in a workgroup environment and when you have selected SQL authentication for *all* database connections, including the configuration database. The database authentication is the user context currently logged onto the Central Administration UI.

- **Search server**   Most installations have only one search server listed. You should always associate the search server with the content database of the Web application. It is important to note that the search server associates with the *content database,* and *not* the Web application. It is possible to create multiple search servers associated with multiple content databases in the same Web application, but they become impossible to manage.

Create a Site Collection at the Root of the Web Application

If you chose a Basic installation, your site collection was automatically created in the root of the Web application. If you decided to give yourself the ability to scale by choosing Web Front End, then you need to create the first site collection in your newly created Web application. You are prompted to create this first site collection as shown in Figure 2-6.

Figure 2-6   You should always create a site collection in the root of a new Web application.

Most organizations create a Team Site in the root (/) of the Web application. We recommend that you always create a site in the root of a Web application to facilitate a collaboration launch point and a place for automated site collection creation. We also recommend an Announcements list to help users find the URL for creating site collections. You must specify at least one Site Collection Administrator, but when creating a root site collection you should specify a secondary Site Collection Administrator as well.

Update IIS Configuration

To assign an IP address to your Web application, you need to configure IIS with the appropriate settings and change the TCP port number in IIS Manager to what was specified during Windows SharePoint Services installation for the load-balanced URL.

Assigning IP Addresses to Web Applications

To assign IP addresses to your Web applications, follow these steps:

1. Add a Host (A Record) in the DNS Management Console.

2. Add the associated IP address to your Windows Server.

3. After an IIS reset, assign the IP address to the Web application in *Web site identification,* as shown in Figure 2-7.

Figure 2-7   To assign an IP Address to a Web application in IIS Manager, right-click on the Web site name, choose Properties, and then choose the Web Site tab.

4. Change the TCP port, if required.

5. Perform an *IISreset /noforce* from the CLI.

6. Modify the internal URL from Central Administration > Operations > Global Configuration > Alternate Access Mappings, and select the internal URL you defined when creating your first Web application. Figure 2-8 shows an example of the modification.

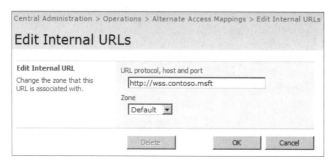

Figure 2-8   If not using the default server name, you should modify the internal URL when assigning IP addresses to Web applications.

Perform a Backup

After your initial configuration is complete and functional, you should perform a backup, including IIS. From Central Administration > Operations > Backup And Restore, create a Full backup using the default settings. Also perform an IIS Metabase backup to a shared location. For details on backing up your server farm, refer to Chapter 14, "Backup and Restore of SharePoint Products and Technologies."

Understanding the Databases Created During Installation

After installation, you will see several databases that are created in SQL Server and that need to be added to your SQL Server maintenance plan:

- **SharePoint configuration**   The SharePoint configuration database (config DB) holds all of your server farm configuration data and is akin to the Windows Server system registry. Any server that uses this installation's config DB is considered a member of the same server farm.

- **Central Administration content**   Because the Central Administration Web application is a custom site collection in a dedicated Web application, it has a corresponding content database. Although this Web application and associated database can be re-created without losing content, it is not a simple task and should be avoided by correctly backing up the server for future restoration.

- **First Web application content database**   During installation the first Web application was created with a corresponding content database. If you installed with the Basic installation type, you were not given the ability to name this content database. Do not try to change this name; simply document the name and be careful to give meaningful names to all future content databases. If you chose the Advanced installation type, you should have given the database a name that is easy to remember and is associated with a similarly named Web application.

- **Windows SharePoint Services search**   When you started Windows SharePoint Services search, a database was created to support these services. This database does not include the actual crawled content, but only the metadata associated with that content. The actual content is stored on each Windows SharePoint Services search server.

Figure 2-9 is an example of a Standard Edition SQL Server 2005 after installation of Windows SharePoint Services.

Figure 2-9   Several SQL Server databases are created during Windows SharePoint Services installation.

Installing the First SharePoint Server 2007 Server in the Farm

Installing SharePoint Server is similar to installing Windows SharePoint Services, but there are some very important differences. For example, the configuration wizard is expanded, and there are many more required post-installation tasks in Central Administration. In addition, even though SharePoint Server installation types are named the same as in Windows SharePoint Services, they are very different. Before beginning the installation process, document your choices thoroughly, and take the time to create all necessary accounts, add IP addresses to your servers, create DNS entries, and install any foundational software. Once again, it is not necessary to install Windows SharePoint Services beforehand because it is installed automatically with SharePoint Server.

The Installation Wizard

By running setup from the installation media, you begin the first of three phases required to install SharePoint Server. Entering the product key is required, and you may copy and paste the product key. After entering your product key, setup requires that you choose either a Basic or Advanced installation. The Basic option always installs SQL Server 2005 Express Edition, in addition to all SharePoint Server services, on a single machine. It does not give you the option to scale in the future or to use robust disaster recovery methods. Therefore, the Basic option is only suitable for very small workgroups or to test functionality. An Advanced installation type is recommended, and although it is possible to host SQL Server Standard/Enterprise on the same server as SharePoint Server, it may be difficult to support or scale out.

Advanced

After selecting an Advanced installation, you are presented with three distinct server installation types:

- **Complete**   This is the preferred server type for an Advanced installation. This type installs all binaries on the server and gives you the ability to run any Web or application service from this machine. Services are started and stopped via Central Administration, so there is no need to manually disable services after a complete install.

- **Web Front End**   A WFE in SharePoint Server is very different from the identically named option in the Windows SharePoint Services setup. Unlike in Windows SharePoint Services, the Web front-end server type in SharePoint Server installs only the binaries to support Web application content rendering and Excel Calculation Services Web proxy. Unless drive space is at a premium, you are better off installing the complete set of binaries and leaving the services disabled (default).

- **Stand-alone**   Selecting a Stand-alone server type gives essentially the same result as a Basic installation type. The primary difference is the requirement to manually set up your first Web application in the farm. Installing Stand-alone is only recommended for very small installations or a lab environment.

SharePoint Products and Technologies Configuration Wizard

After successful completion of the installation, you are prompted to run the SharePoint Products and Technologies Configuration Wizard. If you are imaging systems for rapid restores, you may close the wizard at this point and create your system image. Creating an image from this point allows the server, when restored, to be added to *any* SharePoint Server 2007 server farm in the event of a machine failure. While the wizard is running, you will be prompted for your database server, database names, and your domain server farm user account. Have this information ready, remembering that the server farm user account *must* be in the local administrators group.

Because this is the first server in the farm, do not select the default setting, *Yes, I Want To Connect To An Existing Server Farm*. Instead, select *No, I Want To Create A New Server Farm*, as shown in Figure 2-10.

Figure 2-10   Select No, I Want To Create A New Server Farm when installing the first server in a farm. Doing so creates the configuration database.

Configuration Database Settings   Next you must specify your configuration database settings. The database server must be in the same domain as your SharePoint Server server, and its version must be SQL Server 2000 SP3a or later. If multiple SharePoint products are installed to the same SQL Server server, then change the default name of the database to match the server farm purpose, like *SharePoint_Config_Sales* when installing a server farm to support your sales department. You must provide a username and password to create and permanently connect the config DB. Remember, this account needs to be a local administrator on this machine and have the ability to create and administer databases on the SQL Server instance. Figure 2-11 shows an example of creating a config DB for an organization's enterprise portal.

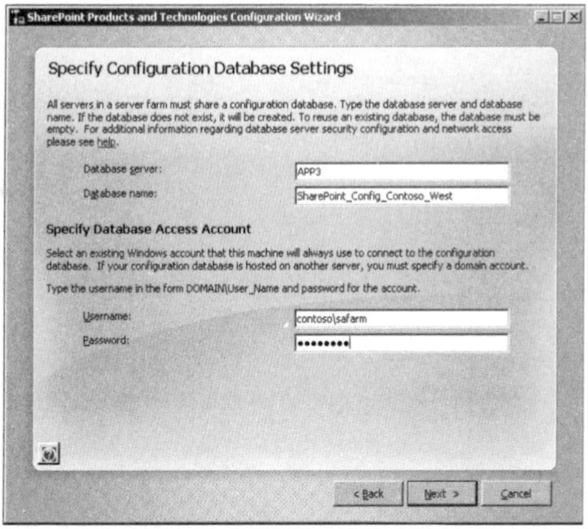

Figure 2-11   Name the configuration database intelligently.

Creating the Central Administration Web Application   There can only be one Central Administration (Central Admin) Web application per server farm. When configuring the SharePoint Central Administration Web application, you must specify the TCP port number used to access the Web application. The number is appended to the Net-BIOS server name you are installing on; for example, *http://Web1:29528* if your server name is *Web1* and the chosen port is *29528*. Remember to open any necessary firewall rules if you are managing your farm from remote subnets.

> **Tip**   The Central Administration port number should never be changed from within IIS Manager. To change the TCP port number, use the CLI tool Stsadm.exe:
>
> `stsadm -o setadminport -port <port#> <-ssl>`
>
> The SSL argument is optional and should only be used if you already have SSL enabled for the Central Administration Web application.

You must also configure your security settings for the Central Admin Web application. If you plan to always manage your server from a centrally located subnet, you may choose to employ Kerberos authentication. Kerberos marginally increases performance and helps secure your Central Admin Web application. It is generally better to use NTLM to authenticate to Central Administration and to disallow any Internet access to the IP address used for that Web application. By default, Central Administration will use All Unassigned in IIS Manager, as shown in Figure 2-12, but this can be changed to the local machine's IP address if desired for greater security.

Figure 2-12   Change the default IP address of the Central Administration Web application.

Best practice is to change the Central Administration IP address to the first IP address in the server's IP stack after installation. Leaving the Web application's IP address as *All Unassigned* opens up the possibility of compromising your administrative interface.

For example, if another Web application is created and its corresponding IP address is open to the Internet through a firewall rule, then your Central Administration TCP port will work on that IP address remotely.

Central Administration Post-Installation Tasks

After the installation wizard completes successfully, you must perform several tasks to have a functional first server in the farm. When you visit Central Administration, you will get a notification that your server farm configuration is not complete. You will also see the administrator task list that can be modified to meet your specific requirements Both Windows SharePoint Services and SharePoint Server search services, along with the Windows SharePoint Services Web application, are required and must be configured. The following are the services available to be enabled:

- **Document Conversions Launcher Services**   The Document Conversions Launcher services are content management feature services that enable the conversion and load balancing of converted documents or generic XML documents to another type of document, HTML, or graphic. These services aren't mandatory in your new SharePoint Server server farm, but are required when using document conversion in Information Management Policies or Web content management.

- **Excel Calculation Services**   Excel Calculation Services is a very powerful service that can help many organizations standardize and centralize their Excel spreadsheets. It is not a required service, however, so enable it it at your discretion. It can always be enabled at a later time.

- **Office SharePoint Server Search**   Before you can create a Shared Services Provider later in the installation process, you must enable SharePoint Server Search. You will also be unable to search any content on your SharePoint Server server(s) unless the search services (Query and Indexing) are enabled. For these reasons, it is best to always enable SharePoint Server Search in the very beginning. When starting the SharePoint Server search service, you must check or answer the following options:

  - ❏ **Use this server for indexing content**   Because this is the first server in your farm, enabling this server for indexing should be checked. You can move the indexing service to another server in the future if needed.

  - ❏ **Use this server for serving search queries**   This is the only server currently capable of serving search queries, so this should also be checked. In-depth details on scaling search and index can be found later in this book.

  - ❏ **E-mail address**   The e-mail address used for e-mail notification should be directed to the person responsible for search and indexing. When search, indexing, or crawling of content fails, this account is notified. This is a farm-wide setting and cannot be changed per query or index server.

❑ **Farm search service account**   This should be a domain account and a member of the local administrators group. For account administration and security, it can be the same account used for the server farm (configuration database access).

❑ **Index server default file location**   For most installations, the default file location is fine. However, if you have large content indexes, you might decide to use another drive for this purpose. Although you can change this drive later, it is much easier to configure it during setup. Changing the drive later forces a re-crawl of all content sources.

❑ **Indexer performance**   If your indexing server hosts other applications, such as Excel Calculation Services (ECS), consider running your Indexer at a Partly Reduced level. Reducing the level further could affect the accuracy and timeliness of query results. If your indexes are quite large, partly reducing the performance level can also help increase the responsiveness of your SharePoint sites by reducing the overhead on the SQL Server instance.

❑ **Web front end and crawling**   By default, all WFEs are used to crawl content sources; that is, all WFEs do the actual crawling of content. If your Index server is dedicated, then you should enable it as the dedicated WFE for crawling content. *If you have other applications, such as ECS, then you should leave it at the default settings.*

> **Tip**   You can modify SharePoint Server search settings from the command line:
>
> ```
> stsadm -o osearch
> -action [list | start | stop]
> ```
>
> When using *start,* you can set the farm contact e-mail and service credentials:
>
> ```
> -role <index | Query | IndexQuery>
> -farmcontactemail <emailaddress>
> -farmperformancelevel <Reduced | PartlyReduced | Maximum>
> -farmserviceaccount <DOMAIN\username>
> -farmservicepassword <password>
> -defaultindexlocation <directory>
> -propogationlocation <directory>
> ```

■ **Windows SharePoint Services search**   Windows SharePoint Services search is only used for indexing Help files in SharePoint Server 2.0, and there is only one per SharePoint Server farm.

■ **Service account**   Using the same account as the SharePoint Server search service makes administration easier and is recommended.

■ **Content access account**   We recommend using a dedicated content access account with a broad scope, but with the least possible privileges. Be careful which account you use for Windows SharePoint Services content access, as it will be assigned Read permissions on every SharePoint item indexed. Do not use an administrator account or one that has Write abilities on any SharePoint account.

■ **Search database** Unless you have very specific requirements, always use the default SQL Server instance. Name the database something easy that differentiates it from other search databases. If you have multiple SharePoint products installed into this SQL instance, name your database to correlate with your SharePoint Server installation. Figure 2-13 shows an example of the Windows SharePoint Services search database configuration on a SharePoint Server server farm that hosts an enterprise portal.

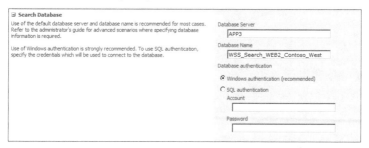

Figure 2-13 When configuring the Windows SharePoint Services search database in a SharePoint Server 2007 server farm, use an easily identifiable name.

■ **Windows SharePoint Services Web application** Verify that the Windows Share-Point Services Web application service is started or you will not see new Web applications in IIS Manager, nor will you be able to see new Web applications other than Central Administration.

Create the Server Farm's Shared Services SharePoint Server Shared Services are a group of highly specialized, CPU-intensive applications. Shared Services are much like your household utilities, such as electricity, gas, and water. They are required services, but you do not want to serve them from multiple locations because of the required processing and administrative overhead. Much of the SharePoint Server feature set will not function correctly without at least one Shared Services Provider (SSP) installed. For detailed instructions, refer to Chapter 8, "Deploying SharePoint Server Shared Services," on creating and administering SSPs.

Create a Web Application for a Site Collection When creating the first server in a SharePoint Server server farm it is always a good idea to create at least one Web application, hosting at least one site collection at the root (/). As shown in Figure 2-14, you begin the process in Application Management when creating a new Web application.

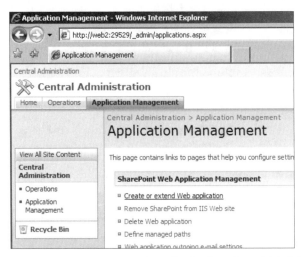

Figure 2-14   You create a Web Application from Central Administration > Application Management > Create Or Extend Web Application.

Select *Create Or Extend Web Application*. A Web application used to be referred to as a Virtual Server. However, with the advent of Microsoft Virtual Server R2, the naming conventions started to be confusing so they are now called *Web applications*. To create a Web application from Central Administration, browse to *http://centraladminurl:tcp#/ _admin/extendvs.aspx*. Remember to change the internal URL if installing with other than the default server name. To create a Web application, complete the following tasks:

- **Create IIS Web site**   Although you can use an IIS Web site created outside of Central Administration, doing so introduces the possibility of user error. For this reason, it is best to create the IIS Web site inside of Central Administration and make changes, such as assigning IP addresses, later.

    Caution   If you decide to use an existing IIS Web site, it must exist on *every* Web front-end server in the farm before continuing.

- **Assign description**   The description you entered also appears as the description in IIS Manager. Because backups, restores, and routine maintenance are performed using this name, choose a description that correctly defines the Web application.

- **Define the TCP port number**   For most implementations the TCP port number is 80. If you are not using host headers, you may need to define a random port and change it after creation of the Web application. Don't forget to change the internal URL address when modifying Web application port numbers.

Tip   To change the internal URL address, open Alternate Access Mappings from Operations > Global Configuration. Once there, select the internal URL you created during Web application creation. Simply modify the URL to match your IIS settings. Don't forget to add the DNS entry for the server!

- **Assign the host header (if required)**   Many organizations use host headers for Intranet web sites. If using host headers, enter the information here. Using host headers makes it easier to create Web applications, but can make it difficult to manage and secure Web application traffic.

- **Create the path for the IIS Web site**   It is recommended that you create a dedicated directory for all SharePoint products Web sites. This dedicated directory eases backup, restore, and general maintenance on IIS Web sites.

- **Choose an authentication provider**   Kerberos is the recommended security configuration for Intranet Web applications. Due to time synchronization issues and the need for clients to see the KDC (Key Distribution Center), many organizations need to enable NTLM for an Integrated Authentication approach in addition to Kerberos. You can enable both Kerberos *and* NTLM, but you must do so using Adsutil.vbs from the CLI.

- **Allow anonymous access**   Unless you plan to serve Web content to the Internet, do not select anonymous access. Anonymous access should only be used when creating a public-facing corporate Internet presence. An exception to this is the use of anonymous access for certain lists, such as blogs and wikis.

- **Enable Secure Sockets Layer (SSL)**   If your organization plans to collaborate via an Internet-facing Web application, enabling SSL is recommended for security.

- **Define a load-balanced URL**   If you are using Network Load Balancing (NLB), then you must define the URL for the VIP (Virtual IP). The URL should be predefined in DNS and should be the FQDN. For example, if your NLB VIP is 192.168.2.120 and the portal name is *portal.contoso.msft*, then the load-balanced URL is *http://portal.contoso.msft*. Don't forget to add the DNS Host Record in DNS Manager for your NLB VIP, or your Web application will fail.

- **Create an application pool**   As with a Windows SharePoint Services 3.0 application pool, you should create separate application pools when possible to isolate processes for security. Creating additional application pools does increase memory utilization, however, so verify that you have the available resources before creating multiple application pools. In any event, you should never use the application pool associated with Central Administration.

- **Create security account for application pool process**   You should create a domain account for every application pool you create, unless all Web applications share a common security boundary. The account used for the application pool must be an administrator on every WFE in the farm.

■ **Create content database**   Every Web application must have at least one associated content database to store content. This content database can be shared with several WFEs, giving you the ability to scale your farm to meet your requirements. Unless you have very large and busy Web applications, you should use the default database server. Be sure to name the database so it corresponds with the Web application, and always use Windows authentication.

Create the First Site Collection   When creating a Web application, you should always create a site collection in the root for ease of administration and to lessen the possibility of confusion if end users browse to the namespace root. When installing SharePoint Server, the most common site collection template for the root is a Publishing Collaboration Portal Template. Alternatively, for an Internet-facing portal, you would apply the Publishing Portal Template. Figure 2-15 shows the option to create a site collection after successful creation of a Web application.

Central Administration > Application Management > Create or Extend Web Application > Create

Application Created

The Windows SharePoint Services Web application has been created.

If this is the first time that you have used this application pool with a SharePoint Web application Services (IIS) Web site has been created on all servers. By default, no new SharePoint site coll To create a new site collection, go to the **Create Site Collection** page.

To finish creating the new IIS Web site, you must run "iisreset /noforce" on each Web server.

Figure 2-15   After successfully creating a Web Application, select the easily overlooked option to create the first site collection.

For the root site collection, it is advisable to assign a primary and secondary site administrator. Verify that you are creating the site collection in the root of the Web application, and give it a meaningful title and description as shown in Figure 2-16.

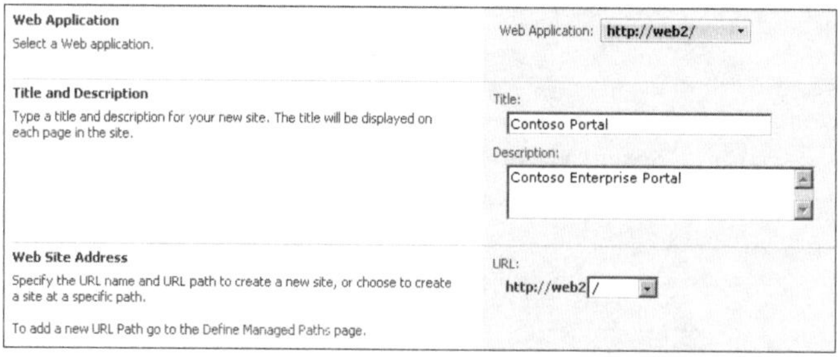

Web Application
Select a Web application.

Web Application: **http://web2/**

Title and Description
Type a title and description for your new site. The title will be displayed on each page in the site.

Title:
Contoso Portal

Description:
Contoso Enterprise Portal

Web Site Address
Specify the URL name and URL path to create a new site, or choose to create a site at a specific path.

To add a new URL Path go to the Define Managed Paths page.

URL:
http://web2 /

Figure 2-16   When you create Web applications, give meaningful names and descriptions to the root site collection.

Configure E-mail Settings   At a minimum, you should configure the outgoing e-mail settings in Central Administration > Operations > Topology and Service > Outgoing E-mail Settings. The outbound SMTP server that you define must allow mail relaying from all your WFE IP addresses.

SharePoint Server Databases Created During Installation

- **SharePoint configuration (config DB)**   The SharePoint configuration database hosts the majority of the configuration data in your farm, including site collection, content database, and Web application definitions. Name the config DB according to the primary function of the server farm; for example, SharePoint_Config_Sales, if sales is the primary function of the server farm.

- **Central administration content**   The Central Administration database is associated with the Web application you created during setup. Take note of the database name created, especially if you are hosting multiple SharePoint installations on this SQL Server instance. The database name looks like SharedPoint_AdminContent_guid.

- **Shared Services Provider content**   The SSP content database is named during installation. The Shared Services DB hosts all content required to render the *http://SSP_name/ssp/admin* site collection and associated applications. SSPs provide many services to a SharePoint Server farm, and these services are contained in this database as well:

  - ❑ User Profiles

  - ❑ Search configuration

  - ❑ Compiled Audiences

  - ❑ Excel Services settings

  - ❑ Business Data Catalog settings

- **Shared Services Search**   This is also called the SharePoint Server search database. The SSP search database hosts all of the metadata for crawled content, as well as a history and search logs. Remember that all indexed content is stored on the query servers' disk drive as an *.edb file.

- **Windows SharePoint Services search**   In SharePoint Server, the Windows SharePoint Services database only stores the associated metadata for the Help files. It is usually named *WSS_Content_Name*.

- **First Web application**   The Web application that you created at the end of setup created an associated database, which should always correlate to the name of the Web application. It should be in the form *WSS_Content_Portal*, if *Portal* is the name of the Web application.

Note   If you created a portal during setup, the portal usage information is stored in the Shared Services Provider content database, not the Portal Application content database.

IIS Web Applications Created During Installation

The following IIS Web applications are created during installation:

- Default Web site
- SharePoint Central Administration
- Office Server Web Extensions
- SharePoint Web Application (Portal)
- Shared Services Provider Web Application

An IIS installation that isolated all facets of SharePoint Server through multiple, dedicated application pools for administration might look like Figure 2-17.

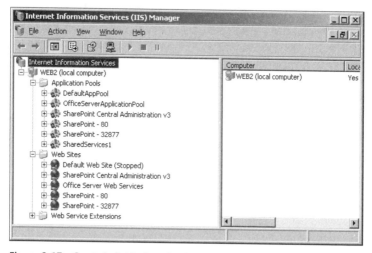

Figure 2-17   Create individual application pools in IIS Manager for a highly secured SharePoint Server installation.

Upgrading Windows SharePoint Services to SharePoint Server

Many organizations upgrade to SharePoint Server from Windows SharePoint Services for search and indexing, Shared Services, and expanded document and business process management. The upgrade process is very painless, and the majority of the decisions are already made for you, based on the type of Windows SharePoint Services 3.0 installation you have. If you have installed Windows SharePoint Services 3.0 with the

Basic option, you may not upgrade to SharePoint Server 2007 with the Advanced option. You also may not upgrade a Windows SharePoint Services 3.0 farm installation to a SharePoint Server 2007 Basic installation. You may only upgrade Windows SharePoint Services 3.0 to the equivalent installation type in SharePoint Server 2007. Figure 2-18 shows the Stand-alone option grayed out when upgrading a Windows SharePoint Services 3.0 Advanced installation to SharePoint Server 2007.

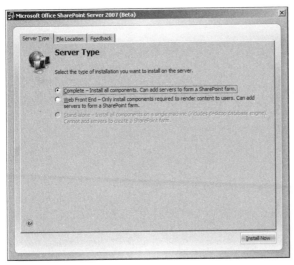

Figure 2-18   You can only upgrade Windows SharePoint Services 3.0 to the SharePoint Server equivalent installation type.

Upgrading from Windows SharePoint Services 3.0 to SharePoint Server 2007 is relatively simple. At the beginning of the installation, the wizard first requires a valid product key.

Important   The installation wizard must first be run on the Windows SharePoint Services 3.0 server hosting Central Administration.

During installation, you will be unable to change the database server, configuration database name, or the installation type to Active Directory account creation mode. Note that you will only upgrade the Central Administration and configuration database on the first server in the farm, but you must still upgrade the binaries on *all* servers in the farm. Not doing so will cause errors until they are successfully upgraded.

Important   If Central Administration is to be hosted on the local machine, choose the *Use This Machine To Host The Web Site* option. The default is not to use the local machine to host the Web site. If Central Administration was hosted on the local machine, choosing not to do so could potentially leave the farm without a Central Administration Web site.

After upgrading, your search server functionality will be extended and the service options will become more granular. If you were using multiple Windows SharePoint Services 3.0 search servers, you need to remove the indexes from all but one, and re-crawl all of your content to ensure a consistent search experience.

Part II
SharePoint Core Administration

Chapter 3
Central Administration

To successfully manage your Windows SharePoint Server 3.0 or Microsoft Office SharePoint Server 2007 installation, you need to become thoroughly familiar with the Central Administration interface. This chapter provides an overview of the Central Administration Web interface, with detailed information on the seemingly disconnected, yet essential administrative tasks that are not specifically covered elsewhere in this book. Many items, such as e-mail settings, logging, reporting, server topology, and document conversion settings, are defined and configured in Central Administration. This chapter is a methodical, easy-to-follow guide, with corresponding command-line tools for scripting and quick administration.

The Central Administration interface can be started from Start Menu > Administrative Tools > SharePoint 3.0 Central Administration. For SharePoint Server installations, the interface can also be started from Start Menu > Microsoft Office Server > SharePoint 3.0 Central Administration. Either choice takes you to the same Web page, and you may also bookmark the site in your browser for future reference. When you open Central Administration, you see three main areas of administration in tabbed format for easy navigation:

- **Home** The Home area, by default, shows all outstanding tasks and a quick launch menu for application and operations management. The Administrator task list contains all of the required tasks for a correctly installed server farm, and the tasks have direct links to the administration URL for a particular task. In large organizations that require input from multiple groups, it is possible and is, in fact, a good idea to create additional tasks here. In addition to the task list, a quick view of the Farm Topology and links to manage the services running in your farm are shown in the Home area. Central Administration can only be enabled on one server in your farm, and it is initially enabled on the first server in the farm. The topology view also allows you to remove servers from the farm (configuration database) when needed.

    Note The Recycle Bin in Central Administration is useful for list items, but does not retain deleted security items, such as groups and accounts.

- **Operations** The Operations tab allows you to navigate to the farm operations Web page containing the majority of the administrative tasks relating to the farm operations. Unlike previous versions, all farm-related tasks are at the same level in the hierarchy, making it easy to navigate. From the Operations screen you can manage your farm topology, services, security, logging, reporting, and disaster recovery.

- **Application Management**   The Application Management page provides a quick and easy interface to configure and manage Web applications and site collections. You can manage content databases, Web application e-mail integration, security, self-service site creation, workflow, and much more.

Server Farm Operations

The server farm operations interface is very similar in Windows SharePoint Services and SharePoint Server. Therefore, in this chapter we discuss server farm operations together, with the differences noted as required. As you progress through the many screens of SharePoint Products management, notice the numerous breadcrumb trail and navigation options that are provided.

After installing Windows SharePoint Services, you must enable several services for full functionality of your server farm. Choosing to disable these services can leave portions of your installation, such as Help, inoperable. Figure 3-1 shows the navigation to access these services.

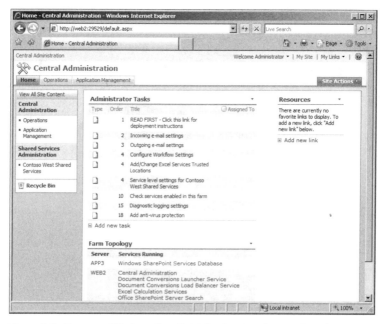

Figure 3-1   To access Windows SharePoint Services topology settings, browse from the Home tab and select a server to view under the Farm Topology Web Part.

The default services after installation are described below:

- **Central Administration**   The Central Administration service is started by default and is required to manage your installation. It is not required, however, for your server farm to serve Web content. Although it is possible to stop the Central Administration Service, *doing so removes any way to manage your installation.* If you need to stop Central Administration for specialized reasons, you must re-run the SharePoint Products and Technologies Configuration Wizard.

- **Windows SharePoint Services Help search**   This is the only Windows SharePoint Services service that requires configuration before it can be started. The configuration items were covered in Chapter 2.

- **Windows SharePoint Services incoming e-mail**   The incoming e-mail service is started by default and should only be stopped if you do not require inbound e-mails. Stopping it removes the ability for document libraries to be e-mail integrated, but might be required for security in some organizations.

- **Windows SharePoint Services Web application**   The Windows SharePoint Services Web application service is started by default, but can stop if errors are encountered during or after setup. Therefore, it is always wise to verify that this service is running before creating Web applications or modifying IIS settings.

Defining SharePoint Server 2007 Farm Services

After installing SharePoint Server, you must enable several services in Central Administration. You may access these services through either the Farm Topology Web Part in Home as shown in Figure 3-1 or through Central Administration > Operations > Topology And Services > Services On Server as shown in Figure 3-2.

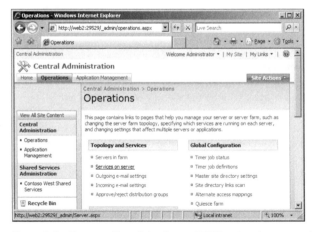

Figure 3-2   To access SharePoint Server 2007 Services, browse to the Services On Server option under Topology And Services.

Once in the Services On Server options page, you can change the current server as shown in Figure 3-3 or select the type of server you want to configure.

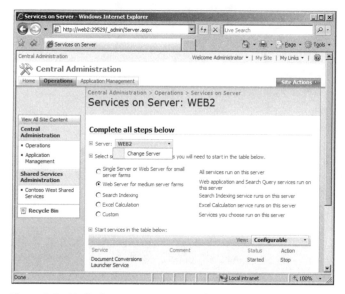

Figure 3-3   Verify that you are managing the correct server before starting or stopping services.

Always verify that you are working with the intended server before changing service status because modifying the incorrect server can cause service outages. Changing the radio button to another server role only modifies the suggested services view; it does not start or stop services.

There are several server roles in SharePoint Server 2007:

- **Single Server or Web Server**   When selecting the Single Server or Web Server server role, you are presented with all service options, except Central Administration. If you wish to run all Windows SharePoint Services services on this machine, except SQL Server, select this radio button and verify that all required services are running. Selecting too many services does not affect base functionality for users, but could affect performance when CPU-intensive roles like Excel Calculation Services are used extensively.

- **Web Server**   The Web Server role for medium server farms is identical to the Single Server option, with the exception of Excel Calculation Services. Although this service can be enabled on a Web front-end (WFE) server, it is usually placed on a dedicated server in medium and large server farms. To function correctly, the Web Server role must have Document Conversions, Document Conversions

Load Balancer (if required), Office SharePoint Server Search, Windows Share-Point Services Help Search, and Windows SharePoint Services Web Application configured and enabled.

- **Search Indexing**   A server servicing the Search Indexing role can be dedicated to provide CPU-intensive processes, like ranking relevancy, compiling indexes, and serving queries; it can enable uninhibited processing without affecting other services. Note that the query and index functions can be further isolated on separate hardware. Refer to Chapter 13, "Scaling Out to a SharePoint Technologies Server Farm," for more information on adding Index and Query servers.

- **Excel Calculation**   The Excel Calculation server role is intended for medium- to large-enterprise implementations that require dedicated Excel Calculation Services. If you enable Excel Calculation Services on an enterprise basis or plan to serve large spreadsheets, consider enabling a dedicated server for this function.

- **Custom**   From the Custom server role view, you have the ability to start and stop all services, including, most notably, the Central Administration service. *Never* turn off this service unless you promote another server in the farm to the Central Administration server. There is no way to turn it back on, so stopping the service removes your ability to manage your server farm. To re-enable this service, run the SharePoint Products and Technologies Configuration Wizard on any farm server, thereby re-associating that server with the Central Administration content database and configuration database.

> **Tip**   To see a list of all running Web and server services, run *stsadm.exe -o enumservices* from the command line.

E-mail Configuration

There are three places to configure your e-mail, two of which are here in farm operations management; the third is in Application Management and is covered in Application Management settings.

Outgoing E-mail Settings

Outgoing e-mail is required for alerts and other e-mail services to function properly. Configuring outgoing e-mail is a straightforward process. You must enter an outbound SMTP server and desired e-mail addresses. The only caveat is that the SMTP server selected for outbound e-mail must allow relaying from the WFE's primary IP address. SharePoint Products and Technologies do not allow for authenticated outbound e-mail.

Incoming E-mail Settings

Incoming e-mail allows documents to be sent directly to document libraries, tasks to be sent from e-mail to task lists, or calendar events to be sent to calendar lists. To implement correctly, incoming e-mail configuration requires several configuration steps. You must (1) make Active Directory Changes when using the Directory Management Service, (2) configure your WFE, and (3) correctly configure incoming e-mail in Central Administration.

> **Caution**   Verify that the server used for incoming e-mail never changes. The contact and list information created in Active Directory are set to a single server address (for instance, *doclib2@wfe01.contoso.msft*), not the farm. Therefore, if you lose that server in the farm, all incoming e-mail flow stops instantly. The incoming e-mail server has to be brought back up with the same name, the SMTP service needs to be installed, and related IIS settings made before incoming e-mail will start working again.

To enable incoming mail, do the following:

■ **Configure Active Directory**   If you wish to integrate with the Directory Management Service (DMS), you must create an Active Directory Organizational Unit (OU). The server farm account defined in setup should be delegated full control in this OU. Figure 3-4 shows an example of an OU created for the purpose of storing e-mail distribution lists and contacts. If you have enabled DMS, these distribution lists can be created automatically when implementing document libraries and lists. If you have not enabled DMS, you must create manually an entry for each mail-enabled document library and list you wish to receive e-mail. There is an option to set the e-mail address on creation of a document library or list. When not using DMS, you should document the address and add the e-mail address to your global address list.

Figure 3-4   You need to create an Organizational Unit in Active Directory for the Directory Management service to create contacts that correlate to Document Libraries and lists.

- **Configure Web front-end server**   Although it is possible to use any SMTP server, it is easier to install and use the Windows Server component SMTP (Simple Mail Transfer Protocol) service. If you choose to use a third-party SMTP service, you must follow the instructions for configuring in Advanced Mode, which are found later in this chapter. The SMTP service is responsible for receiving list-based e-mail. Don't forget to allow mail relaying in IIS Manager so you can accept mail from other SMTP servers.

   For detailed instructions on installing the SMTP service, browse to
   http://www.microsoft.com/technet/prodtechnol/WindowsServer2003/
   Library/IIS/e4cf06f5-9a36-474b-ba78-3f287a2b88f2.mspx.

- **Configure incoming e-mail in Central Administration**   To configure incoming e-mail, browse to Central Administration > Operations > Topology And Services > Incoming E-mail Settings. There are two settings when enabling sites to receive e-mail:

   ❏ **Automatic mode**   This mode configures your system automatically for inbound e-mail. It is the preferred method and should only be changed when you are using a service other than the Windows Server SMTP service to receive incoming e-mail.

   ❏ **Advanced mode**   This mode requires that you specify a drop folder that inbound e-mail will populate. The *SPTimer* will look every 30 seconds for e-mails in that folder and, when found, will send them to the associated Document Library or list. When using third-party e-mail products, refer to their documentation for e-mail drop folders. The account used for the *SPTimer* service needs NTFS *modify* permissions on the drop folder.

- **Configure Directory Management Service**   To enable the automatic creation of contacts in Active Directory for your document libraries and lists, as well as to create SharePoint distribution lists, you must configure the Directory Management Service. This service defines the connection to your Active Directory, allowing distribution lists and contacts to be created automatically in the OU that you specified previously. This service allows users to find these e-mail-enabled Document Libraries and lists in the global address book (GAL). If you do not enable the Directory Management Service, users will be unable to find the e-mail-enabled lists in the GAL unless you add them manually.

   Tip   You can synchronize entire Web applications or individual sites with Active Directory using *stsadm -o refreshdms -url <web application>* or *stsadm -o refreshsitedms -url <web application/path/sitecollection>*

When choosing to use the local server farm for the Directory Management Service, you must enter the OU specified earlier. For the example *SharePointOU*, the correct Active Directory container entry would be *OU=SharePointOU,*

DC=Contoso,DC=msft. Although the SMTP mail server entry for incoming mail should be populated automatically, the entry should be the fully qualified domain name (FQDN) for this machine. Figure 3-5 shows an example of a configuration.

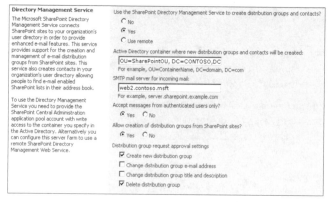

Figure 3-5 Carefully enter the location for the OU to contain distribution lists and contacts, and always use the FQDN for the incoming mail SMTP server.

The following choices must also be made, but unless you are in a highly secure environment, the defaults are usually sufficient.

- **Accept Messages From Authenticated Users Only?** The default is Yes. If you wish to accept messages from nontrusted authentication domains, you may need to change this default.

- **Allow Creation Of Distribution Groups From SharePoint Sites?** The default is Yes. Choosing No disables the creation of distribution lists for e-mail-enabled lists.

- **Distribution Group Request Approval Settings** By default, Create New and Delete Distribution Group are selected. Consider carefully whether to select the *change* option, because selecting that causes any previous e-mails sent on the distributions list to bounce when replied to.

- **Incoming E-mail Server Display Address** You may change the address of the domain displayed to make it friendlier to your users or to conform to DNS and firewall policies.

- **Safe E-mail Servers** By default, mail is accepted from all e-mail servers. To prevent e-mail from other sources from being sent directly to document libraries and lists, you should specify your primary e-mail server as the only safe server. For example, if you want all mail routed through your Exchange Server, you may only want to specify your Exchange Server host as a safe server.

Managing Service Accounts

New in Windows SharePoint Services and SharePoint Server 2007 is the ability to change service and application pool credentials from Central Administration. Exceptions are services managed directly from a dedicated interface, such as Windows SharePoint Search and SharePoint Server Search; these service accounts are managed directly from their respective interfaces. Both of these services are modified by accessing the corresponding hyperlink from Central Administration > Operations > Services On Server. By default, you can manage three Windows Service Accounts from Service Account management:

1. Document Conversions Launcher Service

2. Document Conversions Launcher Load Balancer Service

3. Single Sign-on Service

As a general rule, these services run as the server farm account. They can be changed if you are in an environment that requires frequent password changes or if you develop a customized single sign-on service with specific authentication requirements.

You can also define the username and password for your IIS web application pools. Although it can be done from the IIS Manager snap-in, Central Administration provides a centralized interface on which to make changes. You first need to select a Web service and then the application pool identity you wish to modify. Figure 3-6 shows an example of selecting a Web application pool for modification.

Figure 3-6   To change an application pool identity, first select a Web service and then the desired application pool.

After selecting an application pool identity to manage, you have two choices:

1. *Predefined* defaults are *Network Service* and *Local*. With the exception of Basic or Stand-alone installations, you should use dedicated accounts for Web application pool identities.

2. *Configurable* accounts should have proper access to SQL Server databases and Windows Server services. These permissions were assigned automatically during installation. Changing these identities to accounts not defined during installation can cause service failure. For detailed information on required security account permissions, see Chapter 2.

> **Tip**   You can modify the server farm account using *stsadm -o updatefarmcredentials -identitytype <configurableid | networkservice> -userlogin <domain\name> -password <password>*. You must manually perform an *IISreset* on all members of the farm to update credential caches.

Enabling Information Rights Management

SharePoint Products and Technologies can be integrated with Windows Rights Management Services (RMS). The optional use of an RMS server can restrict the access and distribution of sensitive documents by attaching a security policy, thus limiting the availability of the content to others. RMS integrates with Microsoft Office, Windows SharePoint Services, SharePoint Server, and Exchange Server. RMS, in conjunction with Windows SharePoint Services and SharePoint Server, can create a seamless transition from a client working in a Microsoft Office application to creating a secure workplace in a SharePoint site collection. When a user creates a document workspace in a site collection, the users and their associated rights defined in the document's security policy are transferred to the document workspace created. To configure Information Rights Management correctly, you must do the following:

- Install the RMS Client, with at least SP2, on every Web front-end server (WFE) in your server farm.

- Decide if you will connect to your default RMS server or if you will use an RMS server in another location. Most organizations use the default RMS server specified in Active Directory.

Updating the Farm Administrator's Group

Use caution when adding users to the Farm Administrator's group. Users added to this group can access Central Administration and disable services, causing widespread service outages. When you open the People and Groups interface, you see that the server administrator, server administrator group, and the farm account are administrators. You can add local users and groups or preferably add Active Directory users and groups.

> **Important**   If you decide to use local accounts for Administrative access, be sure to create these accounts on each server in your farm.

The safest course of action is to add only administrators to this group, giving them Full Control (Farm Administrators) access. *Never* modify the default Farm Administrator's group settings. Because Central Administration is simply a specialized site collection, it is possible to granularly control access, but it should be reserved for Site Designers or a custom group.

Note   Central Administration is a site collection and can therefore be modified to extend the interface with your implementation-specific software, or customized to meet your organization's design requirements. Always have a backup of the server farm before modifying the Central Administration site collection.

It might also be used for restricted Helpdesk access or temporary personnel. Figure 3-7 shows the default view when adding users to the Farm Administrator's group.

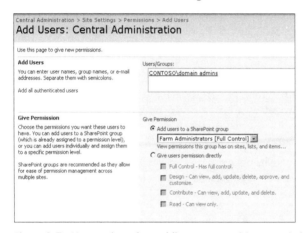

Figure 3-7   Use caution when adding or customizing permissions for server Farm Administrators.

Tip   You can use the CTRL+K combination to verify user and group items.

Understanding Timer Jobs

The Windows SharePoint Services timer, SPTimerV3 (Owstimer.exe), is responsible for scheduling such tasks as notifications, alerts, and content deployment. It is a Windows SharePoint Services application and should always be running on every server in the farm. It should use the server farm account for service log on, with local server administrator privileges. The following is a sample of critical events that are controlled by SPTimerV3:

- Administration Service Timer Job
- Bulk Workflow Processing
- Customer Experience Improvement Program (CEIP) Data Collection
- Logging And Usage Analysis
- Immediate Alerting

- Recycle Bin
- Content Delivery
- Configuration Database Refresh
- Dead Site Deletion
- Disk Quota Notifications
- Expiration Policies (SharePoint Server)
- Indexing Schedules (SharePoint Server)
- Profiles Import (SharePoint Server)
- Record Processing (SharePoint Server)
- Backup And Restore Jobs
- Workflow Processing

As you can see from this list, SPTimerV3 is crucial to the well-being of your farm. In the event of farm configuration replication errors or other unexplained errors, you should check the SPTimerV3 service first. Verify that the service is running and is using the correct credentials with proper permissions and that the service account is not locked out.

You can access the status and definitions of timer jobs from Central Administration > Operations > Global Configuration. You should select Timer Job Definitions to disable or delete timer jobs, as shown in Figure 3-8.

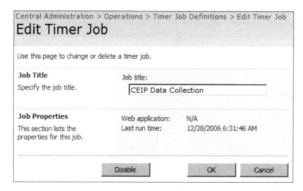

Figure 3-8 You can view and modify current timer job definitions from Central Administration > Operations > Global Settings > Timer Job Definitions.

Alternate Access Mappings

Alternate Access Mappings (AAMs) provide a way to change your Web application URLs, configure Network Load Balanced Web applications, and add additional URLs for alternative access.. For example, if you served content from a single Web application via multiple host headers for security, you would need to map the additional host headers with alternate access URLs. Figure 3-9 shows an example of the Web application *http://portal.contoso.msft* being served securely and externally as *https://external.contoso.msft*.

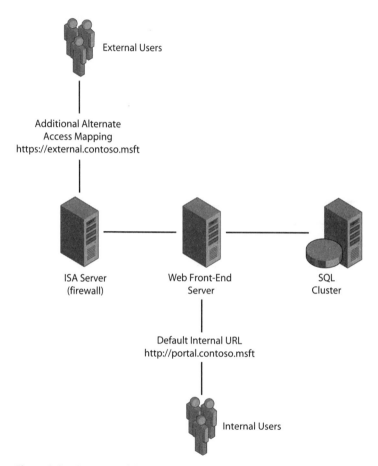

External Users

Additional Alternate
Access Mapping
https://external.contoso.msft

ISA Server   Web Front-End   SQL
(firewall)   Server   Cluster

Default Internal URL
http://portal.contoso.msft

Internal Users

Figure 3-9   You must add an alternate access mapping for each additional URL that you configure for a Web application.

In this example, the internal URL would already exist, but you must add an alternate access mapping for the external URL. If you did not add the alternate access URL, the host field returned in an external user's browser would be incorrect. Therefore, an external user would be returned *http://portal.contoso.msft,* when in fact the user should be returned *https://external.contoso.msft.* In addition, the embedded URLS in alert e-mails would be sent incorrectly.

Caution Absolute URLs (URLs that are hard coded on a Web page or document) cannot be mapped.

There are three choices when modifying AAMs:

■ **Edit Public URLs** You can edit public URLs from the Alternate Access Mapping page, as shown in Figure 3-10. By default, there is no AAM collection selected; this feature is for your protection.

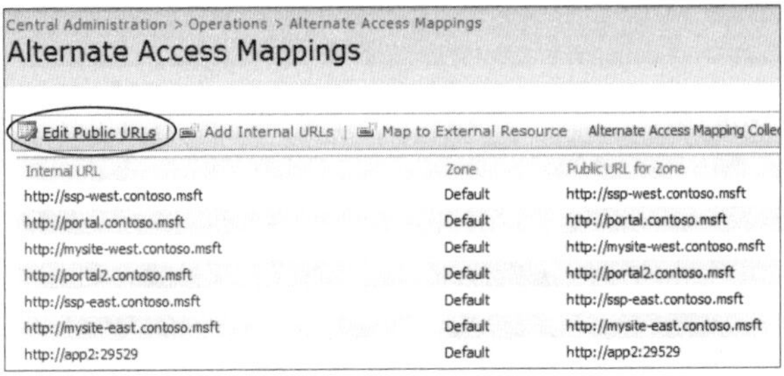

Central Administration > Operations > Alternate Access Mappings

Alternate Access Mappings

| Edit Public URLs | Add Internal URLs | Map to External Resource | Alternate Access Mapping Colle |

Internal URL	Zone	Public URL for Zone
http://ssp-west.contoso.msft	Default	http://ssp-west.contoso.msft
http://portal.contoso.msft	Default	http://portal.contoso.msft
http://mysite-west.contoso.msft	Default	http://mysite-west.contoso.msft
http://portal2.contoso.msft	Default	http://portal2.contoso.msft
http://ssp-east.contoso.msft	Default	http://ssp-east.contoso.msft
http://mysite-east.contoso.msft	Default	http://mysite-east.contoso.msft
http://app2:29529	Default	http://app2:29529

Figure 3-10 To add public URLs for a Web application, choose Edit Public URLs in the Alternate Access Mappings management interface.

After selecting a collection, you have several options for defining the Public URLs. Public URLs fill in the URI (Uniform Resource Identifier) and Authority to correspond with the originating URL from the browser. For example, if a user inputs *http://portal.contoso.msft,* that will be the return address in the browser. Conversely, if a user inputs *https://external.contoso.msft* in the browser, he or she will be directed to that URL. If the user enters a URL that does not exist as an alternate access mapping, the request will fail. For example, if you are using two different IIS virtual servers to publish the same content database(s), and your default internal URL is *http://portal* and your Extranet URL is *https://external.contoso.msft,* then you would configure alternate access URLs as follows:

❑ Default internal URL is *http://portal.contoso.msft.*

❑ Either Internet, Extranet, or Custom URL should be *https://portal.contoso.msft.*

When users visit *http://portal,* they are assumed to be on the internal network and will be returned content to *http://portal.contoso.msft.* Conversely, if they visit *https://portal.contoso.msft,* it is assumed that they are coming from an external network and are returned to *https://portal.contoso.msft* as the correct address.

This being the case, your security should not rely on AAM and zones because they merely supplement your firewall and router policies. Figure 3-11 shows the configuration for the previously defined scenario.

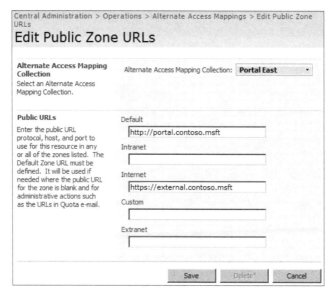

Figure 3-11   You must define an alternate access mapping for every URL to which a Web application will serve content.

■ **Edit Default Internal URL/Add Internal URL**   To edit the default URL, select Add Internal URL, select the AAM collection, and change the URL protocol, host, and port, but do not change the zone. Alternatively, you can simply select the hyperlink of the Web application to reach the same interface. Figure 3-12 shows the hyperlinked selection of an internal URL to edit.

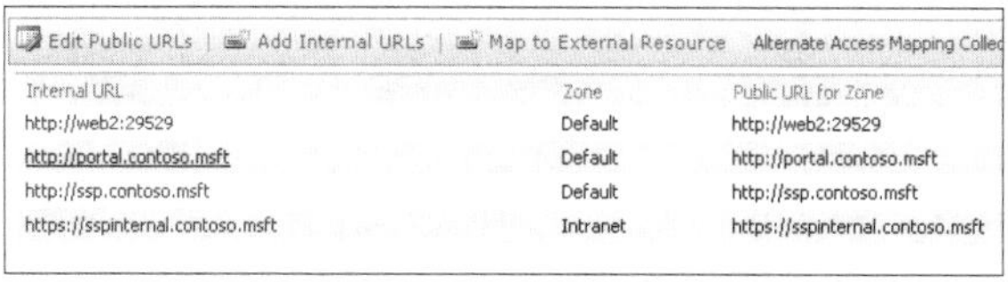

Internal URL	Zone	Public URL for Zone
http://web2:29529	Default	http://web2:29529
http://portal.contoso.msft	Default	http://portal.contoso.msft
http://ssp.contoso.msft	Default	http://ssp.contoso.msft
https://sspinternal.contoso.msft	Intranet	https://sspinternal.contoso.msft

Edit Public URLs | Add Internal URLs | Map to External Resource   Alternate Access Mapping Colle

Figure 3-12   To edit the default internal URL, simply select the hyperlink of the Web application to modify.

■ **Map To External Resources** In addition to mapping server farm URLs, you may also map URLs to external resources. Most installations do not use this feature, but it can be enabled to allow access, through SharePoint, to other IIS Web applications.

> **Tip** You may see all alternate domain mappings at the command prompt by running *stsadm -o enumalternatedomains*.

Quiesce Farm

Quiesce Farm is a new feature in this version that allows a graceful method to disallow new connections to the entire farm, without disrupting active sessions. You may define the amount of time to fully quiesce the farm, but be aware that any sessions still open at the end of that time period will be forcibly disconnected. Using the Quiesce Farm feature is useful for routine maintenance or disaster recovery of a farm. You may still back up, restore, and configure application servers and many other items when a farm is in the quiesced state. Note that the time given to be fully quiesced is in *UTC* (Coordinated Universal Time), and probably not the time zone your server is in. It will continue to show Stop Quiescing until you manually stop.

> **Tip** You may quiesce the farm from the command line by running *stsadm -o quiescefarm -maxduration <duration in minutes>* and see quiesced status by *stsadm -o quiescefarmstatus*. Note that *maxduration* refers to the maximum amount of time to continue connections, not the amount of time to remain quiesced. To unquiesce a farm, run *stsadm -o unquiescefarm*.

The other options in Central Administration > Operations are covered in their respective chapters. Please refer to the index to find their configuration.

Application Management

The third major grouping of administrative tasks is Application Management. This grouping allows you to quickly navigate to configuring and managing Web applications, site collections, shared services, and other application-specific functions.

Creating Web Applications

Creating Web applications is one of the most basic and fundamental aspects of administering SharePoint products. A Web application provides the interface that users interact with from their browsers. Web applications are a combination of IIS virtual servers, associated content databases, and entries for both in the configuration database. Creating a Web application is covered in detail in Chapter 2, so refer there for detailed information on creating a Web application.

Extending Web applications is an interesting feature that is used by those wishing to serve the *same* content databases via multiple Web applications (IIS virtual servers). An example would be an organization wishing to serve content internally via *http://portal* using Windows Integrated Authentication, but serving the same content externally via *https://portal.contoso.msft* using Forms Authentication over the Secure Sockets layer (SSL) for security. You must already have a Web application created and functional before you can extend it. Then, extend a Web application from Central Administration > Application Management > SharePoint Web Application Management > Create Or Extend Web Application > Extend An Existing Web Application. The following items must be configured to extend a Web application:

- **Web Application To Extend**   By default, there is no Web application selected to extend. You must select via the drop-down list box, as shown in Figure 3-13.

Figure 3-13 shows the following:

Central Administration > Application Management > Create or Extend Web Application > Extend Web Application to Another IIS Web Site

Extend Web Application to Another IIS Web Site

Use this page to extend a web application onto another IIS Web Site. This allows you to serve the same content on another port or to a different audience. Learn about creating or extending Web applications.

Web Application
Select a Web application.

Web Application: No selection

Change Web Application

Figure 3-13   Be sure to select the correct Web application from the drop-down menu.

- **Define IIS Web Site**   You have the ability to create an IIS virtual server beforehand, but as in creating a Web application, it is best to create one from Central Administration and make any necessary changes later. Give this site a meaningful description, which makes administration in IIS Manager much easier.

   Note   If you are using host headers, the description changes automatically to the host header + TCP port number.

   If you are not using host headers, leave the port alone for now and change it later in IIS Manager. If you are using host headers, you can change the port to the final configuration now. Use the directory defined during deployment for your path.

   Tip   If you plan to assign IP addresses to Web applications, it is a good idea to enter the host header information now and change the port to 80. You can always add additional host headers as required in IIS Manager. This simplifies the process of adding additional WFE servers to the farm.

- **Configure Security**   Close attention should be given to the security configuration because this is usually the primary reason for extending a Web site. If using Kerberos, don't forget to register the Service Principal Name (SPN) for the original Web application pool identity. Refer to Chapter 7, "Implementing Security for SharePoint Products," for more information on using Kerberos.

> **Caution**   You are not given the option to create another Web application pool. Doing so would break the functionality of the Web application extension. Therefore, *never* change the application pool of an extended site in IIS Manager.

If extending to leverage the security of SSL, be sure to select the option here. Although it can be changed later, it is easier to do it now. Note that you must configure a certificate for this site in IIS Manager after creation before it can successfully serve content via SSL.

> **Note**   SSL certificates and assigned IP addresses are not stored in the configuration database. If you must restore a WFE server for any reason, you will need to reconfigure the Web applications using SSL or assigned IPs. Alternatively, you can restore the IIS Metabase from the last backup.

- **Load Balanced URL**   The Load Balanced URL setting doesn't mean exactly what it says. The URL can be set to a previously defined DNS host name for this Web application, or it can be set to a DNS host name for an NLB IP address. To complete, you must also choose the zone associated with this extended Web application.

To unextend a virtual server in IIS, do so from Central Administration > Application Management > SharePoint Web Application Management > Remove SharePoint From IIS Web Site. Exercise caution when unextending (deleting) a Web application, especially when selecting the Web application to remove. If you need to modify any other settings in IIS, refer to Chapter 2 for details on configuring IIS virtual servers in conjunction with SharePoint products.

Defining Managed Paths

If you have a medium-scale or larger implementation, give serious consideration to extending the default set of managed paths. A managed path is defined as the path in the Uniform Resource Identifier (URI) that is managed by SharePoint products. As an example, *sites* is the managed path in *http://portal.contoso.msft/sites/madison*. Managed paths cannot be limited for use by specific security groups, nor can they be targeted directly with audiences. They are simply a way to organize a large quantity of site collections. When using managed paths, you can have two site collections with the same name. For example, *http://portal.contoso.com/HR/Meetings* and *http://portal.contoso.com/Sales/Meetings*.

When adding a new path, you have the option either to include *only* that path (explicit inclusion) or to specify that path and all subordinate paths (wildcard inclusion). If the path *http://portal.contoso.msft/sites* was specified as an explicit inclusion, content could still be served from the WFE file system at *http://portal.contoso.msft/sites/path*. When creating an explicit inclusion managed path, you can then create a single site collection in the root of that path. If *http://portal.contoso.msft/sites* was specified as a wildcard inclusion, multiple named site collections could be created *under* that path.

Configuring Web Application Outgoing E-mail Settings

The settings for outgoing e-mails are copied from the settings previously defined in Central Administration > Operations > Topology And Services > Outgoing E-Mail Settings. Microsoft has given you the ability to modify these default settings on a per-Web application basis. This feature is useful when segregating e-mails based on workflows or when unique language character sets are required for a given Web application. Always verify that you are in the correct Web application before making changes.

Tip   You can configure Web application outbound e-mail using *stsadm -o email -outsmtpserver <SMTP Server> -fromaddress from@example.msft -replytoaddress <replytoaddress@example.msft> -codepage <codepage> -url <web application URL>.*

Managing Content Databases

Content databases contain all site collection content, including most customization performed in the browser or SharePoint Designer. By default, a single content database is created per Web application. You should create additional content databases to limit the size of your content databases. For example, if your site collection quota is 10 GB and you want to limit your content database size to 100 GB, you would need to create a content database for every ten site collections in the associated Web application. You add additional databases via the Manage Content Databases interface. From here, you can add or manage content databases, as well as view information about a content database, as shown in Figure 3-14.

Important   A database status of *stopped* means the database is not available for new site collection creation. It does not mean the database is down.

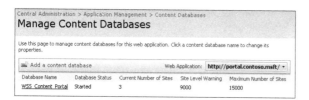

Figure 3-14   To edit the configuration of a content database, single-click the hyperlinked database name.

There are four primary properties that can be modified on a content database:

- **Database information**   The database information section shows the database server name, database name, and status. Changing the status to Offline prevents new site collections from being created in that content database. It also shows the type of authentication that was defined during the associated Web application creation when it is the first content database, or during content database creation for subsequent databases.

- **Database Capacity Settings** You should make an educated decision about the Number Of Sites Before A Warning Event Is Generated and Maximum Number Of Sites That Can Be Created In This Database. For example, if you do not want your content databases to be larger than 100 GB and your site quotas are set to 1 GB, then you need to change the maximum number of sites to 100. The default settings are almost always too high and should be changed.

  > **Note** To force new site collections into a new content database, you can change the Database Status to Offline. Then you must create an additional content database or new site creation will fail.

- **Search Server** It is important to remember that Search Servers are associated with *content databases* and not *Web applications*. Unless you have extremely unusual requirements, you will use the same search server for all content databases.

- **Remove Content Database** There is almost never a reason to remove a content database without removing the entire Web application. But, you might do so when taking sensitive data offline immediately, without losing the data, or re-associating a content database with a new Web application. When removing a content database, all data remain in the database and can be attached to another Web application for access. Re-associating content databases to another Web application should only be performed after thorough testing in a lab.

SharePoint Server Document Conversion

SharePoint Server includes four document converters that allow your users to write content in a format they are familiar with, such as Microsoft Word, and convert those documents to Web pages:

- InfoPath Forms to Web page
- Word Document to Web page (docx)
- Word Document with macros to Web page (docm)
- XML to Web page

The bulk of document conversion configuration is covered in Chapter 10, "Configuring Office SharePoint Server Enterprise Content Management," but some configuration is required in Central Administration. The basics to enable functionality are configured in Central Administration > Application Management > External Service Connections > Document Conversions as follows:

- **Web application** Document Conversion must be configured for each Web application; it is not a farm-wide setting. Always verify the current Web application before continuing.

- **Enable document conversions**   By default, a document conversion is disabled for all Web applications. You must enable document conversions for every Web application desired.

- **Load Balancer server**   If you defined a Document Conversions Load Balancer server during deployment, it will be available in the drop-down menu, as shown in Figure 3-15.

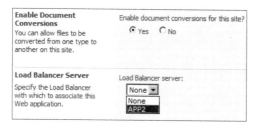

Figure 3-15   If you wish to select a load balancer server, choose it from the drop-down menu.

- **Conversion schedule**   The conversion schedule is set to every minute, but should be tuned according to your specific requirements. Large implementations in which many conversions occur simultaneously should have a reduced schedule or should dedicate hardware for the task. If the Owstimer.exe service consumes a large amount of CPU utilization, check your logs for Document Conversion transactions or errors and adjust accordingly.

- **Converter settings**   You may configure the converter settings on all installed converters. You can enable or disable converter types per server and change the performance settings for each.

Workflow Settings

Workflows are enabled by default for all Web applications. You can modify the global workflow settings from the Workflow Settings option in Central Administration. In the Workflow Settings management interface you can enable or disable workflows for a Web application, and modify task notifications. There are two types of workflow task notifications:

- **Alert Internal Users Who Do Not Have Site Access**   This notification is enabled by default and alerts users who do not have site access permissions when they are assigned a workflow task. The users can then follow the embedded hyperlink e-mailed to them and request permission to access the site. Selecting No only allows workflow tasks to be assigned to users who have prior permission to participate in a given workflow.

- **Allow External Users To Participate In Workflow**   You can also have documents e-mailed to external participants in a workflow. This feature is disabled by default, and if security is paramount in your organization it should be left disabled.

If you are looking for a Central Administration topic not found in this chapter, it is covered in depth in its respective chapter. Please refer to the index to find more information on the configuration options.

Chapter 4

Creating Site Collections

Creating site collections is one of the basic functions performed by SharePoint administrators and users. The ease with which end users can create and customize new sites in SharePoint Products and Technologies is a key to its success and offers a major advantage over building Web sites from scratch. This chapter explores the detailed administration of site collections, particularly the different ways in which they can be created and managed.

Site Creation Modes

When planning a medium- or large-scale deployment, two critical decisions that a SharePoint administrator must make are how and by whom new sites will be created. If an administrator does not give adequate thought to these issues, a SharePoint farm can quickly become unmanageable. Because a new site collection can be provisioned so easily, it is essential to have a well-thought-out strategy to prevent an explosion of sites that have no real organizational hierarchy or management capability. There are two natively supported site creation modes: administratively controlled site creation and self-service site creation. This section clarifies the differences between the two and provides guidance in choosing one or a combination of both to form the basis of your site creation strategy.

Determining Which Mode to Use

Many factors, such as your farm architecture and user base, influence which site creation mode you should use. In the administratively controlled site creation mode, only Farm Administrators can create new site collections because creation is performed exclusively through Central Administration. In an environment in which site collection creation must be controlled tightly, it is usually preferable to limit this ability to Farm Administrators. Power Users (or anyone with Full Control or Hierarchy Manager permissions) can still create subsites directly from parent sites, without needing access to Central Administration. However, if certain users need the ability to create site collections, possibly for informal or temporary use, you can enable self-service site creation. This mode allows specified users to create their own site collections in the Sites directory. Remember that site creation mode is on a per-Web application basis, so you may mix and match modes as required.

One other consideration in determining how sites should be created is the handling of permissions. Site collection permissions must be specified individually, whereas subsites can inherit permissions from a parent. Self-service site creation allows the management of permissions to be delegated to the content owner. The user who creates the site collection is given access by default and can modify the permissions to grant access to other users or groups. Some organizations object to this site creation mode because of the potential for unused and redundant sites to accumulate. However, SharePoint Products and Technologies provide a means of automatically cleaning up these sites through quotas and site use confirmation settings, which are discussed in more detail in the next section.

Enabling Self-Service Site Creation

To enable self-service site creation for a particular Web application, there must be a site already created at the root of the Web application. Otherwise, you will receive an error message when attempting to enable self-service site creation. If there is an Announcements list in the root site, it will get populated with an announcement that links to the URL at which new sites can be created.

1. Open SharePoint Central Administration and go to the Application Management tab.

2. Under the Application Security section, select *Self-Service* site management.

3. Choose the Web application in which you want to enable self-service site creation. Because self-service site creation is enabled at the Web application level, you must specify which Web application's settings you wish to change.

4. Select the option button to enable self-service site creation for the chosen Web application.

5. (Optional) Require that users specify an additional contact name when creating a site by selecting the Require Secondary Contact box. This is useful because if one owner leaves the organization there is still someone who can perform administrative tasks without involving the farm administrator.

6. Click OK to save your settings.

Site Use Confirmation and Deletion

Site use confirmation and deletion provide a method of cleaning up the content database by deleting sites within a Web application that are unused and are no longer needed. When notifications are turned on, site owners automatically receive e-mails regarding sites that have been unused for a specified number of days. They can then confirm that their site collection is still in use or allow it to be deleted if automatic deletion is enabled.

Enabling Site Use Confirmation and Deletion

1. Open SharePoint 3.0 Central Administration and click the Application Management tab.

2. In the SharePoint Site Management section, choose the link to manage site use confirmation and deletion.

3. Because it is enabled on a Web application basis, you must choose a Web application from the drop-down list.

4. Select the box to enable e-mail alerts to owners of unused site collections.

5. Set the notification threshold. The default is 90 days.

6. Choose the frequency for sites to be checked automatically and the time at which to run the checks.

7. (Optional) Check the box to delete the site collection automatically after a specified number of alerts, and enter the number of alerts allowed.

8. Click OK.

Caution   Although the user interface says *unused* site collections, it actually means *all* site collections. If you decide to use this feature, you should consider modifying the e-mail alert and removing the deletion URL.

Creating Site Collections

A *site collection* is a grouping of sites that includes a top-level site and all subsites. Subsites are created from the top-level site through the Site Actions menu and are generally related to the top-level site, as well as to each other. Subsites can inherit their security settings and navigational scheme from their parent, or they can define their own.

Creating a Site Collection from Central Administration

1. Open SharePoint Central Administration.

2. Click on the Application Management Tab.

3. Under the SharePoint Site Management section, select *Create Site Collection*.

4. Choose the Web application in which the site collection will be created from the drop-down list as shown in Figure 4-1.

Figure 4-1   Verify that you are creating the site collection in the correct Web application before continuing.

5. Specify the Title and Description for the site (see Figure 4-2).

6. Specify the URL path to the new site.

7. Choose the template to use for site creation. The template list consists of all installed site templates and site definitions, including those installed with Share-Point Services and any custom templates that have been installed.

8. Specify the Primary Site Collection Administrator.

9. (Optional) Specify the Secondary Site Collection Administrator.

10. Specify Site Quota for the site.

11. Click OK to create the site.

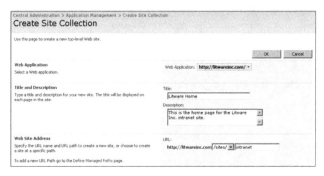

Figure 4-2 Always give your site the shortest name possible because of the 254-character URL limit.

Creating a Site Collection Through the Self-Service URL

1. When an administrator enables self-service site creation, an announcement is added to the top-level site in the site collection with a link to the self-service URL. Find this announcement and click the link for creating a new Web site or, if you cannot find the announcement, contact your administrator for the self-service URL.

2. On the New SharePoint Site page, specify a Title and (optionally) a Description for the new site.

3. Specify the URL for the new site. The first part of the URL has been set by the administrator.

4. Select the site template from which to create the new site.

5. Click Create.

6. The Set Up Groups for this Site page appears, and you can set up the groups that will have access to the site. You can either add users to existing groups or add new ones.

> **Tip** Often, high-profile sites, such as CEO or CIO sites, benefit from the disaster-recovery advantages of being in a standalone content database. If you need a site collection to be in its own content database, you can create a new site collection from the command line using Stsadm.exe.

```
stsadm -o createsiteinnewdb stsadm.exe -o createsiteinnewdb
-url <url> -owneremail <someone@example.com>
```

If needed, you may also add the following optional flags:

```
-ownerlogin <DOMAIN\name> -ownername <display name>
-secondaryemail someone@example.com> -secondarylogin
<DOMAIN\name> -secondaryname <display name> -lcid <language>
-sitetemplate <site template> -title <site title>
-description <site description> -hostheaderwebapplicationurl
<web application url> -quota <quota template> -databaseuser
<database username> -databasepassword <database password>
-databaseserver <database server name> -databasename
<database name>
```

Be aware that any required information not supplied, such as the template, will be asked for on the first visit by an administrator. The site collection will not work for an ordinary user until an administrator supplies the missing information.

Site Collection Quotas and Locks

Site quotas allow an administrator to specify the storage limit for sites in a site collection, as well as the site size that will trigger an e-mail alert. To modify site quota settings for a site collection perform the following steps:

1. Open SharePoint Central Administration and go to the Application Management tab.

2. Under the SharePoint Site Management section, choose Site Collection Quotas and Locks.

3. Choose the desired site collection from the drop-down list.

4. In the Site Quota Information section, select the default quota template from the drop-down list, and check the box if you wish to override the storage limit specified in the quota template. The storage limit must be specified in megabytes.

5. If you wish to override the alert setting of the quota template, check the corresponding box and specify the size that should trigger an e-mail alert to be sent to the site administrator.

Tip   You can set a site lock from the command line by executing:
```
stsadm -o setsitelock -url <site collection url> -lock
<none | noadditions | readonly | noaccess>
```

Quota Template Management

Quota templates are created at the farm level; therefore any new templates are available across the entire farm. However, because they are applied at the Web application level, all site collections in a Web application share the same quota template, unless it is overridden for an individual site. This multitiered approach allows for a great amount of flexibility in the management of quota templates.

Creating a New Quota Template

1. Open SharePoint Central Administration and click the Application Management tab.

2. In the SharePoint Site Management section, choose Quota Templates (see Figure 4-3).

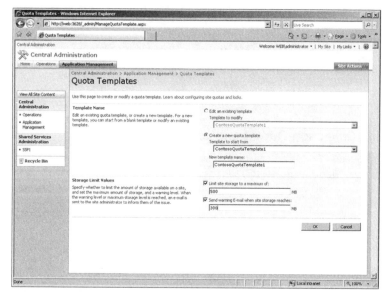

Figure 4-3   When creating a new quota template, choose a name that is easily identified with the function.

3. If there are existing templates, you are given the option to edit one of these templates. Use caution when doing so because the changes will affect all sites already using this template. You should usually select the option to create a new template.

4. If there are existing templates, you can use one as a starting point for your new template. If you choose an existing template in the drop-down list, the storage limit and warning values are filled in according to the chosen template. If there is an existing template that is similar to the one you want to create, choose it; otherwise choose to start from a new blank template.

5. Specify a template name.

6. Specify the storage limit and warning values. Be sure to check the box beside each to include these settings in the new template.

7. Click OK.

Modifying an Existing Quota Template

1. Open SharePoint Central Administration and click the Application Management tab.

2. In the SharePoint Site Management section, choose Quota Templates.

3. Choose to edit an existing template.

4. Select the template to edit from the drop-down menu.

5. Modify the site storage limit, warning value, or both.

6. Click OK.

Site Locks

Site locks provide a means for controlling the operational status and availability of a site and are managed at the site collection level. A site can be in one of four states:

1. Not Locked

2. Adding Content Prevented

3. Read-Only

4. No Access

Not Locked is the default state, in which content can be added, edited, and deleted by anyone with the proper permissions. The Adding Content Prevented lock allows Web Parts and content to be modified or deleted, but nothing can be added. A Read-Only lock prevents any modifications to sites whatsoever, whereas a No Access lock prevents access to the site collection altogether.

Changing the Lock Status of a Site Collection

1. Open SharePoint Central Administration and click the Application Management tab.

2. In the SharePoint Site Management section, choose Site Collection Quotas And Locks, as shown in Figure 4-4.

Figure 4-4 Modify the lock status from Central Administration > Application Management > Site Collection Quotas And Locks.

3. Choose the site collection in the drop-down list.

4. Change the lock status to one of the states described previously.

5. Click OK to enforce the lock.

Follow these same steps any time that you need to change the lock status of a site collection; for example, when clearing a lock set by an application or by exceeding a quota.

Site Collection Administrators

Site collection administrators have full control of a SharePoint site collection and are the recipients of alerts relating to their sites. Only site collection administrators can perform certain functions, such as removing locks because of overrun quotas and emptying or restoring items from the second-stage Recycle Bin. In addition, site collection administrators defined in Central Administration cannot be removed from a site's permissions.

It is possible, and in most cases recommended, to specify both primary and secondary site collection administrators so that if the primary administrator is unavailable for any reason, the secondary administrator will still receive administrative alerts. One change from the 2003 version is that IT administrators, such as local computer and domain administrators, no longer automatically have site collection administrator privileges, unless explicitly given those privileges in SharePoint Services.

Creating Subsites and Workspaces

Users with Full Control or Hierarchy Manager permissions on a particular site can create subsites from that site. Subsites and workspaces can either inherit permissions from the parent or be given a completely independent set of permissions. *Workspace* is the term that is applied to a site created for the purpose of collaborating on a particular task, such as a document or a meeting. For all practical purposes, workspaces are simply sites.

Creating a Subsite or Workspace

1. From the Home page of the parent site, click the Site Actions drop-down menu located in the upper right section of the page.

2. Click Create.

3. On the Create Page, choose Sites and Workspaces from the Web Pages section.

4. On the New SharePoint site page, enter a Title and Description for the subsite.

5. In the Web Site Address section, enter the URL for the new subsite. Notice that the subsite is located underneath the parent site in the URL hierarchy.

6. Specify whether to inherit permissions from the parent site or to use unique permissions. Using unique permissions requires you to explicitly set permissions for the site.

7. In the section labeled Navigation, specify whether to include links to the new site on the Quick Launch and the Top Link Bar of the parent site, as well as whether to display the Top Link Bar from the parent.

8. Finally, select the Basic Meeting Workspace template from the Meetings tab, and click Create.

The new subsite is shown in Figure 4-5.

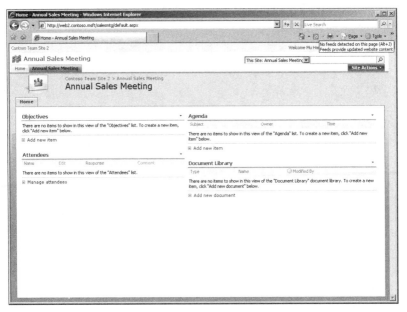

Figure 4-5   A subsite can be created based on any template, like the Basic Meeting Workspace.

Site Settings

Top-level sites, as well as subsites, are managed through the Site Settings page. In a site collection, each subsite has its own Site Settings page, and the top-level site has a Site Settings page that applies to the site collection itself. To access the Site Settings page for any site, simply click the Site Settings link on the Site Actions menu. From the Site Settings page of a subsite or workspace, you can access the Site Collection Settings page from the Site Collection Settings section, where there is a link to the top-level Site Settings page.

Users and Permissions

Security in Windows SharePoint Services 3.0 and SharePoint Server 2007 is greatly improved over Windows SharePoint Services 2.0 and SharePoint Portal Server 2003. Users are managed more easily, and the new security-trimmed user interface means that they only see links to actions they have the permission to perform.

As in the previous version, an object can either inherit permissions from a parent or declare its own permissions explicitly. There are two basic ways to control access to objects:

1. In this version, groups have been simplified to a single type, formerly known as cross-site groups and now called site groups. Permission levels can be specified for a group and then for users given those permissions by being added to the group.

2. Objects have their own permissions collections, which can be managed independently. For example, the permissions for a list can be managed independently of the permissions for the site in which it is contained. This feature allows for more granular management of objects.

> **Important**   One major complaint in previous versions of Windows SharePoint Services was the inability to manage permissions on individual list items and documents. This feedback has been addressed, and individual items, both documents and list items, can have permissions applied independently.

Site groups are collections of individual users that are given the same permissions on a particular site. All sites are created with three basic security groups by default:

- **Owners** Full control
- **Members** Can contribute to existing lists and libraries
- **Visitors** Read only

Creating a Custom Site Group

1. From the site in which you want to create a new group, click the Site Actions menu and choose Site Settings.

2. Click the People and Groups link in the Users and Permissions section.

3. From the New menu, choose New Group.

4. Specify the Name and Description for the group.

5. Specify the group owner.

6. Specify who has permission to see the list of group members and who has permission to add and remove members from the group.

7. Choose whether to allow requests to leave or join the group and, if so, whether to auto-accept the requests. If auto-accept is turned on, users are added or removed automatically from the group when they submit a request.

8. Specify an e-mail address where you can receive requests to join or leave the group.

9. Specify the permission level that users should be granted on the site.

Refer to Chapter 7, "Implementing Security for SharePoint Products," for more information on Permission Levels.

The new site group page is shown in Figure 4-6.

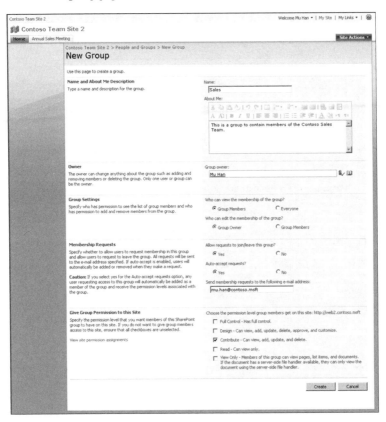

Figure 4-6   Give meaningful names to site groups.

Adding a User to a Site

1. From the Site Actions menu, choose Site Settings.

2. Select Advanced Permissions from the Users and Permissions section.

3. From the Permissions page, you can add individual users to the site or create new groups. To add a user to a site group or assign permissions to the user directly, click New and choose Add Users.

4. Enter user names, group names, or e-mail addresses of users to be added.

5. Choose a group to add the user to, or choose the permissions to assign directly.

6. Click OK.

Tip   When possible, use Active Directory users and groups to populate SharePoint groups. If you must create SharePoint groups, it is a good idea to mail enable the group so the members can be e-mailed as a group.

Modifying User Properties and Permissions

1. From the Site Actions menu, choose Site Settings.

2. Select Advanced Permissions from the Users and Permissions section.

3. Select the box next to the user for whom you want to edit permissions.

4. Click the Actions menu and choose Edit Permissions, as shown in Figure 4-7.

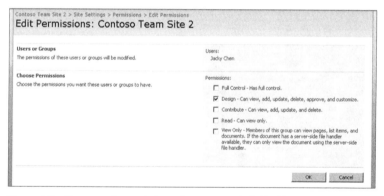

Figure 4-7   You can edit permissions of users on an individual basis when necessary.

5. Modify permissions of user.

6. Click OK to save changes.

Tip   You can enumerate all users in a site from the command line:

```
stsadm -o enumusers -url <site collection url>
```

Regional Settings

Regional settings control how a site behaves, including how lists are sorted and how values such as dates are displayed. Regional settings for a site are based on standards for a particular region of the world. For example, some parts of the world use a 24-hour clock, and others use a 12-hour clock. In addition, some regions of the world use the Gregorian calendar, and other regions use different calendars. The regional settings available to a site are outlined below:

- **Locale:** the world region on which settings should be based
- **Sort Order:** the method used for sorting
- **Time Zone:** the standard time zone
- **Calendar:** type of calendar used, such as Gregorian or Buddhist
- **Secondary Calendar:** settings from an optional alternate calendar to be added to the primary calendar chosen for the site
- **Work Week:** the standard working days of the week for the region; it includes other settings, such as first day of the week and first week of the year, as well as workday start and end times
- **Time Format:** 12- or 24-hour clock

Regional settings for a site can be managed through the Regional Settings link on the Site Settings page of the site.

Creating Document Libraries

Document libraries provide a central location for storing and managing documents. Using SharePoint Products and Technologies, documents can be organized into folder hierarchies as in the traditional network shared folder model, but with much better management capabilities, such as document check in and check out, automatic versioning, and integrated workflow.

Creating a Document Library

1. From the Site Actions menu, click Create.
2. In the Libraries section, choose Document Library.
3. Enter a Name and Description for the document library.
4. Specify whether to display the new document library on the Quick Launch.
5. Specify whether to turn on versioning for the document library.
6. Choose a document template to be used when creating new documents in this library. The default template will work well for most organizations. All of these options are shown in Figure 4-8.

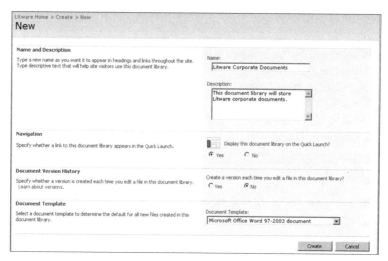

Figure 4-8   The document library creation page.

Note   The document template does not limit the document library to storing only a single type of document. It is simply used to determine the type of document that should be created when a new document is created from the menu. Any types of documents that are not restricted may be stored in the document library. You may enable several document templates per document library when using content types. Refer to Chapter 10, "Configuring Office SharePoint Server Enterprise Content Management," for more information.

Managing Check In and Check Out Settings

In the 2003 version of SharePoint Products and Technologies, files could be modified in a document library without being checked out first. This feature caused many concurrency problems and led to a poorly understood overwrite/merge model. Fortunately this has been corrected in the current version, and you can now set libraries to require a file to be checked out before modifying it. This setting will improve document integrity and make it more straightforward to understand and manage document libraries.

Set a Document Library to Require Check Out

1. From the document library settings page, choose Versioning Settings.

2. In the last section, entitled Require Check Out, select the Yes option button to force a document to be checked out before it can be edited.

3. Click OK to save your settings.

Managing Acceptable Document Types and Sizes

Through the use of the Blocked File Types list, Windows SharePoint Services and SharePoint Server provide the ability to specify the document types that are allowed to be stored and created in document libraries. This list is managed through the Operations tab in SharePoint 3.0 Central Administration. File types can be added to the list for a specific Web application or for the entire farm.

> **Note**   When checking the Blocked File Types list for a file being uploaded or created, SharePoint only looks at the file extension to determine if it is allowed. A clever user could simply rename the file with an unblocked extension to bypass the check. There are products available, such as Microsoft Forefront, that will look into the file itself to determine the type regardless of the extension to provide a much more robust filtering mechanism.

Adding a File to the Blocked File Types List

1. Open SharePoint 3.0 Central Administration and click the Operations tab.

2. Select the Blocked File Types link in the Security Configuration section.

3. Choose the Web application to manage, or choose Global Settings.

4. Add the file extension of the file type to be blocked on a new line in the list.

5. Click OK to save changes.

Figure 4-9 shows the Blocked File Types list management page.

Figure 4-9   Each blocked file type must be on a separate line.

Important   To unblock a file type for a Web application, remove it from the Blocked Files List for both the Web application and the Global Settings if it exists in both places. You can block or unblock files for a Web application from the command line by running:

```
stsadm -o blockedfilelist -extension <extension>
[-add | -delete] -url <Web application url>
```

Setting Size Limitations on Documents

It is possible to limit the size of files uploaded to a Web application. This setting is available from SharePoint 3.0 Central Administration and can be modified in the following way:

1. Open SharePoint 3.0 Central Administration and go to the Application Management tab.

2. Choose Web Application Settings.

3. Set the Maximum Upload Size value to the desired size. The default is 50 MB, and this setting will provide the best performance for the majority of users, but implementations with low-latency, high-bandwidth networks can consider limits in the 200-MB range. Raising the Upload Size value beyond this level can cause upload timeout issues.

4. Click OK.

Note   The maximum upload size setting applies to any single upload, whether of a single file or group of files. Therefore, even if the individual files are below the maximum size, if the combined size of a group of uploaded files exceeds the maximum, you will receive an error message on attempting the upload.

Using Content Types in Document Libraries

Content types are a new feature that provides a means of encapsulating settings and metadata for a particular type of content. A single document library can host one or more content types simultaneously. When a new document library is created, a content type called Document is provisioned with a document template based on the default document type of the document library. For example, if you set the default document type to be Microsoft Excel, the document template for the default Document content type is template.xls.

By default, content types cannot be managed for a document library. To perform actions, such as adding a content type or modifying the default content type, you must first allow management of content types in the Advanced Settings menu of the document library settings.

Adding a Content Type to a Document Library

1. From the document library settings page, choose Advanced Settings.

2. Ensure that the Yes option button is selected to enable management of content types.

3. Click OK to save settings.

4. There will now be a Content Types section on the document library settings page. Click the link to add from existing site content types.

5. Choose a group to filter the available content types, and then add one or more content types by selecting them in the list on the left and clicking the Add button.

6. Click OK.

Figure 4-10 shows the Add Content Types screen.

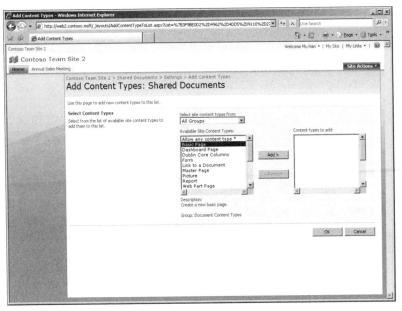

Figure 4-10   You can add multiple content types for use in a single document library or list.

Creating and Managing Lists

Lists are the basic building blocks of SharePoint content. They allow data to be organized logically and manipulated easily. Understanding list creation and management is fundamental to using SharePoint Products and Technologies.

Creating a List

1. From the site where the list will be created, click the Site Actions menu and choose Create.

2. Choose the list template to use to create a new list: for example, Tasks, as shown in Figure 4-11.

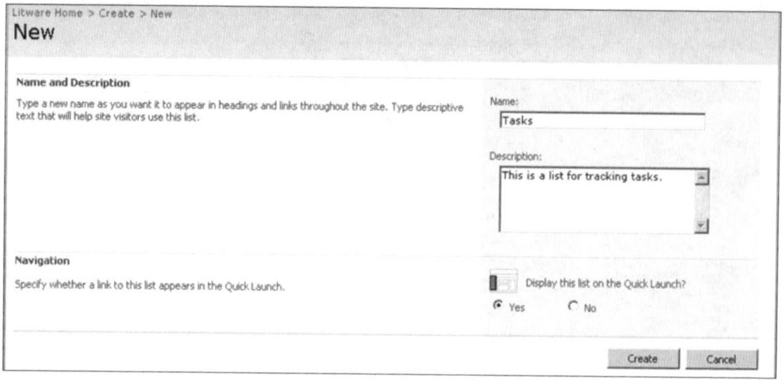

Figure 4-11   You must specify the list template when creating a list.

3. Enter a Name and Description for the list.

4. Specify whether it should be displayed on the Quick Launch Bar.

5. Click OK to create the new list.

> **Note**   The various library types, such as document and picture, as well as discussion boards and surveys, are all just specialized types of lists.

Shared List Columns (Field Definitions)

Shared list columns, also called site columns, provide a column definition that can be reused among lists without redefining the column in each list. The site column is defined once at the site collection level and saved as a template from which lists and content types can reference it. When a site column is added to a list, a local copy of the column is created as a list column. Any changes made to that column from the list are local changes, applying only to the list column.

Creating a Shared List Column

1. Go to the Site Settings page of the site where you want to create a shared list column.

2. In the Galleries section, click the link to the site columns gallery.

3. This gallery contains all of the site columns for the site. Click Create to create a new site column.

4. Specify a name for the column, and choose the type of information that the column will contain.

5. Specify a group for the column to belong to, as shown in Figure 4-12, or create a new group. Groups are a way to organize site columns to make finding them easier.

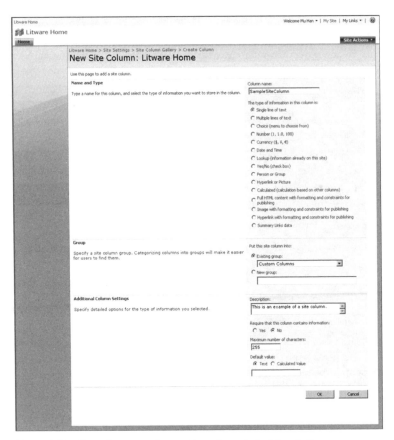

Figure 4-12   Site columns can be used in a site and all of its subsites.

6. Add a description for the column.

7. Specify whether the column is required.

8. If applicable, enter the maximum number of characters the column may contain.

9. (Optional) Specify a default value for the column.

10. Click OK to create the column.

Adding a Shared List Column to a List

1. From the list settings page, scroll down to the Columns section.

2. Click the link to add from existing site columns.

3. Select the columns to add from the list of available site columns, and click the Add button.

4. To add the columns to the default view, check the box in the Options section.

5. Click OK and the columns will be added.

Content Types

Content types are one of the most important new features of SharePoint Products and Technologies. As stated previously, content types encapsulate settings and metadata for a particular type of content in a template that can be reused and is independent of any particular list or library. Content types can include one or more of the following:

- Content metadata, represented by columns, that will be added to the list or library on addition of the content type

- Custom forms, used for New, Edit, and Display functions

- Workflows that can be designed to start automatically based on some event or condition or can be started manually by a user

- The document template on which to base the documents created from this type (for document content types only)

- Custom information stored as XML files

Just like site columns, content types are scoped at both the site and the list level. Content types are created at the site level and then are available to the containing site and any subsites beneath it. When a content type is added to a list or document library, a local copy of the content type is created. This is known as a list content type, and any changes made to it directly only apply to the list where it resides. Changes made to a deployed site content type can be easily pushed down to list content types that were created from it.

Creating a New Content Type

1. From the Site Actions menu, choose Site Settings.

2. In the Galleries section, click the link to the Site Content Type gallery.

3. Click the Create button.

4. Specify a Name and Description for the new content type.

5. Content types created through the Site Settings page must inherit their initial settings from another content type. Choose the group from which the parent content type should be chosen.

6. Choose the parent content type.

7. Choose the group to put the content type into, or specify a new group.

8. Click OK to create the new content type.

Figure 4-13 shows the New Site Content Type page.

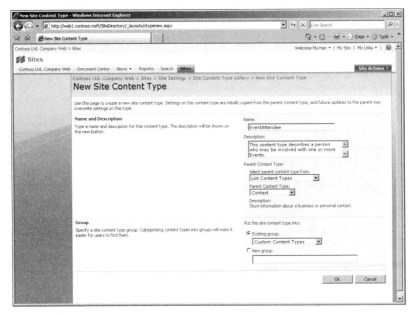

Figure 4-13   Carefully name new content types.

Adding the content type to a list can be accomplished the same way as adding a content type to a document library. After a content type has been added, the content type will be available on the New menu when creating new list items. Figure 4-14 shows the New menu of the Calendar list with a custom content type called EventAttendee added.

Figure 4-14   The New menu of the Calendar list now shows the EventAttendee content type.

User Alerts

As the number of sites and presumably the number of lists and libraries in your SharePoint farm grows, it becomes much more difficult to keep up with the changes to lists and libraries across various sites and Web applications. This is where alerts come in.

Alerts provide notification by e-mail when a particular type of change happens in a list or library. With alerts, lists and libraries can be created and then essentially forgotten until an event occurs that triggers the associated alert action.

Creating an Alert

1. Go to the list for which you want to be alerted.

2. Click the Actions menu and choose Alert Me.

3. Enter a title for the alert, which will be included in the subject of the e-mail alert.

4. Enter the users to be alerted. Notice that the user creating the alert is added automatically, but other users can be added as well. Enter names or e-mail addresses separated by semicolons.

5. Select the change type that will trigger the alert (see Figure 4-15).

Figure 4-15   Select the type of alert you wish to receive.

6. Specify how the alert should be filtered, or to be alerted for any changes that are of the type specified in Step 5, choose Anything Changes, as shown in Figure 4-16.

Figure 4-16   You can filter alerts based on task assignments and modifications.

7. Specify the schedule for alerts. E-mails can be sent immediately, or you can choose to receive a daily or weekly summary. If you choose a daily or weekly summary, you can specify the exact time it should be sent.

Managing Alerts for the Current User

1. From any page on the site where you want to manage alerts, click the welcome message at the top right-hand corner of the page, as shown in Figure 4-17.

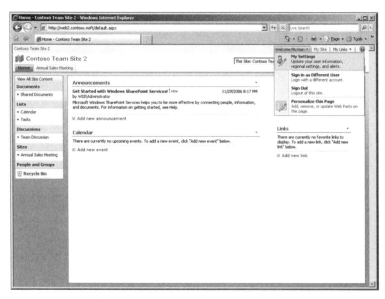

Figure 4-17   To manage alerts for the currently logged in user, go to My Settings from the user action drop-down menu.

2. Choose My Settings.

3. On the User Information page, click the My Alerts link on the menu bar. You will be presented with a list of your alerts for the site (see Figure 4-18).

Figure 4-18   You can manage your personal alerts from a single location.

4. To modify an alert, click the link for the alert name. To delete one or more alerts, select the checkbox next to each, and click the Delete Selected Alerts button in the menu bar.

5. If modifying an alert, make changes to the alert and click OK to save changes.

Discussions

A discussion is essentially a specialized list that uses the Thread and Message content types to provide functionality similar to a Web newsgroup or discussion board. A new thread is created in the discussion list with a subject and body, and then replies can be added. The topics are displayed by subject, but when clicking on a topic, the replies can be viewed in a flat or threaded view. Figure 4-19 shows an example of the flat view.

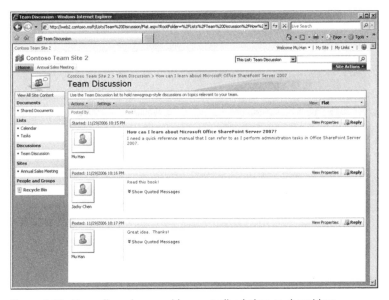

Figure 4-19   Team discussions provide a centralized place to share ideas.

Creating a Discussion

1. From the Site Actions menu, click Create.

2. From the Communications section, choose Discussion Board.

3. Specify a Name and Description for the new discussion board.

4. Specify whether it should be displayed on the Quick Launch of the site.

5. Click Create.

Creating a Discussion Topic

1. Go to the discussion in which you want to create a new topic.

2. From the New menu, choose New Topic.

3. Specify the Subject for the new topic.

4. Enter the body text for the new topic.

5. Click OK.

Posting a Reply to a Discussion Topic

1. From the discussion board where the topic resides, click the topic link.

2. Choose the message to reply to, whether it is the original message or an existing reply, and click Reply from that message.

3. Notice that the subject field is missing. This is because you cannot change the subject of a message when you reply to it. You can only enter text for the body of your reply. Enter the body text.

4. Click OK to post reply.

RSS (Really Simple Syndication)

The dynamic nature of SharePoint content makes it a perfect candidate for RSS. RSS provides the ability to monitor changes to SharePoint content in a simple and straight-forward way, with the latest changes being downloaded automatically and moved to the top of your chosen RSS feed reader, such as Internet Explorer 7 or Outlook 2007. In SharePoint Server, RSS is really simple because it is accomplished automatically for every list and document library created.

Viewing a List Using RSS

1. Go to the list that you want to view as an RSS feed.

2. From the Actions menu, choose View RSS feed.

3. The XML generated by RSS will be automatically transformed into a readable Web page using Extensible Stylesheet Language Transformations (XSLT).

4. If you are using Internet Explorer 7 you can click the link in the yellow box at the top of the page to subscribe to the feed using your browser.

The RSS settings for a list can be modified from the List Settings page by clicking the RSS settings link in the Communications section. Table 4-1 shows the available settings.

Table 4-1   RSS Settings

Setting	Description
Allow RSS for this list?	Yes or No
Truncate multi-line text fields to 256 characters?	Yes or No
Title	Title channel element of RSS feed definition
Description	Description channel element of RSS feed
Image URL	Image URL channel element of RSS feed
Columns	List columns to be included in RSS feed
Maximum items to include	Integer representing the maximum number of items to be included in the RSS feed
Maximum days to include	Maximum number of previous days to include in RSS feed

Recycle Bin

The Recycle Bin is a much-anticipated feature of SharePoint Products and Technologies 2007 that was missing from previous versions, although many organizations resorted to third-party solutions to provide the missing functionality. It provides similar functionality to that of the Windows Recycle Bin, allowing deleted documents or list items to be preserved for a period of time before being destroyed permanently. At any time while a document or list item resides in the Recycle Bin, it can be restored to its original location.

User-Level Recycle Bin

The Recycle Bin in SharePoint Products and Technologies 2007 actually exists on two levels. The first of these levels is the user level. When a user deletes an item from a list or library, the item is sent to the user-level Recycle Bin where it remains until it is purged by either the user or automatically based on administrative settings.

Administrator-Level Recycle Bin

After an item is purged from the user-level Recycle Bin, it is moved into the administrator-level Recycle Bin. This Recycle Bin is maintained for a site collection, and all documents purged by users in all subsites as well as the top-level site are moved here. This second layer of recoverability allows the administrator to restore files that have been deleted by users and even purged from their Recycle Bin. This is a huge improvement over the 2003 version, which required a complete restore of a site to recover a single document that was accidentally deleted.

Restore an Item from the User-Level Recycle Bin

1. From the home page of the site, click the Recycle Bin link in the left navigation pane.

2. Check the box next to the item to be restored.

3. Click Restore Selection.

Delete an Item from the User-Level Recycle Bin

1. From the home page of the site, click the Recycle Bin link in the left navigation pane.

2. Check the box next to the item to be deleted.

3. Click Delete Selection and confirm that you want to delete the selected item.

Managing the Site Collection Recycle Bin

The site collection Recycle Bin can be managed from the top-level site settings page. There are two views available for this Recycle Bin: one for viewing items located in user-level Recycle Bins throughout the site collection and the other for managing items that have been purged from user-level Recycle Bins and are now located in the administrative Recycle Bin; the first view is the default view.

From the site users' view you can see all of the items deleted by users within the site collection. From here you can delete individual items, sending them to the administrative Recycle Bin, or you can empty the users' Recycle Bins all at once by clicking Empty Recycle Bin. Using either method, the deleted items end up in the administrative Recycle Bin. From here they can be deleted permanently or restored to their original locations.

Recycle Bin Settings

The Recycle Bin functionality is managed on a Web application basis through Central Administration. Use the following steps to manage the Recycle Bin for a Web application:

1. Open SharePoint 3.0 Central Administration and click the Application Management tab.

2. In the SharePoint Web Application Management section, choose Web application settings.

3. Scroll down to the last section, which is Recycle Bin.

Chapter 5
Customizing Sites

Each default site, page, and Web Part can be customized in many ways. In turn, every customization contains the promise of further enhancements. This chapter familiarizes you with the tools to customize Windows SharePoint Services and SharePoint Server 2007 to meet both your present and future business requirements.

You can customize sites using the browser interface (no code) or with SharePoint Designer 2007 (limited code) and Visual Studio 2005 (custom code development). This chapter focuses almost exclusively on customization using the browser interface, with a section on how to import custom Web Parts.

Using the Default Site Collection Templates

The default site templates fulfill common organizational needs and serve as a foundation for solutions specific to your organization and environment. They are grouped into four categories: Collaboration, Meetings, Enterprise, and Publishing.

> **Tip** An additional 40 templates, which will be added to a tab labeled "Applications," are available from *http://www.microsoft.com/technet/windowsserver/sharepoint/wssapps/v3templates.mspx*. They include such templates as Board of Directors, Call Center, IT Team Workspace, and Time Card Management.

The Collaboration and Meetings templates are available with Windows SharePoint Services, but the Enterprise and Publishing templates require SharePoint Server 2007. All of the templates are described in this chapter, along with the Web Parts and resources that they include.

Collaboration Site Templates

Collaboration Site Templates are the ones that are used most often and are probably the most useful. The following templates are included with Windows SharePoint Services and SharePoint Server:

- **Team site**   Team sites are used to create, organize, and share information. Team Site templates contain a Shared Document Library, Announcements, Site Image Web Part, Calendar, and Discussion list.

- **Blank site**   Blank sites are team sites without any initially displayed Web Parts, document libraries, or lists.

- **Document Workspace sites**   Document Workspace sites manage collaboration on a single document or possibly a group of similar documents. The Document Workspace template includes a Shared Document Library, Announcements, Calendar, Link list, Tasks list, Discussion list, and a Site Users Web Part.

- **Wiki site**   Wiki sites are used to create repositories of knowledge tailored to the people who use it. Users can add, edit, and link Wiki pages, and these pages can be linked using key words. A history of changes is maintained, allowing restoration of pages if required. A Wiki Site template includes the Wiki Pages Document Library.

- **Blog site**   A Blog site provides online journals in which users can share ideas and information. Users can record comments about blog entries, and these comments are organized in chronological order. The Blog Site template includes a Shared Documents Library, Announcements, Calendar, Links list, Team Discussion, and Site Users Web Part.

Meeting Site Templates

Windows SharePoint Services and SharePoint Server provide Meeting Site Templates. These templates are designed to organize meetings and the resulting tasks, including agendas, documents, and attendees. The following is a brief description of the Meeting Site Templates:

- **Basic Meeting Workspace**   A Basic Meeting Workspace organizes a meeting with team members. Members can set an agenda, define objectives, record attendees, and manage documents related to the meeting. A Basic Meeting Workspace includes a Document Library, Agenda list, Attendees list, and Objectives list.

- **Blank Meeting Workspace**   A Blank Meeting Workspace is much like the blank collaboration site. It has the same features as a Basic Meeting Workspace, but they have not yet been added to the site.

- **Decision Meeting Workspace**   A Decision Meeting Workspace adds the ability to track tasks and decisions.

- **Social Meeting Workspace**   The Social Meeting workspace includes a Picture Library, Attendees list, Directions, Things to Bring, and Discussion Board.

- **Multi-Page Meeting Workspace**   The Multi-Page workspace is the same as a Basic Meeting workspace, but includes two extra tabbed pages to manage multiple meetings.

Enterprise Site Templates

Enterprise sites, such as a Document Center or Records Center, require SharePoint Server 2007. The following Enterprise Site Templates are included:

- **Document Center**   The Document Center template should be used as a central document storage site and is available only as a subsite.

- **Records Center**   The Records Center site is for official file storage and management. Although it can be created as a subsite, it does not accept routed documents when created as such. It includes specialized document libraries for the purpose of classifying data and placing "holds" on documents to prevent them from being expired when they are required for auditing, investigation, or litigation.

  The Records Center also includes Announcements and Tasks.

- **Personalization Site**   A Personalization Site includes Web Parts that integrate with your My Site and provide connections to the portals of which you are a member.

- **Site Directory**   The Site Directory is a specialized site to allow navigation of numerous sites, including your portal. It includes several custom Web Parts and is covered in detail in Chapter 9, "Configuring SharePoint Server Portals."

- **Report Center**   The Report Center should only be used as a subsite. It contains many features that organize and present business intelligence data, such as dashboards and Key Point Indicators. It includes the Team Site Web Parts, in addition to sample dashboards and workflow tasks.

- **Search Center with Tabs**   This site template is used to create multiple tabbed interfaces for custom searching. It includes custom tabbed results lists, in addition to the Basic and Advanced Search Box Web Parts.

- **Search Center**   The Search Center provides the Basic and Advanced Search Box Web Parts.

Publishing Site Templates

Publishing Site Templates are new to this version of SharePoint Server and provide robust functionality enabling Web Content Management. Although any site in a SharePoint Server farm can be upgraded to a Publishing Site, you can use the extended in-browser editor when creating a Publishing Site from these templates only:

■ **Publishing Portal** The Publishing Portal is used as your Internet-facing Web site template. It provides extensible and easily customized navigation, search, and content editing functionality. It includes workflow, search, sample press releases, and forms-based authentication. The Publishing Portal also provides an easy-to-use in-browser editor, as shown in Figure 5-1.

Figure 5-1 The built-in editor enables nontechnical personnel to edit and maintain Web content.

■ **Collaboration Portal** The Collaboration Portal is used most often in the root of a Web application to provide centralized aggregation, organization, and presentation of pertinent enterprise content. This Site Template includes a Sample News Article, Employee Lookup Web Part, Tasks Web Part, and the following tabbed subsites:

❑ Document Center

❑ News Center

❑ Report Center

❑ Search Center

❑ Site Directory

- **Publishing Site**   The Publishing Site template is similar to a team site, but includes the native Publishing Site versioning, Editor, navigation, and workflow.

- **Publishing Site with Workflow**   This Site template extends the Publishing Site template with native approval systems.

> **Tip**   The Publishing and Publishing Site with Workflow templates may only be created as subsites, and only beneath sites that have the Office SharePoint Server Publishing Infrastructure feature activated. To activate this feature navigate to Site Actions > Site Settings > Site Collection Administration > Site Collection Features.

- **News Site**   A News Site can only be a subsite; it is used to present information via News articles or the RSS (Really Simple Syndication) News Web Part. It also includes the This Week in Pictures Web Part.

- **My Site Host Site**   The My Site Host Site is commonly applied to the root of a Web application that will host My Sites.

> **Important**   Enabling the Office SharePoint Server Publishing Infrastructure in other than Publishing Sites is done at the site collection level. Browse to Site Actions > Site Settings > Site Collection Administration > Site Collection Features. From there you can activate the Office SharePoint Server Publishing Infrastructure feature.

Customizing the Default Templates

Building on the default site templates, you can create custom site templates by saving a modified site as a site template. This functionality means that, whenever you modify a site, you are creating the basis of a custom site template. These custom templates are basically macros that contain any changes from the native templates.

Modifying the Common Look And Feel

As the name suggests, the Look And Feel settings control appearance and user interactions across the site as a whole. To modify the look and feel of a site, browse to Site Actions > Site Settings, as shown in Figure 5-2. On entering site settings, you find the options shown in Figure 5-3 under Look And Feel.

Figure 5-2   The Site Actions menu is available only to users with elevated permissions.

Figure 5-3 The Look And Feel settings contain basic customization options.

Title, Description, and Icon

The title, description, and icon page allows you to change settings that were originally defined during site creation.

- **Title** Changing the title for a top-level site changes the text throughout the site and all subsites. However, changing the title for a subsite only changes the text displayed next to the site icon of the subsite.

- **Description** The description is the text displayed on the Home tab of a top-level site or subsite.

- **Icon** To display a custom logo icon in place of the default icon, enter an appropriate URL. If the image cannot be displayed, the URL description displays an alternative text in place of the image. You can specify different logo images for each site within a collection. By default, the images selected are displayed at their full size, and there is no mechanism to resize them.

- **Alternate Web Site Address** The URL Name textbox sets the URL to reference the subsite. This option is not available for top-level sites.

Tree View

The *Tree View* is a very useful navigation tool, but can take up significant page space. For this reason, use it sparingly.

- **Enable Quick Launch** By default, the Quick Launch is enabled when a site is created.

- **Enable Tree View** Unlike the Quick Launch and Top Navigation Bar that simply facilitate access to a site, the Tree View displays the relationships among the sites within a collection and allows navigation.

Site Theme

Themes alter the visual elements of a site, such as colors and fonts, but do not alter the site's content, layout, or functionality. Select the desired theme from the drop-down list and click Apply. Site theme settings do not propagate to child sites and are not automatically applied to subsequently created child sites. To create a consistent look and feel across the site collection, you must apply the theme to each site.

Top Link Bar

The Top Link Bar provides a place that is highly visible to all users and can link to any number of sites. You can use it to provide links to SharePoint sites or external URLs.

> **Important**   If you activate the Publishing Infrastructure feature, Top Link Bar and Quick Launch functionality are transferred to the newly created Site Navigation settings object in Look And Feel.

- **Edit or delete a link**   Click on the icon next to the link that you wish to edit or delete. The URLs of sites added by default cannot be changed.

- **New link**   To create a new link, enter its appropriate URL and a description to appear in the Top Link Bar. If a site link has been removed, an easy solution is to browse to the site from Quick Launch > View All Site Content and then copy its URL. Only the relative URL is needed. For example, for the site *http:// hr.contoso.msft/meetings/default.aspx,* only */meetings/default.aspx* is required.

- **Change order**   To change the order of a link, select the desired position from the associated drop-down list. Remember that changing the order of a link may affect the order of other links.

- **Configuring a custom Top Link Bar for a subsite**   To enable a custom Top Link Bar for your subsite, browse to the subsite's Site Actions > Site Settings > Top Link Bar and click *Stop Inheriting Links.* New sites created beneath this site will be added to the Top Link Bar. New sites created beneath the custom Top Link Bar can also have custom Top Link Bars. This means that every site can have custom top link navigation. To inherit the parent site's Top Link Bar, click *Use Links From Parent.*

Quick Launch

The Quick Launch provides another navigation option for site collection administrators to expose content and links. Add items to the Quick Launch sparingly, as having too many items reduces its effectiveness.

> **Tip**   To enable or disable the Quick Launch, use the Tree View interface.

- **New link**   To create a new link in the Quick Launch, select New Link and enter the URL and the description for the link to be displayed in the Quick Launch. Select the heading that the link will appear under and click OK.

- **New heading**   Although it is not required, headings and links should have a relationship similar to that between sites and subsites. Preferably, clicking on a heading should send you to a high-level site, and clicking a link under that heading should send you to a lower level site. To create a new heading, enter the URL of the site and enter a description to be displayed in the Quick Launch.

■ **Edit and deleting headings or links**   To edit or delete a heading or link, click on the icon to the left of the appropriate item. You can change the URL and description of headings, as well as the heading selections of links. Deleting a heading also deletes any links associated with it.

■ **Change order**   To change the order of the Quick Launch headings, click *Change Order* and select the appropriate values from the drop-down lists. The order of headings can be changed, as well as the order of links within headings, but you cannot move links between headings. To move a link from one heading to another, you must edit the link as described earlier.

■ **Add or remove a list from the Quick Launch**   By default when you create a new library or list, it is added to the Quick Launch. However, you can override this action from the Navigation option at site creation. A library or list may also be added to or removed from the Quick Launch from the items Settings > General Settings > Title, description, and navigation settings.

Saving a Site as a Template

To create a custom template, browse to Site Actions > Site Settings > Look And Feel > Save Site As Template. Give the new template a file name, template name, and description. Use meaningful values for all three properties, and be specific with descriptions. Using a consistent naming convention and thorough descriptions makes future reuse much easier.

Caution   Site templates can contain sensitive information, such as farm URLs and account names. Be certain of what information you are saving within a template and only share templates with trustworthy groups.

When saving a site as a template you can elect to save the site's content along with the site. Doing so saves all of the site's libraries and lists within the site's template, which increases the amount of storage space required for the template. Remember that the maximum size for a template, whether it is a site or list template, is 10 MB. Some customizations, such as workflows, cannot be saved within a template if *Include Content* is selected. After the site template is created, it is available when creating new sites within the site collection and can be viewed by browsing to Site Actions > Site Settings > Galleries > Site Templates.

Resetting a Site

If you no longer want the customizations that are applied to a site, you can reset the site to its original definition. Resetting the site removes only the customizations added to the site and its Web Parts; it resets the site to the default template, as if it had been freshly installed. Browse to Actions > Site Settings > Look And Feel > Reset Site To Definition. To reset a specific page within the site, enter the page's URL in the *Local URL For The Page* text box. To reset all the pages within the collection, select the *Reset All Pages In This Site To Site Definition Version* option button.

> **Tip**   If you use SharePoint Designer 2007 to reset a site, a backup copy of the site is created automatically before the site is reset.

Managing the Site Template Gallery

The Site Template Gallery serves as a central repository of custom site templates for an entire site collection. Sites saved as templates are added to the site template gallery of the collection to which they belong. Sites within the gallery can be exported for use in other site collections. Likewise, sites from other site collections can be imported into the site template gallery. To manage the Site Gallery, browse, from the top level of the site collection, to Site Actions > Galleries > Site Templates, as shown in Figure 5-4.

Figure 5-4   Choose Site Templates from the Galleries settings.

Exporting a Site Template

Within the site template gallery, click on the name of the site template you wish to export and use the Save As dialog box to save the template file. Take care when exporting to a different farm. The Site Template on which the custom template was based, which is also called a *site definition*, must exist on all servers in the target farm or the template will fail.

Adding a Site Template

Within the site template gallery, select *Upload Document* from the Upload drop-down list. Enter a URL in the name text box, or click Browse to select a file to add to the gallery. The site definition must exist on the Web front-end server, or the site will not function. After clicking OK you are taken to the template's edit page.

> **Tip**   If you need to add the same template to more than one site collection, consider adding the template to the Central Template Gallery.

Editing and Deleting Site Templates

Clicking the Edit icon of a template in the template gallery allows you to change the template's name, title, and description, as shown in Figure 5-5. You may also Delete or Check In/Out the template.

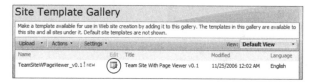

Figure 5-5   The Edit icon in the template gallery is similar to the icon used in the Web Parts gallery.

Managing the Central Template Gallery

In an environment with many site collections, adding a template to each collection is both a tedious and error-prone process. As the number of collections increases, it becomes progressively more likely that you may overlook a collection. Fortunately, a central repository is maintained that provides templates to all the sites in a farm.

Listing the Templates in the Central Gallery

To view all of the templates contained in the Central Gallery, use the command:

```
stsadm.exe -o enumtemplates [-lcid <language>]
```

Adding a Template to the Central Gallery

To ensure that the template is available across site collections you can use the Stsadm.exe command with the syntax:

```
stsadm -o addtemplate -filename<template filename>
-title <template title> [-description <template description>]
```

The description parameter is optional.

> **Note**   If a template exists with the same title as the template that is being added, it must be deleted before the addition of the new template will succeed.

Deleting a Template from the Central Gallery

When a template no longer needs to be available to all site collections or it must be removed to make room for a newer template, it can be deleted using Stsadm.exe as follows:

```
stsadm.exe -o deletetemaplate -title <template title>
[-lcid <language>]
```

Important   Sites that are already provisioned using the template are not affected by deleting the template. Likewise, existing sites are not affected by replacing an existing template with another template of the same title. Deletion of the site definition in the *12 Hive*, however, does disable all site templates based off that site definition.

Web Part Pages

Web Part pages enable related content to be consolidated into a unique page that is optimized for a specific purpose. For instance, you can consolidate related information into a single page to provide an overview. Web Part pages provide a container for Web Parts. They collect and organize Web Parts to create a custom layout and functionality.

Each Web Part page is divided into zones, and each zone has a unique title, such as header, left, or right. The Web Part zones control the layout of the page and are therefore one of the most basic aspects of the page's look and feel. Choose the layout with care, because after the layout is selected, the only way to alter it is with SharePoint Designer or custom coding. Through the Web interface you can only alter the layout by creating a new Web Part page with a different layout.

Note   By using SharePoint Designer, it is possible to add Web Parts to Web Part pages outside the Web Part zones. Doing so allows a Web Part page to possess the necessary functionality of a Web Part while keeping the Web Part hidden.

Creating a Web Part Page

To create a Web Part page, browse to Site Actions > Create > Web Pages > Web Part Page. Enter a meaningful file name for the Web Part page, and choose whether you want to overwrite an existing Web Part with the same name.

Note   If you choose to overwrite an existing Web Part, all versions of the Web Part will be deleted from the document library and not moved to the Recycle Bin. For this reason, it is wise to delete Web Part pages only from within their document libraries and not during the creation of a replacement page.

To finish creating a new Web Part page, select the document library in which the page will be stored and click Create. Remember that a Web Part page will not be displayed on a site unless a link to it is created, possibly from the Quick Launch or Top Link Bar.

Note   You can also organize and create Web Part Pages by creating a document library for them. Browse to Site Actions > Create > Document Library, and create a library with a template type of Web Part Page. Selecting New from this library creates a new Web Part page within the library.

> **Tip** By carefully selecting a name for your Web Part page document library you can create groups of Web Part pages that have a more intuitive URL structure. The shorter the name, the better. SharePoint URLs have a character limit of 254, so shorter URLs allow for a deeper site structure.

Editing a Web Part Page

After the Web Part page has been created, it is displayed in Edit Mode. Figure 5-6 shows an example of editing an existing page by selecting Edit Page from the Site Actions toolbar.

Figure 5-6   Enter Edit Page from the Site Actions toolbar.

When editing a page, notice the Version label in the upper left-hand corner. A Web Part page is always viewed as either the shared version or a personalized version. The shared version is the default view of the Web Part page that is seen by everyone. The personalized view is created on a per user basis and allows users with the appropriate permissions to customize their views of individual pages. If you want users to be able to create personalized views, be aware that they must have the Add/Remove Private Web Parts and Update Personal Web Parts rights to do so.

> **Tip** To see all the content in a site, even if View All Site Content is not available in the Quick Launch, go to the site's URL plus */_layouts/viewlsts.aspx*. For example, if your Web site has a URL of *http://it.contoso.msft/Basic_Meeting/default.aspx*, go to *http://it.contoso.msft/Basic_Meeting/_layouts/viewlsts.aspx*.

Editing the Web Part Page Title Bar

Each Web Part page has a title bar that by default displays a title and generic icon. To edit the title bar and add properties not set by default, click on the *Edit Title Bar Properties* link. There you will find the following properties.

- **Title**   Changing the title alters the text of the title displayed on the Web Part page.

- **Caption**   The caption text appears above the title in a smaller font. By default, no caption text is used.

- **Description**   When the cursor is over the title or caption, the description text is displayed as a tool tip.

- **Image link**   Enter a URL for the desired image file. There is no option to check the validity of the URL, so click Apply and see if the image is displayed. The image is displayed full size and cannot be resized, so be sure to pick an appropriately sized image.

Adding Web Parts on Web Part Page

To add a Web Part to a page, click *Add A Web Part* in the desired Web Part zone, and select a Web Part from the list that is provided. Under *Advanced Web Part Gallery And Options* there are three major divisions: Browse, Search, and Import. The control is easily missed, so look for Browse directly beneath Add Web Parts. Clicking on the down arrow to the right of Browse allows you to navigate to the Search and Import interfaces, as shown in Figure 5-7.

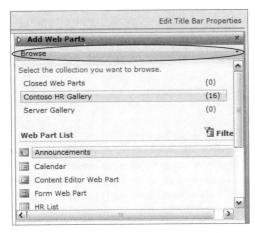

Figure 5-7   The Browse drop-down list box allows you to select among Browse, Search, and Import.

Add Web Part Advanced Options

Web Part Advanced Options allow you to browse Web Parts by collection or to search by Web Part name. After selecting Advanced Options, the Web Part list appears on the right side of the screen, but on a partially minimized browser it is sometimes hidden.

- **Select The Collection You Want To Browse**   Selecting this option displays a list of the available Web Part galleries from which to choose Web Parts. These galleries are described in detail in the Web Part galleries section of this chapter.

- **Web Part List**   The Web Part list displays a list of Web Parts much like the one available from the default Add Web Part dialogue. The advanced option also includes a filter to limit the types of items displayed.

- **Add To**   Selecting a Web Part zone from the drop-down list causes the Web Part to be added to that zone.

- **Search**   Search attempts to find a Web Part matching the search criteria in the available galleries. You can search using a partial name. For instance, a search for only the letter *e* (wild cards are not required) returns all Web Parts that have the letter *e* in their names.

- **Import**   To import a Web Part, browse to or enter the location of the Web Part's definition file and click Upload. The Web Part's binary (.dll) file must exist on the server for the Web Part to function. Select a Web Part zone for the Web Part from the drop-down list and click Add. Note that importing a Web Part to a given Web Part page adds the Web Part only to that single page. To make a Web Part available throughout the site collection, refer to the section on Web Part galleries in this chapter.

Tip   You can drag and drop a Web Part between zones.

Web Parts

Web Parts provide a portable and customizable means of adding functionality to pages. They can be shared among site collections and farms, allowing them to be reused and adapted easily. Each Web Part is designed to provide a specific function, and they can be combined, connected, and customized to meet a wide variety of needs. You can customize Web Parts as part of branding your site or to give the site a new look and feel. You can design completely new Web Parts via custom code development to meet virtually any requirement. Connecting Web Parts allows you to integrate data from multiple data sources or to display the same data in multiple forms. In addition to being able to customize and connect Web Parts, you can personalize them. Within the constraints of the Web Part code, users can further modify Web Parts to meet their individual preferences. Different users can have personalized views of the same Web Part, on the same page. Web Parts can also be targeted to specific audiences. This allows different audiences to see different combinations of the same Web Parts on the same page. This means that Web Parts exist in four distinct varieties:

- **Shared**   A Shared Web Part is added to the page in shared view and is visible to all users.

- **Personalized**   A Personalized Web Part is a Shared Web Part that has been personalized by a particular user.

- **Private**   A Private Web Part is one that has been added to a user's personal view of a page and is seen only by that user.

As an administrator, you can control who is permitted to alter Shared Web Parts, personalize Web Parts, and add Private Web Parts.

Editing Web Parts

To begin customizing Web Parts, go to the page that the Web Part resides on and select Site Actions > Edit Page. Click Edit on the Web Part you wish to edit and then select *Modify Shared Web Part.* Although each Web Part has properties specific to its function, several properties are common to most Web Parts. The Appearance, Layout, and Advanced property groups should remain fairly consistent among differing Web Parts and are summarized below. Figure 5-8 shows the menu item, Modify Shared Web Part.

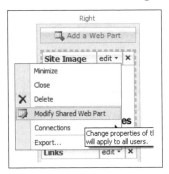

Figure 5-8   To edit a Web Part, select Modify Shared Web Part from the edit menu.

Note   Developers can elect not to implement some of these properties. Any given Web Part will almost certainly have properties unique to it.

Appearance

- **Title**   This changes the title displayed in the Web Part's title bar.

- **Height**   If you select No, the Web Part automatically sizes to the Web Part zone.

- **Width**   To set a fixed width for the Web Part, select Yes, and enter a width in centimeters, inches, millimeters, points, picas, or pixels. To have the Web Part adjust to the Web Part zone automatically, select No.

- **Chrome State**   To display only the Web Part's title bar, select Minimized. To display the full Web Part, select Normal.

- **Chrome Type**   This feature determines how the Web Part's title and border are displayed.

Important   Remember that the entire Web Part zone will be resized to accommodate both the widest and highest Web Parts within the zone.

Layout

- **Hidden**   If the functionality of a Web Part is needed, but it is visually unnecessary, select Hidden.

- **Direction**   This feature specifies whether text will be written left-to-right or right-to-left within the Web Part. Different languages use different directions. English is a left-to-right language; Hebrew and many Asian languages are read right-to-left. Select *None* to use the language direction specified by the language setting of the site. Select *Left to Right* to display text from left to right; choose *Right to Left* to display text from right to left. It may be necessary to have differing language directions on a page that contains links to pages written in multiple languages.

- **Zone**   This determines within which Web Part zone the Web Part is located. Changing the zone changes the location of the Web Part on the page.

- **Zone Index**   The Zone Index moves the order in which the Web Part is displayed within the zone. You may select zone indices of any value, and the Web Parts are displayed in numerical order. However, any Web Part added to the zone is placed at the top of the Web Part zone. If any Web Part is moved by dragging and dropping, the zone is reordered, beginning with an index of 1.

Note   Each Web Part in a Web Part zone must have a unique zone index. Therefore, changing the zone index value of one Web Part may affect the values of some or all of the Web Parts in the zone.

Advanced

- **Allow Minimize**   Certain Web Parts may need to be prominently displayed. To ensure that the Web Part is not minimized, clear the *Allow Minimize* check box.

- **Allow Close**   To guarantee that a Web Part will not be closed, clear the *Allow Close* check box. To permit a Web Part to be closed, select Allow Close.

- **Allow Hide**   If you do not wish a Web Part to be hidden, clear the *Allow Hide* check box. To allow the Web Part to be hidden, select Allow Hide.

- **Allow Zone Change**   To ensure that the Web Part remains within a single zone, clear the *Allow Zone Change* check box. If you wish the Web Part to be moveable, select Allow Zone Change.

- **Allow Connections**   If you would like this Web Part to be able to interact with other Web Parts on the page, select *Allow Connections*. To isolate this Web Part from connections with other Web Parts, clear the Allow Connections check box.

- **Allow Editing In Personal View**   To allow Web Part personalization, select *Allow Editing In Personal View*. To maintain the shared view for all users, clear the Allow Editing In Personal View Web Part.

- **Export Mode**   If you wish Web Part properties flagged as controlled by the Web Part developer to be exportable, select *Export All Data*. To protect controlled properties, select *Non-Sensitive Data Only*.

- **Title URL**   The specified resource is displayed in a separate browser window when the Web Parts title bar is clicked.

- **Description**   The description is displayed as a tool tip when the mouse hovers over the title or icon.

- **Help URL**   Enter an URL that will be displayed when a user clicks on the Web Part's down arrow and selects Help. The help URL is displayed according to the settings specified in the *Help Mode* property.

- **Help Mode**   Selecting *Modeless* opens a separate browser window and allows the user to continue working with the current window. Selecting *Modal* opens a separate browser window that must be closed before the user can interact with the original window. Choosing *Navigate* redirects the user to the help information in the current browser window.

- **Catalog Icon Image URL**   The catalog URL will be associated with the Web Part and displayed when the Web Part is added to a page. Images may be of any size, but large images will be reduced significantly. Experience has shown that images of approximately 32 × 32 pixels are displayed quite clearly.

- **Title Icon Image URL**   Enter the URL of an image to be displayed in the title bar. The image is sized to fit the title, which means that large images become unrecognizable. Experience has shown that images of approximately 32 × 32 pixels work well.

- **Import Error Message**   This sets the error message displayed if there is an error importing the Web Part. Consider using this property to direct users to either people or resources that will help them resolve problems with the Web Part.

Connecting Web Parts

Web Parts provide a means of connecting to data sources and integrating information from different data sources without programming. They can be connected to lists, libraries, and to each other to reveal and manipulate data. Connecting Web Parts allows you to present the same data in different forms. For example, a common use of connected Web Parts is to provide a general view in a list, as well as a detailed view of one item in the list. To save space, a general list of users might contain only their names and e-mail addresses, whereas a more detailed view could display all of a single user's information.

To create a Web Part connection, click on the Edit drop-down list and select Connections. There you will see the list of connections that a particular Web Part can make.

Not all Web Parts are capable of making connections, and not all Web Parts support the same types of connections. For instance, the image Web Part is able to make only a single type of connection, *Get Image From*.

Now consider a Web Part page that contains an image Web Part and a list called *Eighth Wonder*. The list Eighth Wonder displays two columns: *Title* and *URL*. The URL column contains hyperlinks to images. Connecting the Web Parts is as simple as clicking on the Edit drop-down list of the image Web Part and selecting Connections > Get Image From > Eighth Wonder, as shown in Figure 5-9.

Figure 5-9   Select Connections to get the image from the Eighth Wonder list.

Once you choose a list, you can then select a column in the list from a pop-up dialog, box as shown in Figure 5-10.

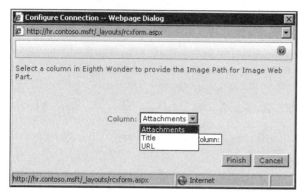

Figure 5-10   After selecting a list, you can then select from the column choices.

Specifying URL and clicking Finish complete the process of connecting the image Web Part. Selecting one of the rows in the Eighth Wonder list will display the corresponding image in the image Web Part.

Caution You are able to create connections between Web Parts that do not generate an error, but are meaningless. If the Title column of the Eighth Wonder list had been linked to the image Web Part, the image Web Part would have attempted to interpret the Title value as an URL. This would not have caused an error message, but no image would have been displayed. Always check Web Part connections to ensure that they function as expected.

Tip The list and image Web Parts could also have been connected from the list. To do so, go to the list's Edit > Connections > Provide Row To > Image Web Part and select the URL column.

Web Part Galleries

Web Part galleries serve as a central location for storing and managing Web Parts. Because Web Parts are essential to your site, it is critical that they be managed carefully. Nonfunctioning Web Parts can keep pages from displaying. Poorly written or improperly configured Web Parts can adversely affect site functionality and availability. In addition, Web Parts from unknown third parties may pose the risk of malicious code execution. Carefully consider which Web Parts you will make available and to whom you will make them available.

The default gallery for your site collection is listed in the form of *Site Name* Gallery. For instance, if your site collection is named *Contoso HR*, your default gallery is named *Contoso HR* Gallery. In addition to the default gallery there are two other important galleries:

- **Closed Web Parts** This gallery displays the Web Parts that remain on the page, but are not visible because they have been closed. The closed Web Parts remain on their Web Part pages and are available to be opened at any time. However, they do require additional system resources, so it is wise to remove unneeded closed Web Parts.

- **Server** The Server gallery makes Web Parts available across site collections and is managed using the Stsadm.exe command. There may also be one or more custom galleries available.

Managing Web Parts

By browsing to Site Actions > Site Settings > Galleries > Web Parts, you can preview Web Parts, add Web Parts to the gallery, import and export Web Parts, and edit properties of Web Parts. Figure 5-11 shows where to manage your Web Parts.

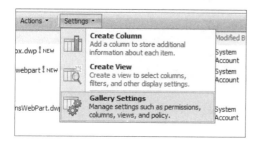

Figure 5-11   To manage your Web Parts, browse to the list's Settings > Gallery Settings.

Previewing a Web Part

Many Web Parts allow you to preview how they appear on the page by clicking on the Web Part's name. Selecting the edit icon allows you to view the Web Part's properties.

New

New allows you to add a Web Part that has been deployed on the site collection to the Web Part gallery. Select the Web Part or Parts you wish to add to the gallery and click *Populate Gallery*. When Web Parts are added using Stsadm.exe, they must be added to the gallery using New.

Editing Web Parts

By clicking on a Web Part's Edit icon, you can preview, delete, export, view the XML code of the Web Part, and manage the properties of the Web Part.

Deleting a Web Part   To remove a Web Part from the gallery, click *Delete Item*. A default Web Part that is deleted from the gallery can be replaced by using New in the Web Part gallery.

Exporting a Web Part   Every Web Part has at least two resource files: a Web Part description file (.wpd or .webpart) and a Web Part assembly file (.dll). Web Part assembly files contain the logic that makes the Web Part work. Web Part description files are simply XML descriptions of the Web Part; they contain the default and personalized properties for a given Web Part. Therefore, they are small and can be e-mailed, which makes their distribution simple.

Clicking *Export* allows you to save Web Part description files only. For Web Parts that are included with SharePoint Products and Technologies, the description is all that is needed. For Web Parts from third parties, you must install the appropriate .dll file, as well as import the description file. To export a file, click Export and specify where the file should be saved using a meaningful file name.

> **Caution**   Many Web Parts require Web Part resource files, in addition to description and assembly files, for them to function properly. Also, some Web Parts reference more than one Web Part assembly file and therefore require all of the assemblies they reference to function.

Viewing a Web Part's XML   The Web Part's XML description file contains the Web Part's properties and references to all of the assemblies on which the Web Part is dependent. Blank properties indicate that the Web Part uses the default. The <assembly> property references the Web Part assembly file for the particular Web Part file.

Managing Web Part Permissions   Web Part permissions are handled in the same manner as permissions for any list or list items, which are covered in Chapter 4, "Creating Site Collections." To set permissions for an individual Web Part, click on its Edit icon. By default the Web Part gallery inherits permissions from the Site Settings > Advanced Permissions. If the Web Part gallery is still inheriting permissions and you select *Manage Permissions of Parent* you will be directly altering the Advanced Permissions. If the Web Part gallery has its own unique permissions, you will be altering the Web Part galleries permissions. Take care to ensure that you alter only the desired set of permissions. To manage gallery-level permissions, browse to Settings > Gallery Setting > Permissions And Management > Permissions for this gallery, as shown in Figure 5-12.

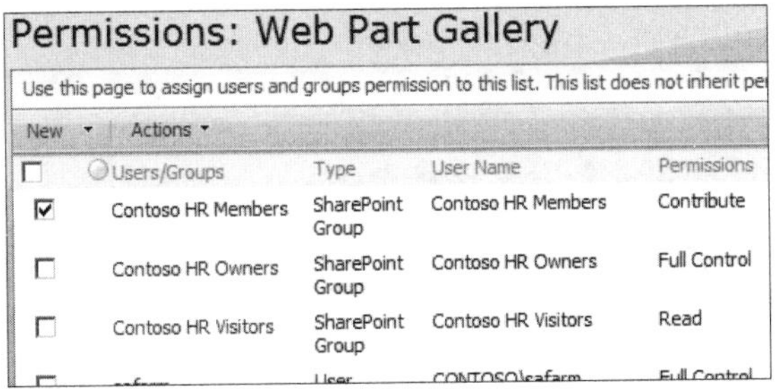

	Users/Groups	Type	User Name	Permissions
☑	Contoso HR Members	SharePoint Group	Contoso HR Members	Contribute
☐	Contoso HR Owners	SharePoint Group	Contoso HR Owners	Full Control
☐	Contoso HR Visitors	SharePoint Group	Contoso HR Visitors	Read
☐	...farm	User	CONTOSO\safarm	Full Control

Figure 5-12   Select the object to manage and choose Remove, Edit, or Inherit from the Actions menu.

Importing Web Parts

To import a Web Part, select *Upload Document* from the Upload drop-down list of the Web Part gallery. Enter the path for, or browse to the file that you wish to import. If you wish to overwrite existing files, select the *Overwrite Existing Files* check box. After clicking OK, the *Edit Item* page for the Web Part is displayed. You can change the Web Part's File Name, Title, Group, and Quick Add Group values. The *Quick Add Group* adds the Web Part to a list of recommended Web Parts for a given Web Part zone.

Important   Only Web Part description files are uploaded to the Web Part gallery. If the Web Part's assembly file isn't already on the server, it must be added to the *http(s)://<webapp>/bin* directory or the Global Assembly Cache (GAC).

Importing Web Part Assembly Files

All Web Parts require both a Web Part description file (.dwp or .webpart) and an assembly file (.dll). Uploading Web Parts to the Web Part gallery or importing them to a page only retrieves the Web Part description file. The assembly must also be added for the Web Part to function. Web Part assemblies must be added either to the Bin directory of the site collection on which they will be used or to the global assembly cache (GAC). Web Part assemblies located in the Bin directory must be registered as Safe Controls in the Web.config file. Web Part assemblies located in the GAC must be strong-named to function.

Adding Web Parts Using Stsadm.exe

Of the several ways in which to deploy Web Parts, using Stsadm.exe is perhaps the most straightforward. Adding Web Parts with Stsadm.exe has two significant advantages. Because the Web Part deploys from a Cabinet (.cab) file, all of its resources are also deployed. In addition, deployment using Stsadm.exe is a simple two-step process.

The syntax for deploying a Web Part using Stsadm.exe is:

```
stsadm.exe -o addwppack -filename <Web Part Package filename>
or -name <name of Web Part Package> [-lcid <language>]
[-url <url>] [-globalinstall] [-force] [-nodeploy]
```

- **-filename**   Specifies the location of the .cab file to be deployed.

- **-name**   If the Web Part package has already been added to a site collection, it can be added to others without using the .cab file. Instead of the filename, use *-name* and the name of the Web Part package.

   Tip   *Stsadm -o enumwppacks* lists all of the Web Part packages on a server.

- **-lcid**   Specifies the language code identification number.

- **-url**   Is the URL of the site collection to which the Web Part will be added. If you do not specify a URL, the Web Part is added to all Windows SharePoint Services–enabled virtual servers on the computer.

- **-globalinstall**   Installs the Web Part in GAC. Only strong-named assemblies can be installed in the GAC. Assemblies that are not strong-named are added to the Bin directory instead.

- **-force**   Causes already installed Web packages with the same name to be overwritten.

- **-nodeploy**   Prepares the Web Part pack to deploy using the *stsadm -o deploywppack* command.

Tip   Web Part Packs can be deployed and retracted according to a schedule using:

```
stsadm.exe -o deploywppack -name <Web Part Package name>
[-url <virtual server url>] [-time <time to deploy at>]
[-immediate][-local] [-lcid <language>]
[-globalinstall] [-force]
```

and

```
stsadm.exe -o retractwppack -name <Web Part Package name>
[-url <virtual server url>] [-time <time to retract at>]
[-immediate][-local] [-lcid <language>]
```

After the Web Part has been added using Stsadm.exe, it still must be added to the Web Part gallery using the New function.

Deleting Web Part Packages Using Stsadm.exe

A Web Part package can be removed from a virtual server using *stsadm -o deletewppack*, which has the syntax:

```
stsadm.exe -o deletewppack -name <name of Web Part Package >
[-lcid <language>] [-url <url>]
```

- **-name**   Specifies the name of the Web Part pack to be removed.

- **-lcid**   Specifies the language code identification number.

- **-url**   Specifies the virtual server from which the Web Part pack will be removed. If no URL is specified, it will be removed from all Windows SharePoint Services-enabled Virtual Servers on the computer.

After deleting the Web Part pack, you must manually delete its Web Part gallery entry.

Adding Web Part Assembly Files to the Bin

The process for adding a Web Part to the Bin directory is relatively straightforward and has four steps. It is much easier to do than describe and should become second nature with practice.

1. Identify the assembly name in the Web Part description file (.dwp or .webpart).

   Use Notepad to open the Web Part description file of the Web Part that you wish to import. Find the Web Part's assembly tag. Copy the portion between the <Assembly> and </Assembly> tags as shown in Figure 5-13. Keep this copy of Notepad open, because it is needed again in Step 2.

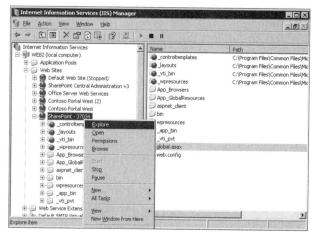

Figure 5-13 Copy the assembly tag in the Web Part description file.

2. Add the assembly name from the Web Part file to the safe controls list in the Web.config file.

    ❑ The Web.config file for the site collection is located in the root directory of the site collection virtual server. Using IIS Manager, find the site collection you wish to add the Web Part to under Web Sites. Right-click on the Web site's name and choose Explore as shown in Figure 5-14.

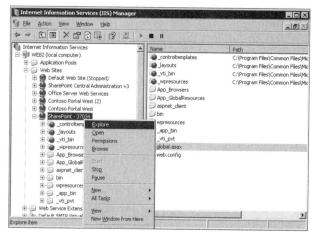

Figure 5-14 You can open the Web.config file using IIS manager.

    ❑ Open the Web.config file with Notepad. Find the <SafeControls> section of the Web.config file. Copy the first <SafeControl> entry. It is easier to adapt a copy than type the entry by hand. Simply highlight and copy, as shown in Figure 5-15.

Figure 5-15 Copy the first Safe Control entry in the Web.config file.

❑ Paste the copy of the <SafeControl> entry at the beginning of the list, and separate it from the list with a carriage return for easy reference, as shown in Figure 5-16.

```
<webPartCache Storage="CacheObject" />
<webPartControls DatasheetControlGuid="65BCBEE4-7728-41a0-97BE-14E1CAE36AAE" />
<SafeControls>

  <SafeControl Assembly="System.Web, Version=1.0.5000.0, Culture=neutral, PublicKeyT(

  <SafeControl Assembly="System.Web, Version=1.0.5000.0, Culture=neutral, PublicKeyT(
  <SafeControl Assembly="System.Web, Version=1.0.5000.0, Culture=neutral, PublicKeyT(
```

Figure 5-16   Paste the copy of the Safe Control into the Web.config file.

❑ Replace the value of Assembly= "..." in the Web.config file with the value between <Assembly> </Assembly> that was located in Step 1, as shown in Figure 5-17.

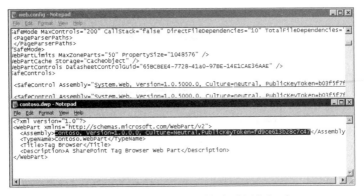

Figure 5-17   Replace the underlined text with the highlighted text.

❑ After updating the <Assembly> tag in the Web.config file, there is still some work to be done. Change the Namespace so that it matches the assembly name.

> **Note**   If you have been given a Namespace for a Web Part other than its assembly name, use it and not the assembly name.

❑ Change the TypeName value to TypeName="*". Make sure that Safe has the value Safe="True". If you would like a design package such as SharePoint Designer to be able to modify the Web Part, set AllowRemoteDesigner="True".

❑ Finally, check the safe control structure, for a Web Part description that contains the following.

```
<Assembly>Contoso, Version=1.0.0.0, Culture=Neutral,
PublicKeyToken=fd9ce613b28c7c47</Assembly>
```

You should have a SafeControl entry that looks like:

```
<SafeControl Assembly="Contoso, Version=1.0.0.0,
Culture=Neutral, PublicKeyToken=fd9ce613b28c7c47"
Namespace="Contoso" TypeName="*"
Safe="True" AllowRemoteDesigner="True"/>
```

3. Place the Web Part's assembly file (.dll) in the Bin directory of the SharePoint collection.

   Using IIS Manager, find the Bin directory of the Site Collection's virtual server. Right-click on the Bin directory and choose Explore. Copy the Web Part assembly file to the Bin directory. As seen in Figure 5-18, verify that you are in the correct virtual server.

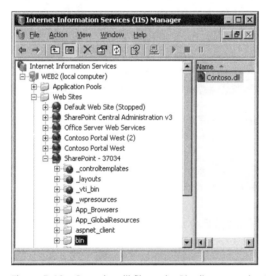

Figure 5-18   Copy the .dll file to the Bin directory using IIS Manager.

4. Add the Web Part to a page or the Web Part gallery

   Import the Web Part description file to a page, or add it to the Web Part gallery just as you would any other Web Part.

Web Part Maintenance View

If a Web Part is placed on a page where it does not work properly, a Web Part Page Maintenance page can be used to remove the problem Web Part. No link to this page is available under normal circumstances. However, when a page fails to load, the Maintenance

Page should open automatically, or an error message should contain a link to the maintenance page. The page can also be reached by appending *?contents=1* to the URL of the broken page. For instance, for the URL *http://hr.conotso.msft/default.aspx*, entering *http://hr.conotso.msft/default.aspx?contents=1* causes the Web Part Maintenance Page to be displayed, as seen in Figure 5-19.

Figure 5-19   The Web Part Maintenance page allows you to remove Web Parts from a broken page.

Using the Maintenance page, you can remove problem Web Parts and reset all of the personalizations on the page to shared values. If the problem is only with your personal view, you can select *Switch To Personal View.*

> **Tip**   You can deploy custom Web parts and features to the entire farm using Solutions. For more information on deploying Solutions, please visit *http://msdn2.microsoft.com/en-us/library/aa544500.aspx.*

Chapter 6
Using Workflows and Information Management Policies

One of the challenges that organizations face is how to accurately monitor and guide the flow of information in their business processes. To meet this challenge, SharePoint Server 2007 provides Information Management Policies that enable you to define a set of rules that govern content labeling, auditing, and expiration of documents and list items. SharePoint Server 2007 also includes a set of built-in workflow templates that allow you to program the sequence of steps that a document or list item must go through for approval or completion.

Automating Document Management in SharePoint Server 2007

Many of your business processes can now be automated using the document management features of SharePoint Server 2007. Although it is possible to create workflows in Windows SharePoint Services implementations, the built-in workflow templates are only available with SharePoint Server. To create custom workflows for either Windows SharePoint Services or SharePoint Server, you must use SharePoint Designer to create basic workflows with custom logic, or Visual Studio to create unique workflows that can include .NET code modules.

Workflow Automation

The purpose of adding workflow to your sites is to automate repetitive operations and ensure that critical tasks are assigned to the appropriate person and then completed. Workflows can be configured so that users can start them manually, but most are scheduled to start when a document or list item is created or when it is updated. Combining the automatic triggering of a workflow with business logic that evaluates conditions on an item allows you to create workflows that only take effect after specific criteria are met.

There are several workflow templates available with SharePoint Server 2007, and each is covered in this chapter. The standard workflows and their functions are described below:

- Approval Workflow: routes a document for approval
- Three-State Workflow: tracks items in a list
- Translation Management Workflow: manages document translation
- Collect Feedback Workflow: routes a document for review
- Collect Signatures Workflow: gathers digital signatures needed to complete a Microsoft Office document
- Disposition Approval Workflow: manages document expiration and retention

Note There is also a Group Approval workflow that is available only in East Asian versions of SharePoint Server 2007, and therefore it is not covered in this chapter.

In addition to the pre-installed workflow templates, you can also create new workflows and attach them directly to lists and libraries using SharePoint Designer 2007. When you need to implement more complex logic than is provided by the pre-installed workflow templates listed above, then consider using SharePoint Designer to create custom workflows. A custom workflow allows you to specify complex criteria that permit the workflow engine to execute business logic against a document or a list item. Workflows built with SharePoint Designer are stored in the site, but are always assigned directly to a specific SharePoint list and cannot be used for items in another list. Using Visual Studio 2005, it is possible to create true custom workflow templates that can be installed as Features on the server and made available to all sites and lists. Building custom workflow templates involves writing custom code and is outside the scope of this chapter.

Whether customizing a pre-installed workflow template or creating a custom workflow with SharePoint Designer, you can program the workflow to start automatically under specific conditions, such as when a document is first created or when it is changed. Workflows started in this way can be used to incorporate business practices and policies into your SharePoint environment and to ensure that certain procedures are always followed.

To determine which type of workflow you need for your organization, refer to Table 6-1.

Table 6-1   Common Workflow Scenarios

If you want to do this	Use this workflow
Add workflow for draft document approval in a document library	Approval
Authorize the publication of a Web page on your Intranet or Internet site	Approval
Route a document to others for review and comment	Collect Feedback
Obtain digital signatures on a document	Collect Signatures
Schedule a document to be reviewed for deletion when it expires in the Records Center	Disposition Approval
Track the handling of an issue	Three-State
Manage the routing of documents for translation to other formats or languages	Translation Management
Build multistep workflows or include specific business logic	Create a custom workflow

Information Management Policies

Many organizations need to implement controls on their information to remain in compliance with government regulations, such as HIPAA and the Sarbanes-Oxley Act of 2002, or to meet other legal requirements. Information Management Policies in SharePoint Server 2007 can be applied to lists and content types to help you meet these requirements. An Information Management Policy represents a set of rules governing one or more of the following:

- Label policy: automatically generate a text label that can be embedded in a document
- Audit policy: log some or all user activities on list items and documents
- Expiration policy: set a specific duration for a document or item and the method for deleting it when it expires
- Barcode policy: automatically generate a barcode that can be embedded in a document

Creating and Configuring Workflows

Configuring a workflow in SharePoint Server 2007 involves two steps: defining a customized instance of a workflow template and associating it with a list, library, or content type. To customize a workflow template you need to have the Manage Lists permission, which is included in the Design permission level. In most sites the only group that has this permission is the site owners group; however, in a publishing site, a Designers group also may have this permission. The Manage Lists permission also grants the ability to create custom workflows with SharePoint Designer. Associating a workflow with a list or library makes that workflow available only to items or documents in that list. Associating a workflow with a content type makes the workflow available to all documents that are based on that content type.

Creating a New Workflow

Although the steps for fully configuring each workflow vary depending on the type of workflow, the initial configuration is the same for all:

1. Browse to the list or library on which you want to create the workflow.

2. On the Settings menu, click *Document Library Settings* (or click *List Settings* for a list).

3. Under Permissions and Management, click *Workflow Settings* (shown in Figure 6-1).

> **Note**   If this is not the first workflow for this list, then you next see the Change Workflow Settings page, and you need to click *Add A Workflow* to go to the Add A Workflow page.

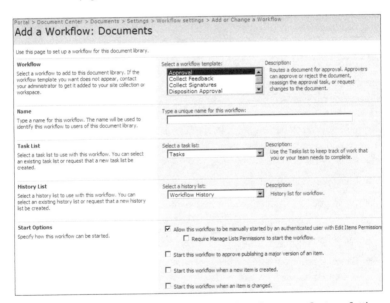

Figure 6-1   To create a new workflow, browse to Site > Document Center > Settings > Workflow Settings > Add Or Change A Workflow.

4. In the Workflow list, choose the workflow template on which to base your workflow.

5. In the Name box, enter a name for the workflow that is unique within the list or library.

6. In the Task List drop-down box, select the Tasks list that will be used to track the workflow steps as they are assigned to users. If you do not want to use an existing Tasks list, then select *New Task List.*

> **Tip**   If the workflow involves a document that is in a restricted library or the subject of the workflow is sensitive, then it is advisable to use a new Tasks list for the workflow. For greater security, create the new Tasks list manually, and modify its permissions to restrict access only to those involved in the workflow.

7. In the History List drop-down box, select the *Workflow History List* that will be used to track workflow steps as they are completed. If you do not want to use an existing list, then select *New History List.*

8. In the Start Options section you can choose from four options that determine how the workflow will be initiated:

   ❑ The first option allows users who have Edit permissions on the list to manually start the workflow. This permission is assigned to anyone in the site Members group. You can additionally restrict this right only to those with Manage Lists permissions.

   ❑ The second option triggers the workflow to start when a user saves a document as a major version or selects the Publish a Major Version command. This option is only available for the Approval workflow and requires that Content Approval be enabled on the library. This option overrides the option to start a workflow when a document is created or changed, and the following two options will no longer be available. If the option is dimmed, then Major and Minor Versioning have not been turned on for the library.

   To enable Content Approval: (a) Browse to the document library you want to configure. (b) From the Settings menu, choose Document Library Settings. (c) Under General Settings, click Versioning Settings. (d) Under Content Approval click Yes to require content approval for submitted items. (e) Click OK.

   > **Important**   Only one Approval workflow can be configured to start automatically when a major version is published.

❑   The third option starts the workflow when a document is created and only runs once. If the Require Check Out feature has been enabled on the document library, then the workflow will not start until the document is checked in the first time.

❑   The fourth option starts the workflow when a document is modified. This option starts the workflow when either the document or one of its properties is changed. If the document is first checked out, then the workflow will not start until the document is checked in again.

9. Click Next or OK.

> **Note**   There may be an additional page of configuration for some types of workflow. For further details, see the section on each workflow later in this chapter.

Starting a Workflow

If a workflow is configured to allow users to start it manually, then any user with the Edit item permission can launch the workflow as needed. To start a workflow, do the following steps:

1. Browse to the list or library containing the workflow that you want to run.

2. From the item or document drop-down menu, click *Workflows* as shown in Figure 6-2. The Workflows selection page then appears, similar to the one shown in Figure 6-3. The specific set of workflows available varies depending on the workflows that have been configured on the list and content type.

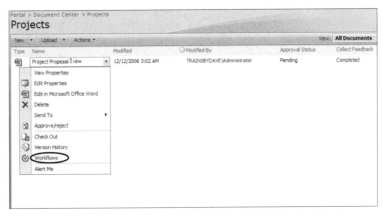

Figure 6-2   You can start a workflow on an individual item by selecting Workflows in the drop-down menu.

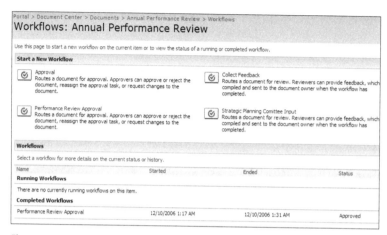

Figure 6-3   Create a workflow from the Workflows selection page.

3. Click the workflow that you want to start. The workflow Start page then appears, similar to the one shown in Figure 6-4.

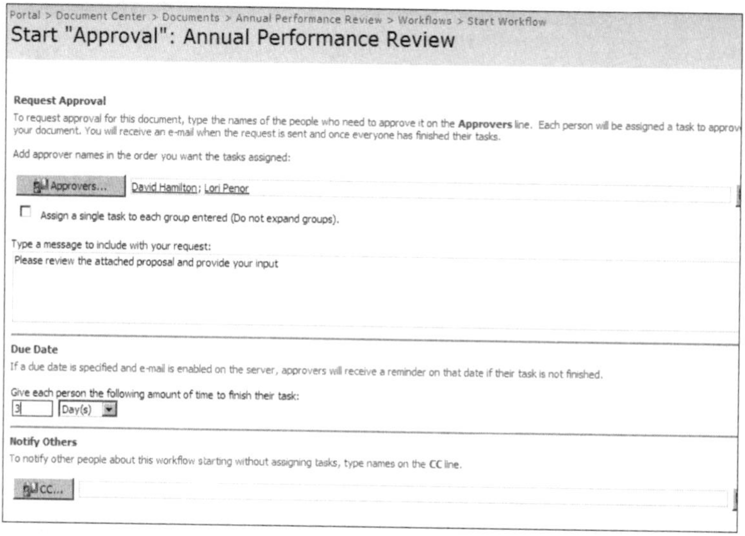

Figure 6-4   Start a workflow from the workflow Start page.

4. Enter the account names of those users who will be assigned to the workflow, if defaults have not been supplied.

5. Enter a message that will be included in the e-mail sent to users assigned to this workflow and that will appear in the tasks created for users in the Tasks list.

6. Enter a Due Date for each user to finish his or her task in the workflow. If the workflow is assigned as a set of serial tasks (as is the default Approval workflow shown in Figure 6-4), then enter the number of days or weeks that each user will have to complete the task. If the page shows a parallel workflow, then enter the final due date for all users to complete their tasks.

7. Click Start. SharePoint Server 2007 will start the workflow.

Completing a Workflow Assignment

SharePoint Server 2007 assigns workflow steps to users by creating a task item in a Tasks list in the same site as the workflow being processed. Users who are included in a workflow will receive an e-mail informing them that they have been assigned a task, as shown in Figure 6-5.

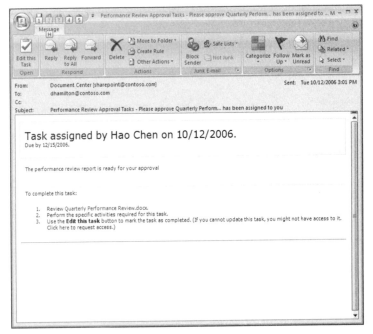

Figure 6-5 Users receive workflow assignment e-mails with a link and instructions to the task.

To open the task assignment a user can either click the *Edit This Task* option button as shown in Figure 6-5, or browse to the Tasks list in the site and edit the task directly.

After a user clicks the Edit This Task button, the task details screen opens, similar to the one in Figure 6-6.

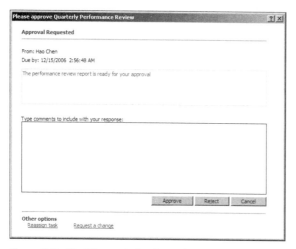

Figure 6-6   Workflow task details can be opened from e-mail.

From this screen a user can complete the task according to the type of workflow that has been started. In this example, an Approval workflow is underway, which offers the user the options to Approve or Reject the document in question. If the user has been granted the right to reassign the task or request a change to the task, then these links are also shown. The Reassign Task link allows users to redirect the task to another user, and the Request A Change link allows users to respond to the originator of the workflow with a comment or question. Once the user completes the task in the workflow, SharePoint Server 2007 marks the task completed in the workflow history table and continues to process the next step in the workflow.

Canceling a Running Workflow

1. On the document that is currently running the workflow, click the drop-down menu and select *Workflows*.

2. Under the Running Workflows section, click the workflow that you want to cancel.

3. Click *Cancel This Workflow*.

Approval Workflow

The Approval workflow is used to direct a document or list item to a series of users who can review and determine if it should be approved for further disclosure. Its primary purpose is to provide a robust method for managing the content approval process on a list or library. When content approval is enabled for a list, then all items that are saved to the list must be approved by an administrator or a user with approver permissions before they can be viewed by other users. Requiring content approval on a list does not, by itself, require that a workflow be used to administer the approval process. Items can be manually approved by a user with the appropriate rights, but without a workflow in place, the approvers do not receive any notification that items are ready for approval.

A basic Approval workflow is already configured to be available on any document that is associated with the Document content type, and it can be started by any user with Edit rights on the list item. The basic Approval workflow is configured as a serial workflow and requires users to start the workflow manually whenever they want to have an item approved. To ensure that a workflow starts automatically, you need to configure a workflow that starts when a specific condition is met. In this case the condition would be when an item is published as a major version. Only one workflow on a list or library configured to start automatically when an item is published.

Enabling Content Approval on a List or Library

1. Browse to the main page of the list or library.

2. On the Settings menu, click *List Settings* (or Document Library Settings).

3. Under General Settings, click *Versioning* settings.

4. Under Content Approval, click the Yes option.

5. For a Document Library, under Document Version History, click the option to *Create Major And Minor (Draft) Versions*.

6. Under Draft Item Security, click the option to allow Only users who can approve items to see drafts.

7. Click OK.

Configuring an Approval Workflow

To create a customized Approval workflow, begin by following the steps for creating a workflow, described earlier in this chapter. After clicking *Next* on the Add A Workflow page, the Customize Workflow page appears. Follow the steps below.

1. On the Customize Workflow page, make selections in the Workflow Tasks section, shown in Figure 6-7.

   ❑ Choose whether to assign tasks all participants at once (parallel workflow) or to assign tasks to one participant at a time (serial workflow). When you choose serial workflow, each user who receives a task must complete it before it can be assigned to the next user.

❑   Choose the option to allow users to reassign the task to another person when you cannot guarantee that every document will be processed in the same way. Providing this option can allow the workflow to be re-routed to the most appropriate person for the task.

❑   Choose the option to allow users to request a change before completing the task if it would be better to let users make suggestions about a document before completing their task on it.

Figure 6-7   You can route tasks serially or in parallel, but not both.

2.   Enter values in the Default Workflow Start Values section, shown in Figure 6-8. If the workflow can be started manually, then these default values can be modified by users when they start the workflow. When the workflow starts automatically, then these values are used without modification.

3.   Enter the specific users or groups who should be assigned tasks in the workflow. When you check the box to assign a single task to each group, then the entire group is treated as one user for the purposes of task assignment. Only one task is created, and any member of the group can respond to it.

4.   Uncheck the option to allow changes to the participant list if you plan to allow the workflow to be started manually but do not want users changing the routing list.

5.   Enter a message to send to users in the e-mail that SharePoint Server 2007 will generate when they are assigned a task.

6.   If you chose to make this a parallel task, enter a date by which all users assigned the task must respond. Note that the workflow will not finish automatically; if not finished, it simply sends e-mail reminders. If you chose to make this a serial task, then enter the number of days or weeks. The duration for both must be between 1 and 999.

7.   (Optional) Include a list of users to be notified about the workflow in the Notify Others field. These users will receive an alert but not a task assignment.

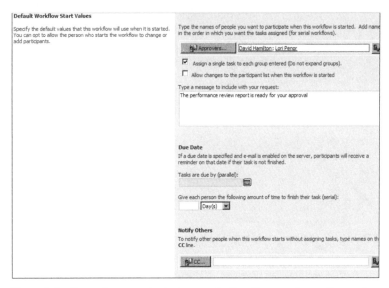

Figure 6-8   If you allow users to start manually, then they can change these values.

8. In the Complete The Workflow section, shown in Figure 6-9, indicate what conditions will dictate that the workflow is either completed or canceled. For a serial workflow it is assumed that all users must complete their tasks for the workflow to be completed. In the case of a parallel workflow, you can elect to have the workflow declared complete when a specific number of users have completed their tasks. The workflow can be cancelled automatically either when a user Rejects the document or when someone changes it.

9. In the Post-completion Workflow Activities section, shown in Figure 6-9, you can choose to have the workflow automatically update the approval status of the document based on the results of the workflow. If you leave the Update The Approval Status box cleared, then any further action on the document will have to be done manually.

10. Click OK.

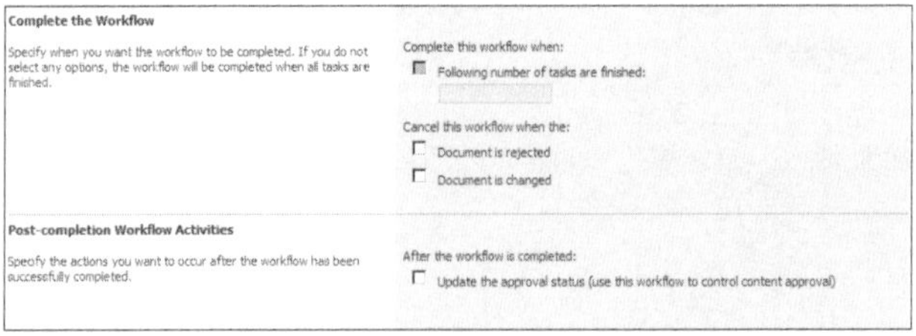

Figure 6-9   Indicate when to cancel the workflow, if required.

Note   If a user who has approval permissions on a document uses the Approve/ Reject command on the document to approve it, rather than responding to the workflow task, then the workflow is cancelled automatically.

Collect Feedback Workflow

A Collect Feedback workflow is similar in behavior to an Approval workflow. In both cases, a document or list item is routed to a set of users for review and consideration. Both types of workflows can be used to approve the publishing of a major version, but only the Approval workflow can start automatically when the item is published. The Collect Feedback workflow is used for the same purpose as routing a document for review via e-mail: to disseminate information and solicit input. The advantage of using a workflow is that it enables you to do all these tasks more easily: set a deadline for responding, monitor who has responded, and view all the comments in one place when the workflow is completed.

To create a customized Collect Feedback workflow, follow the steps for creating a workflow described earlier in this chapter and configure the workflow to start either automatically or manually, as needed. To start the workflow, follow the steps for starting a workflow described earlier in this chapter.

Once the Collect Feedback workflow has run, you can view the feedback by opening the Workflow History page:

1. Browse to the list or library hosting the workflow.

2. On the list or document drop-down menu, click *Workflows*.

3. Under Running Workflows section, click the Collect Feedback workflow that has completed.

On the Workflow Status page, you can view the Workflow History, which will look similar to Figure 6-10.

Workflow History

■ View workflow reports
The following events have occurred in this workflow.

Date Occurred	Event Type	User ID	Description	Outcome
12/12/2006 3:23 AM	Workflow Initiated	Hao Chen	Collect Feedback was started. Participants: David Hamilton, Lori Penor	
12/12/2006 3:23 AM	Task Created	Hao Chen	Task created for David Hamilton. Due by: 12/15/2006 12:00:00 AM	
12/12/2006 3:23 AM	Task Created	Hao Chen	Task created for Lori Penor. Due by: 12/15/2006 12:00:00 AM	
12/12/2006 3:27 AM	Task Completed	David Hamilton	Task assigned to David Hamilton was completed by David Hamilton. Comments: I agree with the objectives of the proposal and the timeline. I recommend we allocate more testing resources to phase 3 to ensure that the deadline is met.	Reviewed by David Hamilton
12/12/2006 3:30 AM	Task Completed	Lori Penor	Task assigned to Lori Penor was completed by Lori Penor. Comments: Sections 1 and 2 look good. I suggest we try to add more details to section 3 so we can be certain we have covered all the issues there.	Reviewed by Lori Penor
12/12/2006 3:30 AM	Workflow Completed	Hao Chen	Collect Feedback was completed.	Collect Feedback on Project Proposal has successfully completed. All participants have completed their tasks.

Figure 6-10   View workflow status on the Workflow History page.

Collect Signatures Workflow

The Collect Signatures workflow is used to gather digital signatures from a group of people using Microsoft Office 2007. Unlike other workflows, this workflow must be started from within either Microsoft Word 2007 or Microsoft Excel 2007 and cannot be started automatically when an item is created or changed. To start the workflow the user must first prepare the file by inserting one or more digital signature lines into the document. These lines are Microsoft Office 2007 placeholders that allow users to digitally sign a document in a specific place. Once the document is digitally signed, it will become read-only and any attempts to modify the document will invalidate the signatures.

To create a customized Collect Feedback workflow, follow the steps for creating a workflow, described earlier in this chapter, and configure it to start either manually or automatically.

Adding a Digital Signature Line to a Document

1. Browse to the document library that contains the file.

2. From the document drop-down menu, click *Edit* in Microsoft Word (or Microsoft Excel).

3. Inside the document, place your pointer in the location in your document where you want to add a signature line.

4. On the Insert tab, in the Text group, click the arrow next to Signature Line, and then click *Microsoft Office Signature Line*.

5. In the Signature Setup dialog box, shown in Figure 6-11, fill out the suggested signer information. Enter the suggested signer's name, title, e-mail address, and any instructions for the signer. If you want to allow the signer to add a comment and to show the date when the signature is added in the signature line, then check the appropriate boxes.

6. Click OK.

Figure 6-11 You must fill out the information for suggested signer, suggested signer's title, and e-mail address.

Starting a Collect Signatures Workflow

1. Open the document that requires signatures and make sure that there is at least one signature line in the document and that the document is currently checked in.

2. From the Microsoft Office button, click *Start Workflow*.

3. In the Workflows dialog box, locate the Collect Signatures workflow and click *Start*.

4. In the Collect Signatures dialog box, shown in Figure 6-12, review the names of the people who are assigned to sign the document and make changes to the Suggested Signers if necessary. You may need to click the Check Names button to the right of each signature to validate the e-mail addresses.

5. To route the signature requests in serial order, select the *Request Signatures In The Order Above, Rather Than All At Once* check box. This option is only available when the document contains more than one signature line.

6. Click *Start*.

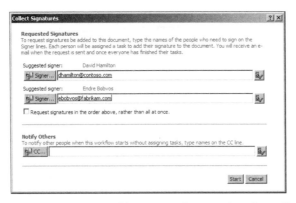

Figure 6-12 You can add a manager, for example, to be notified when workflows begin.

When the workflow starts, the requested signers receive e-mails inviting them to sign the document. The e-mail contains a link to the document that the user can click to open it. A document does not need to be checked out from the document library to be signed. In fact, checking out the document and saving it again invalidates any signatures already in the document. To sign the document, users can double-click the signature line reserved for their use and either type their name or select a signature image from a file. Once the document has been signed, the signers must mark the task as completed in the SharePoint Server 2007 Workflow Task page.

Three-State Workflow

The Three-State Workflow is the most flexible and powerful of the out-of-the-box workflows provided with SharePoint Server 2007. It is designed to track the resolution of open issues in an Issues list, such as Helpdesk calls or order fulfillment. The workflow allows you to specify three different status levels or states for every item in the workflow: an Initial state that the item has when the workflow starts, a Middle state that it takes when its status is updated to indicate that some action has been taken, and a Final state to indicate that the issue is completed or closed. The first two states can be configured with custom routing and a custom e-mail message with instructions to the assignee. Although the Three-State Workflow works well for tracking issues, it can also be used to track items in any list or library.

> **Real World**   For example, a Three-State Workflow could be used to process a backordered product in a warehouse. When a product is backordered, an item is created in an Issues list, which starts the workflow. The state of the workflow is maintained in the Status field. Creating a new issue item sets the Initial state to "backordered," which sends an e-mail to the warehouse staff asking them to ship the product when it becomes available. After the product is eventually shipped, a warehouse staff member edits the Issue item and changes the Status field to "Shipped." This signals that the issue has reached its Middle state, and in response, the workflow sends an e-mail to the sales staff indicating that the product is on its way. The sales staff member follows up with the customer to ensure that the product has arrived and then changes the Status field of the item to Fulfilled, indicating that the issue has reached its Final state, which terminates the workflow.

Configuring a List for the Three-State Workflow

Although you can apply a Three-State Workflow to any type of list, the workflow requires at least one field to be a Choice data type that can be used to indicate the different states of the workflow. The Issue Tracking list is automatically provided with three Choice columns: Issue Status, Priority, and Category. Any of these columns can be used to track workflow state, or you can create a custom column to use for that purpose.

Adding a Custom Choice Column to a List

1. Browse to the main page of the list or library.

2. On the Settings menu, click *Create Column*.

3. In the Column name box, enter a name for the column.

4. Click *Choice* (menu to choose from).

5. In the Additional Column Settings section, click *Require That This Column Contains Information*.

6. Select the existing choices in the choice list and delete them; then type at least three new values in the box.

7. Click OK.

Configuring a Three-State Workflow

To create a customized Three-State Workflow, begin by following the steps for creating a workflow, described earlier in this chapter. After clicking *Next* on the Add A Workflow page, the Customize Workflow page appears. Follow the steps below.

1. On the Customize the Three-State Workflow page the first section is the Workflow States section, shown in Figure 6-13. In the first drop-down list, select the column that will be used to track the workflow state. In the next three drop-down lists, select the values in that column that will be used to track the Initial state, the Middle state, and the Final state, respectively.

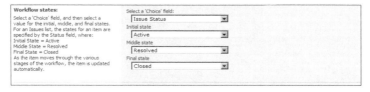

Figure 6-13   Select the choice and initial status for each state of the workflow.

2. Under the Specify What You Want To Happen When A Workflow Is Initiated section, shown in Figure 6-14, provide details about the task to be generated when the workflow starts. Under the Task Details section, enter a custom message that will appear in the Title of the first task that will be created for the workflow. This first task is the one issued to the user specified in the Task Assigned To setting lower down in the section. To append a value from one of the columns in the list item that started the workflow, check the box *Include List Field* and select the column from the drop-down list.

3. Under Task Description, enter the text that will appear in the Description column of the task. To include a field value in this description, check the box *Include List Field*, and select the field from the drop-down list. To include a hyperlink for the user to browse directly to the item in this list, check the *Insert Link To The List Item* check box.

4. Under Task Assigned To, you can assign the task to the value of any column in the list that holds a "Person or Group" data type. All lists have the Created By and Modified By columns, and some, such as the Issues Tracking list, have additional columns like Assigned To. Optionally, you can select a specific user to assign the task to.

5. In the E-mail Message Details section, check the box *Send E-Mail Message* to create an e-mail message in addition to the task that will be created. In the To box, enter the e-mail address of the person to whom the e-mail should be sent, and check the *Include Task Assigned To* box to send the e-mail also to the assignee of the task. In the Subject box enter a subject for the e-mail and check the *Use Task Title* box to include the task title specified in the Task Details section above. In the Body box enter the message for the body of the e-mail and to also include a hyperlink to the item in this list, check the *Insert Link To List Item* check box.

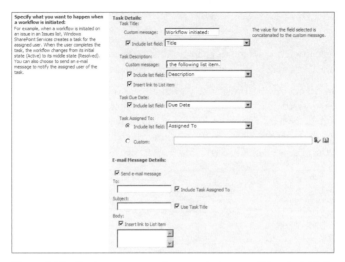

Figure 6-14 You have very granular control when specifying the initiation behavior.

6. The Specify What You Want To Happen When A Workflow Changes To Its Middle State section, shown in Figure 6-15, follows the same format as the previous section. Complete the settings here to assign a task to a user when the status of the list item changes to the value specified in the Middle State setting at the top of the page.

7. Click OK.

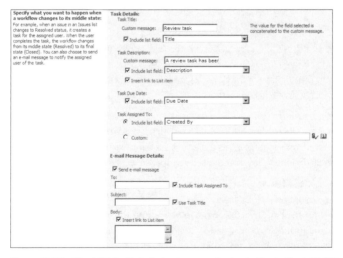

Figure 6-15 The Middle State behavior page looks similar to the Initial State page, but use caution when creating the custom message, as it should be clear which stage the user is in.

Translation Management Workflow

A Translation Management workflow is used to manage and track the work associated with translating documents to different languages. This workflow is available only inside a Translation Management Library which is a special type of document library available only in Office SharePoint Server 2007. Before you can use this workflow you may have to activate it as a Feature within the site.

Activating the Translation Management Workflow

1. From the Site Actions menu, select *Site Settings*.

2. Under Site Administration, click *Site Features*.

3. If the Status of the Translation Management Library is not marked as Active, click *Activate*.

After activating the workflow in the site, you can create a Translation Management library by clicking *Create* under the Site Actions menu and selecting *Translation Management Library* under Libraries. The library creation screen gives you the option to add a Translation Management workflow to the library, or you can add it later.

Configuring a Translation Management Workflow

To configure a workflow, select either the option when a Translation Management library is created or click *Add A Workflow* from the Workflows settings page. Begin by following the steps for creating a workflow described earlier in this chapter. After clicking *Next* on the Add A Workflow page, the Customize Translation Management Workflow page, shown in Figure 6-16, appears. Follow the steps below.

1. In the Lists Of Languages And Translators section you can either use an existing Translators list or create a new one. Create a new one if no Translators table has been created yet.

2. If the Due Date is disabled, then the workflow is not set to start automatically. If it is enabled then you can specify the number of days that users have to complete the translation.

3. In the Complete The Workflow section, you can elect to have the workflow marked as complete as soon as the document is changed or wait until all tasks are completed.

4. Click OK.

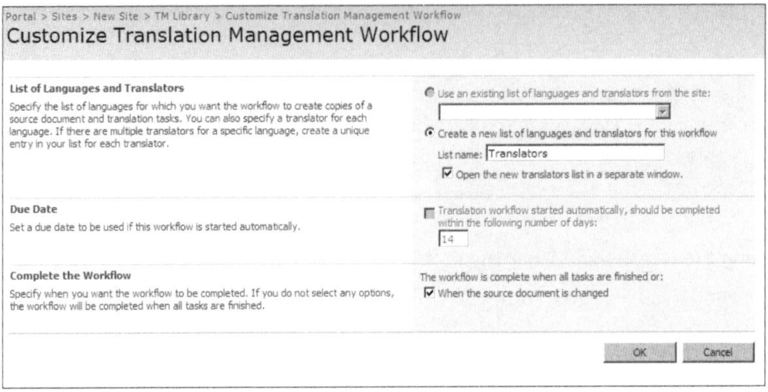

Figure 6-16   Translation management workflows are used to track translations of documents and Web pages.

The Translators List

The Translation Management workflow depends on a special list to track those users who will be performing translation on documents. The Translators list contains three columns of information related to translations: the Translating From and Translating To columns, which track the source and destination languages, respectively, and the Translator, which lists the person doing the translation. The Translators list is created automatically when you configure the workflow. Before a workflow can be started on a document, you need to populate the Translators list with at least one translator who can translate from the current language of the document. When a translation workflow starts, a task is issued to every translator whose From property matches the current language of the document. A copy of the document is made in the library for each language that it is translated into, based on the To languages of the translators who are available to translate.

Starting a Translation Management Workflow

When a Translation Management workflow starts, it assigns tasks automatically to all the appropriate translators based on the Language column value of the document, which is a required column in the library. When you complete the work of translating a copy of the document, save the work and mark the task as complete.

1. Browse to the library that contains the document to be translated.

2. From the Microsoft Office Button, click *Start Workflow.*

3. In the Workflows dialog box, locate the Translation Management workflow and click *Start.*

4. Under Request Translation, enter the date by when the translations should be complete.

5. Type a message to send to the translator of the document.

6. Click *Send*.

Disposition Approval Workflow

The Disposition Approval workflow is a special-purpose workflow that is used to manage the deletion of documents that expire through an Information Management Policy. Although the Disposition Approval workflow is most often used inside a Records Center site to track the automatic deletion of old content, it can be used in any site in which an Expiration Information Management Policy has been configured. When a document expires you can configure the document library to launch a Disposition Approval workflow to seek approval for the permanent deletion of a document. When a document is routed through the Disposition Approval workflow, it is held without being deleted until the users assigned to approve it have responded to the workflow. If deletion is approved then the document is permanently deleted from the site without going through the Recycle Bin. If deletion is not approved, then the document is held in the library without being deleted. The Expiration policy is discussed more fully in the Information Management Policy section later in this chapter.

Configuring a Disposition Approval Workflow

To use a Disposition Approval workflow you must (1) configure an instance of it on a document library or content type; (2) follow the steps for creating a workflow, described earlier in this chapter; and (3) do not configure the workflow to start either when the document is created or when it is modified. The workflow will be automatically started when the document expires. Unlike other workflows, you do not configure a routing list of users who will be assigned tasks for this workflow. Any user with Contribute permissions can respond to the task and approve the deletion.

> **Best Practices**   Because tasks are not assigned directly to individuals, it is important that any user who will be approving document deletions set an Alert on the Tasks list used to track Disposition Approval workflow tasks. Doing so ensures notification when the item expires.

Starting a Disposition Approval Workflow

If the Disposition Approval workflow is associated with an Information Management Policy, then it will start automatically. If you configured the workflow to allow users to start it manually, then it can be started using the following steps.

1. Browse to the list or library containing the workflow that you want to run.

2. From the item or document drop-down menu, click *Workflows* and select the Disposition Approval workflow that was configured for this list. The workflow will start and create a single task in the associated Tasks list.

Completing a Disposition Approval Workflow

To respond to a Disposition Approval task, a user must have Edit permissions in both the list that holds the item being deleted and in the Tasks list containing the task created by the workflow. When a user edits the task and selects *Delete Item*, as shown in Figure 6-17, the item is permanently deleted from the site. To retain log records of the item, check the box *Retain A Copy Of The Item's Metadata In The Audit Log*. When a user selects *Do Not Delete This Item*, the workflow ends, and the document or list item is marked as Exempt from expiration policies.

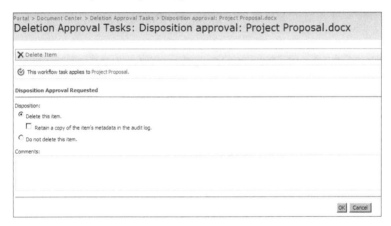

Figure 6-17   Disposition Approval Workflow Task.

> **Tip**   If you need to approve multiple disposition tasks then you can save time by selecting *Process All Tasks* from the Actions menu in the Tasks list. Doing so allows you to approve all tasks simultaneously.

Custom Workflows

If you need a workflow that provides more logic or control than you find in the out-of-the-box workflows to this point, you can create a custom workflow to meet your needs. Custom workflows can be developed in two ways. Using Visual Studio 2005 a developer can create workflows that directly interact with the Windows Workflow Foundation code library on which all workflows in SharePoint Server 2007 are based. This allows the developer to create virtually any type of workflow and to include custom code to perform actions that are not supported natively. Another way of creating custom workflows is by using SharePoint Designer 2007 to build a workflow for a specific purpose in a document library or list. SharePoint Designer does not require any coding, and workflows are deployed automatically to the list on which they are created. This chapter focuses on custom workflows created with SharePoint Designer.

SharePoint Designer 2007 allows you to connect to a SharePoint site and create a custom workflow associated with a library or list. SharePoint Designer provides you the ability to build complex workflows that involve conditional business logic and execute a variety of actions that are not available through the standard workflows in SharePoint Server 2007. For example, you can create a workflow to send an e-mail notification to the project manager on a team when a team member sets the Status column on a task item to Completed and, at the same time, create an item in an Announcements list to notify others as well.

Workflows created with SharePoint Designer can only be assigned to a single list or document library. Once a workflow has been created in SharePoint Designer it can only be modified using SharePoint Designer or through initiation variables created at design time.

Actions are the basic units of a workflow, with each action being a pre-built set of functionality, such as sending an e-mail or moving a list item.

Creating Workflows Using SharePoint Designer

To create a workflow in SharePoint Designer, follow these steps:

1. Launch SharePoint Designer 2007 and from the File menu select *Open Site* and enter the URL of the site where you will create the workflow.

2. From the File menu, select *New* and then select *Workflow*.

3. On the Define Your New Workflow page, shown in Figure 6-18, enter a name for the workflow, and select the list to which to apply the workflow from the drop-down list of available lists on the site. Select the options for starting the workflow.

> **Important**   SharePoint Designer only allows you to create Sequential workflows that execute completely once they are started. You cannot create state-based workflows that can pause and wait for a particular condition or event to occur and then resume. State-based workflows can only be created with Visual Studio 2005.

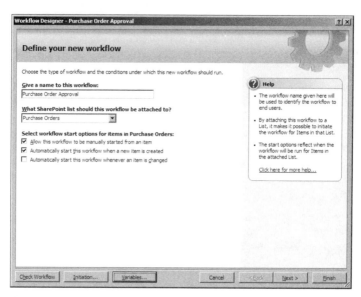

Figure 6-18   You can create custom workflows in SharePoint Designer 2007.

4. At the bottom of the screen, click the *Initiation* button, shown in Figure 6-19, to add an input field that users can fill in when they start the workflow. This input field can then be referenced by actions inside the workflow.

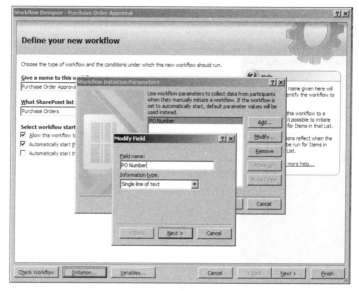

Figure 6-19   When creating custom workflows you can define initiation parameters.

5. At the bottom of the screen, click the Variables button, shown in Figure 6-20, to add local variables that can be used to store values temporarily as the workflow progresses.

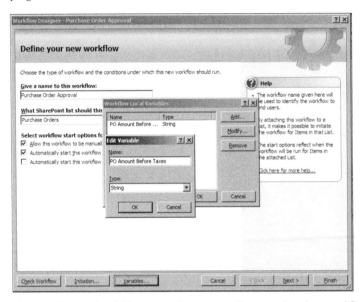

Figure 6-20   Local variables are used to temporarily store values for a workflow.

6. Click *Next*.

On the workflow steps configuration screen, shown in Figure 6-21, you can configure multiple sets of conditions and the actions that should follow them. You can also create additional steps to group sets of conditions and actions together.

7. Click *Conditions* and select one of the available conditions to evaluate against the workflow item. If the condition evaluates to True then the selected action(s) will be executed.

8. Click *Actions* and select one of the available actions to execute. You can select additional actions to take effect after the first one finishes. If you would prefer to have all actions run simultaneously, then click the small arrow button to the right of the Conditions section and select *Run All Actions In Parallel*.

9. To create additional sets of conditions and actions, click the link *Add 'Else If' Conditional Branch*.

10. To add further steps to the workflow, click the *Add Workflow Step* at the far right of the screen.

11. Click the *Check Workflow* button at the bottom of the screen to validate the workflow for errors.

12. Click *Finish*.

The workflow will now appear in the Workflow Settings of the list or library. No further configuration is required to start the workflow according to the start settings selected in the workflow configuration.

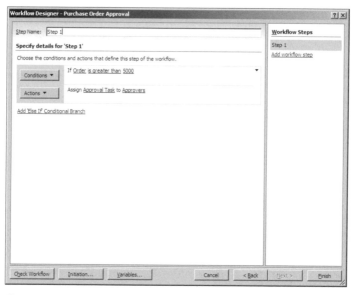

Figure 6-21 Be sure to intelligently name the workflow step so that users can quickly identify it.

Monitoring and Reporting on Workflows

There are several ways to track the status and performance of workflows at the item, list, and site collection level.

Viewing the Status of a Single Workflow

To view the status and progress of an open or completed workflow:

1. Browse to the list or library hosting the workflow.

2. On the list or document drop-down menu, click *Workflows*.

3. Under Running Workflows or under Completed Workflows, click the workflow that you want to monitor.

The Workflow Status page then appears, similar to Figure 6-22.

Figure 6-22   The Workflow Status page displays general information, tasks, and workflow history.

Viewing the Performance of All Workflows on a List

To monitor the performance and success of all workflows on a list:

1. Browse to the list or library hosting the workflows.

2. From the Settings menu, click *List Settings* (or *Document Library Settings*).

3. Under Permissions and Management, click *Workflow Settings*.

4. Click *View Workflow Reports*.

The View Workflow Reports page gives you access to Activity Duration Reports and Cancellation & Error Reports for each type of workflow configured to run on the list.

Monitoring Workflows in the Site Collection

Site Collection Administrators have access to a workflows report that displays the number of workflows in the site collection that have been associated with a list or content type and the number of instances that are in progress, as shown in Figure 6-23. To view the workflows report:

1. Browse to the top-level site in the site collection.

2. On the Site Actions menu, click *Site Settings* and then click *Modify All Site Settings*.

3. In the Galleries section, click *Workflows*. The page then displays the current number of lists and content types that workflows are bound to, along with the number of running workflows.

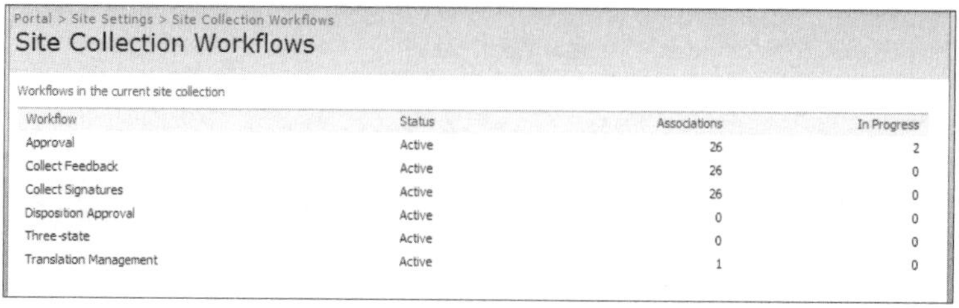
Portal > Site Settings > Site Collection Workflows

Site Collection Workflows

Workflows in the current site collection

Workflow	Status	Associations	In Progress
Approval	Active	26	2
Collect Feedback	Active	26	0
Collect Signatures	Active	26	0
Disposition Approval	Active	0	0
Three-state	Active	0	0
Translation Management	Active	1	0

Figure 6-23 Current site collection workflows can be seen from Portal > Site Settings > Site Collection Workflows.

Defining Information Management Policies

Information Management Policies are a set of rules that can be applied to a list or content type to help enforce document management procedures in an organization. Information Management Policies are not available in Windows SharePoint Services installations. They are only available on Microsoft Office SharePoint Server 2007 servers. Information Management Policies can be used in any site and on any list, although they are most often applied to document libraries. When an Information Management Policy is created on a document library it applies to all documents in that library unless a document is attached to a content type that has a separate Information Management Policy assigned to it.

Label Policy

This policy allows SharePoint Server 2007 to automatically generate a text label for each document in a library, and it requires that the label appear in the document when it is saved or printed. Labels consist of a combination of static text and dynamic field data that can be inserted from the document metadata. For example, a law firm may require that a descriptive label which, includes the case number and filing date, be inserted into every document printed. These two values may be stored in separate columns in the document library and will be automatically queried and entered into the label at the time the label is generated.

Auditing Policy

The Auditing policy allows you to specify which user actions you want to log to an audit trail that can be reviewed and reported on later. The audit log tracks the event name, the date and time that it occurred, and the account name of the user taking the action.

Expiration Policy

An Expiration policy provides a way to automatically delete documents and items that are no longer needed or to purge information that has exceeded its legal life-span. This policy is useful for meeting regulatory requirements in some industries. The retention period can be set based on some length of time from the value of any Date column in the list, such as the Date Created, or it can be set later through the execution of a coded event or workflow. The options to delete the item at the expiration point include Delete, which puts the item in the Recycle Bin of the site, or Delete Record And Submission Information, which deletes the record completely without putting it in the Recycle Bin. A third alternative is to initiate a workflow, such as the Disposition Approval workflow described earlier in this chapter.

Barcodes Policy

A Barcodes policy generates a standardized bar code that can be inserted into a document to allow it to be scanned and tracked using standard barcode readers. Barcodes provide a way of generating a unique identity for every document that does not include the title or filename of the document so that document identifiers can be listed and catalogued without exposing any sensitive information. The barcodes generated by this policy conform to the Code 39 standard (ANSI/AIM BC1-1995), but SharePoint Server 2007 also supports installing custom and third-party barcode generators.

Creating Policies

Policies can be created on individual lists and libraries, on content types, and at the site collection level as policy templates. You can only define one policy for a specific list, but you can support multiple policies on different content types within a site collection. Users require at least the Manage Lists permission to edit the policy settings for a list or library.

To Create an Information Management Policy

1. Browse to the list or library where you will create the policy.

2. From the Settings menu, click *List Settings* (or *Document Library Settings*).

3. Under Permissions And Management, click *Information Management Policy* settings.

4. In the Specify The Policy section, click *Define A Policy*.

5. Click OK.

6. On the Edit Policy page, shown in Figure 6-24, in the Name And Administrative Description section, enter a description of the policy.

Name and Administrative Description	Name:
The name and administrative description are shown to list managers when configuring policies on a list or content type.	Document
	Administrative Description:
Policy Statement	Policy Statement:
The policy statement is displayed to end users when they open items subject to this policy. The policy statement can explain which policies apply to the content or indicate any special handling or information that users need to be aware of.	
Labels	☐ Enable Labels
You can add a label to a document to ensure that important information about the document is included when it is printed. To specify the label, type the text you want to use in the "Label format" box. You can use any combination of fixed text or document properties, except calculated or built-in properties such as GUID or CreatedBy. To start a new line, use the \n character sequence.	
Auditing	☐ Enable Auditing
Specify the events that should be audited for documents and items subject to this policy.	
Expiration	☐ Enable Expiration
Schedule content disposition by specifying its retention period and the action to take when it reaches its expiration date.	
Barcodes	☐ Enable Barcodes
Assigns a barcode to each document or item. Optionally, Microsoft Office applications can require users to insert these barcodes into documents.	
	OK Cancel

Figure 6-24 Always enter an easy-to-understand description when creating policies.

7. In the Policy Statement section, enter a text description that users see when they open documents or items controlled by the policy. A policy statement can be up to 512 characters long.

8. To require that documents have labels, click *Enable Labels.*

9. To require users to add a label to a document, select the *Prompt Users* to insert a label before saving or printing check box.

10. To make the label read-only so that it cannot be changed, select the *Prevent Changes To Labels After They Are Added* check box. Doing so also prevents the label from being updated automatically when the properties of the item change.

11. In the Label format box, type the static text that will appear in the label along with column references in curly braces. These column references will be replaced by data from the list item or document when the label is generated. Labels can contain up to 10 column references. You can also format the font, font size, style, and justification of the label, as well as its overall dimensions. The label will inserted into the document as a movable element that can be positioned by the user.

12. Click *Refresh* to preview the label content.

> **Tip** To add a line break in the label text, type **\n** where you want the line break to appear.

13. To enable auditing for documents and items in the list, click *Enable Auditing,* and then specify which events you want to audit. You can audit the following events:

    ❑ Opening, viewing, or downloading documents and items, and viewing their properties

    ❑ Editing items and documents

    ❑ Checking out or checking in items and documents

    ❑ Moving or copying items and documents within the site

    ❑ Deleting or restoring items and documents

14. To define a retention period for documents and items in the list, click *Enable Expiration,* and then select a retention period and expiration action. To set the expiration date based on a date value, click *A Time Period Based On The Item's Properties* then select one of the date fields from the list and then enter the number of days, months, or years from that date that the item will expire. To set the expiration date through a workflow, click *Set* programmatically.

15. Under When The Item Expires, select either to delete the item immediately or to start a workflow to approve the deletion. Any custom workflows configured on the document library will be available in the list under *Start This Workflow.*

16. To require that documents or items in the list have barcodes attached to them, click *Enable Barcodes,* and then click the *Prompt Users* to insert a barcode before saving or printing check box. The user will insert the barcode into the document as a movable element that can be positioned as desired.

17. Click OK.

Creating Policy Templates

A policy template allows you to pre-configure a set of policy settings at the site collection level that can be applied to individual lists or to custom content types. By using this feature you can configure policy settings in one location and apply the same settings to every document library or list in every site in the site collection.

Creating a Site Collection Policy Template

1. Browse to the top-level site in the site collection.

2. From the Site Actions menu, select *Site Settings.*

3. Under Site Collection Administration, click *Site Collection Policies.*

4. Click *Create.*

5. Configure the policy according to the instructions under creating Information Management Policies earlier in this chapter.

Applying a Site Collection Policy

1. Browse to the list or library where you will create the policy.

2. From the Settings menu, click *List Settings* (or *Document Library Settings*).

3. Under Permissions and Management, click *Information Management Policy Settings*.

4. In the Specify The Policy section, click *Use A Site Collection Policy* and select the policy from the drop-down list.

5. Click OK.

Using Content Types

A content type is a template that stores a group of settings that define how a document or list item should behave and be managed. Content types are extremely flexible in that a single content type can be applied to many different types of documents. As soon as the content type is associated with a document, all of the settings configured on the content type immediately apply to that document. Among the settings that content types can manage are the following:

- Columns (metadata)
- Custom forms
- Workflows
- Information Management Policies
- Document conversions

Understanding Content Types

Content types are built in a hierarchy that allows one content type to inherit settings from its parent and to supplement these with its own settings. Content types are defined centrally at the site level, and the content types of a parent site are inherited by its child sites. Therefore, custom content types can be defined at the site collection root site that will propagate down to all the child sites in the collection. For more information on content types, see Chapter 10, "Configuring Office SharePoint Server Enterprise Content Management."

Configuring Workflows on a Content Type

By configuring a workflow on a content type, any document that adopts the content type is automatically subject to that workflow. This feature allows two documents in the same library to be using two different workflows at the same time.

Associating a Workflow with a Content Type

1. Browse to the site where the content type is defined.

2. From the Site Actions menu, click *Site Settings.*

3. In the Galleries section, click *Site Content Types,* and then select the content type that will hold the workflow.

4. Under the Settings section, click *Workflow* settings.

5. On the Change Workflow Settings page, click *Add A Workflow.*

6. Follow the steps for creating a workflow, described earlier in this chapter.

7. Click OK.

Configuring Information Management Policies on a Content Type

Configuring an Information Management Policy on a content type provides the same level of centralized flexibility that attaching a workflow to a content type does. Any change made to the policy on the content type is immediately reflected in those documents to which the content type is applied.

Associating an Information Management Policy with a Content Type

1. Browse to the site where the content type is defined.

2. From the Site Actions menu, click *Site Settings.*

3. In the Galleries section, click *Site Content Types,* and then select the content type that will hold the workflow.

4. Under the Settings section, click *Information Management Policy* settings.

5. On the Information Management Policy Settings page, choose to either define a new policy or select a site collection policy.

6. Click OK.

Tracking Information Management Policy Use

You can view reports at the site collection level, which gives you detailed information about user activity on sites in the site collection in which auditing is enabled.

Viewing the Audit Reports

1. Browse to the top-level site in the site collection.

2. From the Site Actions menu, select *Site.*

3. Under Site Collection Administration, click *Audit Log Reports.*

The reports are grouped into four sections as shown in Figure 6-25.

Figure 6-25   To view auditing reports, browse to the Site Collection > Site Actions > Audit Log Reports.

- **Content Activity Reports**   These reports display edits, additions, deletions, and viewing of documents and items in the lists and libraries to which the audit policy has been applied.

- **Custom Reports**   These reports give you the flexibility to design a custom report that can show any combination of information from other reports, as well as filter the details to show only a single user or a date range.

- **Information Management Policy Reports**   These reports display the events associated with the Expiration policy and all events that involve modifying Information Management Policies on a site.

- **Security and Site Settings Reports**   These reports do not depend on any policies being enabled in lists or libraries and always show any changes to auditing settings and security settings applied to the site.

Office SharePoint Server 2007 provides a means of tracking the implementation of Information Management Policies in the server farm through centralized reporting. All reports are outputted in XML-formatted files that can be opened in Excel 2007 or another XML viewer. By default the policy reporting is not turned on and must be enabled to generate and view reports.

Enabling Information Management Policy Usage Reporting

1. Open SharePoint 3.0 Central Administration and click on the Operations tab.

2. Under Logging And Reporting, click *Information Management Policy Usage Reports.*

3. To have Office SharePoint Server 2007 generate reports on a scheduled basis, check the box to enable recurring reports and specify the report schedule.

4. In the Report File Location text box, type the URL address for the document library that will hold the reports. This is a relative address such as "/IMReports."

5. To apply a custom template to the report generation process, type the URL address to the template in the Report Template box.

6. To generate reports immediately, click *Create Reports Now.*

Viewing Policy Reports

1. Browse to the document library designated to hold the reports.

2. Click on the report that you want to view. It will open in Excel 2007 if that software is installed on your workstation; otherwise you can download it.

Chapter 7

Implementing Security for SharePoint Products

Implementing security for Windows SharePoint Services and SharePoint Server is a multifaceted exercise. Although it is impossible to completely secure any network server, you can implement controls to mitigate the most common risks. The controls discussed here are a basic set of practices to begin your secure design and implementation; they do not guarantee security. Your environment may require greater security than discussed here, or practices described in this chapter could possibly break your current implementation. For these reasons, it is important to always test new access, authentication, and authorization controls in a test environment before implementing these controls in your production installation.

For in-depth information on securing your Windows infrastructure, see http://msdn.microsoft.com/practices/Topics/security/default.aspx.

New in Windows SharePoint Services 3.0 and SharePoint Server 2007 is the security-trimmed user interface (UI). It prevents users from viewing lists, documents, and management options not available to them. For example, SharePoint Portal Server 2003 allowed all users to see the Site Settings hyperlink. The new version of SharePoint Server hides Site Actions, the Site Settings equivalent in SharePoint Server 2007, from users who do not have permissions to manage the site.

Securing Web Applications

Web applications contain all of your valuable user content and also provide the bedrock for the security of your site collections. The foundation of security is authentication, and SharePoint products authentication is usually provided by Internet Information Services (IIS), but can be provided by ASP.NET via pluggable authentication.

Internet Information Services

If your SharePoint servers are Intranet only and therefore private, then you may not need to secure traffic. If your SharePoint servers are Internet-facing, however, you should consider encrypting the inter-server and client-server traffic. Collaborative sites that are Internet-facing sites should always use Secure Sockets Layer (SSL) for communication. Using SSL helps ensure that external traffic does not expose proprietary or confidential organizational content, and it protects user authentication.

Secure Sockets Layer

Secure Sockets Layer (SSL) was developed to transmit data over networks securely. The use of SSL is encouraged for most Web applications, but does add some complexity to your implementation. In addition, because SSL can also affect server performance; always test your design before implementing it on a large scale. To enable SSL for a Web application during creation, check the Use Secure Sockets Layer (SSL) option button and then install the SSL certificate in IIS Manager. To enable an existing Web application for SSL, you must do the following:

1. Open Central Administration from the Start Menu.

2. Go to Operations > Global Configuration > Alternate Access Mappings.

3. Locate the Web application you wish to enable with SSL and edit the default internal URL by clicking the name under Internal URL.

4. Change the URL protocol, as shown in Figure 7-1.

5. Click OK.

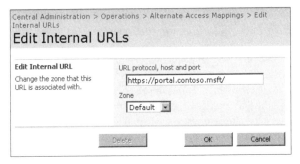

Figure 7-1   To edit the default Internal URL, select the hyperlink.

6. From IIS Manager, add the certificate to the Web application's IIS virtual server.

Note   If your servers need to communicate sensitive data over a public network, as is the case with Inter-Farm Shared Services, you should strongly consider using SSL for every Web server that connects to the Internet.

Integrated Authentication

Integrated authentication provides a transparent authentication mechanism for Intranet and limited Extranet SharePoint applications. Integrated authentication hashes the current username and password and then sends the hash to the authenticating server. When using integrated authentication, the hashing and authentication are done automatically using the currently logged-on username and password. This process increases the transparency to the user because no input is required to visit SharePoint servers. There are two types of integrated authentication:

- **Kerberos**   Kerberos is the preferred authentication mechanism for internal SharePoint Web applications. Because both the client and IIS server must see the Key Distribution Center (KDC), Kerberos does not work with most Internet-facing SharePoint solutions. To enable Kerberos, simply choose the option during Web application creation. Remember, to use Kerberos, you must configure a Service Principal Name (SPN) for the Web application pool identity. To configure an SPN, follow these steps:

  1. Download the Setspn.exe tool from *http://www.microsoft.com/downloads/details.aspx?FamilyId=6EC50B78-8BE1-4E81-B3BE-4E7AC4F0912D.*

  2. From the command prompt, execute *setspn.exe -A HTTP/ServerName Domain\username.* The username should be the Web application pool identity.

  3. Perform an IISReset.exe from the command line.

To enable Kerberos for an existing Web application, perform the following steps in addition to setting the SPN:

1. Find your Web application's IIS virtual server ID. Go to the IIS Manager Web Sites folder, and look for ID in the identifier column.

2. From the command line, execute

```
Cscript c:\intepub\adminscripts\adsutil.vbs set
w3svc/<ID>/root/NTAuthenticationProviders
"Negotiate,NTLM"
```

If possible, it is a good idea to enable both Kerberos *and* NTLM. Doing this ensures user authentication if Kerberos fails. Unfortunately, this dual enabling cannot be done from Central Administration. The preceding list explained how to enable Kerberos (Negotiate) and NTLM from the command line. This action must be performed on each server that will serve content via the Kerberos-secured Web application. Note that IIS authenticates from the most-secure protocol to the least-secure protocol. Therefore, your users will authenticate with Kerberos first, if both protocols are enabled.

- **NTLM**   NTLM works with most Windows SharePoint Services and SharePoint Server installations without further configuration. However, NTLM isn't as secure as Kerberos and should be considered insecure unless password lengths are longer than 14 characters. NTLM can also fail when traversing proxy servers, because it is connection-based and proxies don't always sustain connections. Additionally, not all browsers support NTLM and Kerberos and will require basic authentication support on the servers.

Basic Authentication

For remote users, users behind proxy servers, or non-Windows clients or to accommodate a custom program, you may implement Basic Authentication. Basic Authentication supports most browsers and works from almost anywhere on the Internet. Its downside is that the username and password are sent as Base64 clear text. This information is easily compromised, unless it is secured using encryption. Therefore, *always* use Basic Authentication in conjunction with an SSL-secured Web application. This sufficiently protects the username and password from compromise. To enable Basic Authentication, do the following:

1. Enable SSL, as shown earlier.

2. Open Central Administration, and browse to Application Management.

3. In Application Security > Authentication Providers, choose the Web application to manage, as shown in Figure 7-2.

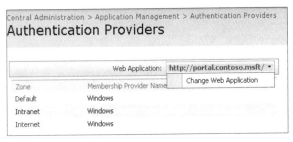

Figure 7-2   Verify the Web application before modifying authentication providers.

4. Select the zone to modify, usually Default.

5. From the bottom of the page, check *Basic Authentication (Password Is Sent In Clear Text)*.

6. Click Save.

Enabling Anonymous Access

Care should be taken when enabling anonymous access. Although security is always important in a site collection when creating users and groups, it is particularly important when anonymous access is enabled in the Web application and site collection. Be sure to limit access for users with anonymous access. If a site collection is primarily used for collaboration, you should strongly consider limiting anonymous access when possible. Always perform authentication provider changes from Central Administration, not from IIS Manager. To enable anonymous access, you must do so on the Web application and the site collection. To enable anonymous access for a Web application, browse to Central Administration > Application Management > Application Security > Authentication Providers > Edit Authentication. After enabling anonymous access for the Web application, you must then enable anonymous access for a site collection using these steps:

1. From the site collection, open Site Actions > Site Settings.

2. In the Users and Permissions column, select Advanced Permissions.

3. On the Settings menu tab, select Anonymous Access in the drop-down menu. If you do not see Anonymous Access listed, then Anonymous Access is not enabled for the hosting Web application.

4. Select the portion of the site to which you will allow anonymous access: Entire Web site, Lists and Libraries, or nothing.

If you enabled List and Libraries previously, for example, follow these steps to enable anonymous access on a document library:

1. Browse to the document library on which you would like to enable anonymous access.

2. From the Settings drop-down menu, select Document Library Settings.

3. Under Permissions and Management, select Permissions for this document library.

4. If not already done, you must break inheritance by selecting Edit Permissions from the Actions drop-down menu.

5. Select OK when warned that you will create unique permissions for this document library.

6. From the Settings drop-down menu, select Anonymous Access.

7. Select the permission you wish to grant anonymous users.

Configuring User Permissions for Web Applications

When modifying user permissions for Web applications in Central Administration, be aware that changes are applied immediately and can cause site collection failure. User permissions are managed on an individual Web application basis so you may have a unique policy for each Web application. Always verify that you are modifying the correct Web application before modifying permissions. Many an administrator has accidentally modified the wrong Web application.

The permissions available from Central Administration > Application Management > Application Security > User Permissions For Web Applications are those that are available in site collections contained within that Web application. If you disable *Delete Versions*, for example, that option will not be available to site collections in the selected Web application. Figures 7-3 and 7-4 show the correlation between Web application security settings and site collection security settings.

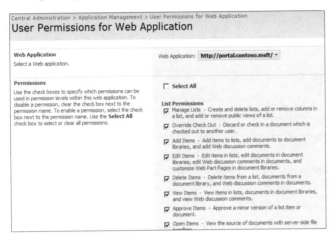

Figure 7-3 Changing the Web application security settings affects what permission levels are available for site collections within that Web application.

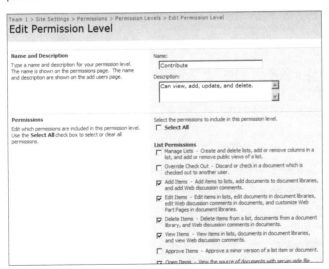

Figure 7-4 If a permission level isn't available, check the Web application security settings for the host Web application.

Re-enabling a permission level for a Web application in Central Administration allows the level to be used once again in all site collections contained in the selected Web application. Be cautious when making changes to large Web applications because every site collection contained in it is then modified by the system. This modification can cause a very large spike in CPU utilization, which possibly may deny service to users.

Configuring Antivirus Settings

The installation of a correctly configured antivirus program is essential to protecting content in your SharePoint environment. To configure antivirus settings, you must have a SharePoint-aware antivirus program. A standard antivirus version for Windows Server 2003 will not scan items in SharePoint databases. When installing the SharePoint antivirus program, the program must exist on all WFE servers before continuing configuration. To configure antivirus for SharePoint products, perform these actions:

1. Open Central Administration from the Start Menu.

2. Browse to the Operations interface, Security Configuration, and select Antivirus.

3. Configure **Antivirus Settings.**

   These settings allow you to define whether files are scanned on upload, download, or both and to define actions taken on infected documents. It is wise to prohibit users from downloading infected documents, except in special circumstances, such as mission-critical environments.

4. Configure **Antivirus Time Out.**

   The default is set to 300 seconds, but this length of time should probably be reduced. If your server performance is suffering and you are antivirus-enabled, consider starting at a 60-second time out duration and increasing until performance again decreases.

5. Configure **Antivirus Threads.**

   The default is set to 5 threads, which is a good choice for medium-scale implementations. If you have a robust hardware environment, you can increase this number. Conversely, you may decrease this value to fit your installation if performance is an issue.

Managing Single Sign-on

The single sign-on (SSO) service has been removed from Shared Services and is now a standalone component. It is now possible for developers to use any SSO provider they choose. To configure the SSO that is included with SharePoint Server, you must first enable the service. Figure 7-5 shows where to configure and start the service in the MMC Services snap-in.

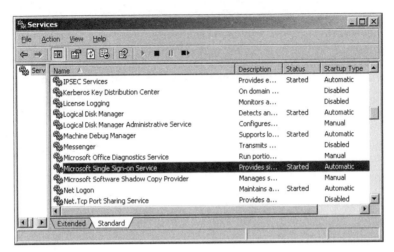

Figure 7-5   You must define the logon account and set the service to automatic.

The specific Log On As: service account depends on the connection you make with the SSO service, but must be a member of the local administrators group on the encryption key server. If connecting to an Enterprise Resource Management system, check with the administrator of that service for an account recommendation. Keep in mind that this account also connects to your default SQL Server installation and must be a member of the SQL Server Security Administrators group and the DB Creator group. SSO allows connections to third-party systems and eliminates the need for the users to enter multiple passwords.

After configuring the SSO service, you must configure the settings for SSO in Central Administration > Operations > Security Configuration > Manage Single Sign-on. From there, you can manage the SSO administrator, which is usually the same account as the service account, and assign an administrator for managing enterprise application definitions. Enterprise application definitions are used in conjunction with the Business Data Catalog (BDC), part of a Shared Services Provider.

For more information on configuring the BDC, see http://msdn2.microsoft.com/en-us/library/ms583986.aspx.

Before you are finished, you must also create an SSO database by specifying a SQL Server and database name. Most implementations use the same database server as the SharePoint server farm, but yours may vary. After creating the database, you can remove the Database Creator permission from the SSO service account.

Configuring Blocked File Types

From Central Administration > Operations > Blocked File Types you can configure, on a per-Web application basis, the types of files that can be uploaded. The default list is too extensive to list here, but a few default blocked file types warrant mentioning:

- **.cer**   These files are usually certificate files and can pose a minor threat if allowed to be served from your SharePoint installation. The downside to blocking .cer files is the inability to post root Certificate Authority certificates for users to install in their local browser.

- **.com, .dll, and .exe**   These file name extensions should *never* be allowed on your SharePoint installation. Allowing .com or .exe files can cause catastrophic security consequences should a hacker find and execute code, such as a cross-domain (site) scripting attack, on your server.

- **.pst**   It is unwise to allow users to upload .pst files to any site collection. Doing so can take significant amounts of storage. In addition, users cannot use a .pst over HTTP in Microsoft Outlook.

Tip   Blocked file types can also be managed from the command line:

```
stsadm -o blockedfilelist -extension <extension> - [add | delete]
-url <web application URL>
```

Note   Users can change the extension of any file and circumvent your blocked file type configuration. To prevent uploads of file types based on the binary and not the file extension, consider a Content Policy software suite, such as Microsoft ForeFront.

Updating the Farm Administrator's Group

By default, the local administrators are part of the farm administrators group. This is not required in the new versions, however, and you may remove them. You can also add Active Directory groups as farm administrators, which eases administration. One downside to using Active Directory groups is that domain administrators can easily escalate their privileges by adding themselves to the farm administrator's Active Directory group. To update the farm administrator's group, browse to Central Administration > Security Configuration > Update Farm Administrator's Group and select New > Add Users.

Site Collection Security

After a user is authenticated, you then can *authorize* that user to view or modify existing content in addition to creating content. SharePoint technologies authorize users at the site collection level, including the Central Administration site collection. For example, you might authorize a user to read documents in a document library, but not grant him or her the ability to change documents. Within a site collection, authorization can be specified on a per-object basis, such as a document or folder.

Site Collection Administrators

Site collection administrators are assigned when a site collection is created. There must always be at least one site collection administrator, and this account cannot be an Active Directory group. For reasons such as Unused Site Confirmation and enabling administration in the event that the administrator leaves, it is always best to define at least two site collection administrators. You can view site collection administrators from two different management interfaces:

- **Central Administration**   From Central Administration > Application Management > SharePoint Site Management > Site Collection Administrators, select the site collection to manage. The selection menu for the site collection isn't intuitive at first, so be careful when selecting site collections to modify.

  Tip   If several content databases are associated with a single Web application, the *Select Site Collection* interface shows the database that a given site collection is in, as shown in Figure 7-6.

Figure 7-6   The Select Site Collection Web page shows the association of content databases and Site Collections.

- **Site Collection Settings**   If you want to add more than two site collection administrators, you must do so from the Site > Site Settings > Permissions > Site Collection Administrators Web page.

Permission Levels

Permission levels are the building blocks for authorizing users to access or modify objects in a site collection. Permission levels should always be named the same across multiple sites, and you should *never* modify an existing permission level. Modifying an existing permission level could cause a document, list, or page owner to accidentally grant access to unauthorized users. Always create a new permission level, create a correlating group with the same name, and populate that group with users. Doing this assures you of an easy-to-use permission level and group environment. To create a new permission level, do the following:

1. Open the site to manage in your browser.

2. Select Site Actions > Site Settings > Users and Permissions > Advanced Permissions.

3. From the Settings tab, select Permission Levels, as shown in Figure 7-7.

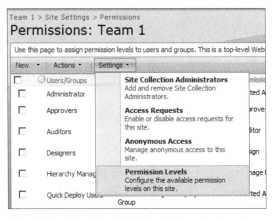

Figure 7-7   Select Permission Levels from the drop-down menu.

4. Select the Add A Permission Level tab.

5. Enter a name for the permission level.

6. Enter a description.

7. Select the required permissions for this permission level and associated group.

Remember, the only available permissions are those that are defined in Central Administration > Application Management > Web Application Security.

> **Caution**   You should develop a consistent naming convention for permission levels across all site collections. Otherwise, users will not know what permissions are associated with each permission level. For example, if you modified the default *View Only* permission level and granted the *Edit Items* permission, users would falsely assume they were giving read-only access to a user or group.

Users and User Groups

Although you can add users directly to almost any object, this process becomes very difficult to manage and can make it nearly impossible to manage security in a site. Use the following guidelines when granting rights, and only assign permissions directly to single users if required, such as online presence:

1. Create an Active Directory group (when using Active Directory for authentication).

2. Create a matching permission level (if custom permission levels are required).

3. Create a matching new site group, and grant it the previously created permission level.

4. Grant the new site group access to an object, such as a document, list, or Web page.

Site Access Groups

By default, there are three site access groups in a site. You can add additional groups as you wish, but the default site access groups are added by default and can be modified by doing the following:

1. Open Site Settings from the Site Actions menu.

2. In the Users and Permissions column, select People and Groups.

3. From the Settings menu, select People and Groups from the drop-down menu, as shown in Figure 7-8.

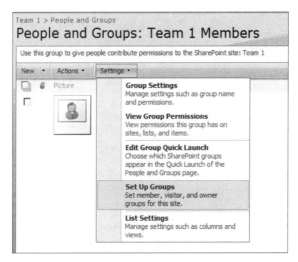

Figure 7-8 You must select People and Groups from the drop-down menu to manage the default site groups.

Each of the following groups can be changed to an existing site group, or you can create a new group from this interface.

- **Visitors**   The Visitors group should grant read-only access to members of this group. Adding additional permission levels is inadvisable because users could mistakenly grant escalated permissions to members. The Visitors group is also the only group to which you can add all authenticated users. This is done by selecting Create a New Group and choosing the Add All Authenticated Users hyperlink, as shown in Figure 7-9.

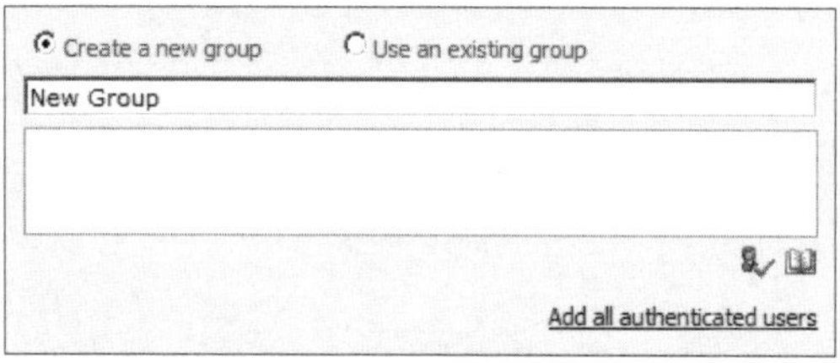

Figure 7-9   You can only add All Authenticated Users to the Visitors group.

- **Members**   The Members group grants contributor rights by default, but can be modified to meet your organizational standard for contributors. Unique to this site group when creating a new group is the option of creating an e-mail distribution list. This option is not available to the Visitors or Owners site groups.

- **Owners**   The Owners site group should not be modified in most circumstances. You can, however, create a new site group and use it for the Owners site group. This action is usually taken after the creation of a subsite, when wishing to break the inheritance from the parent site.

Tip   You can modify Site Access Groups in a subsite, but by default, the changes will have no effect. You must break the inheritance from the parent site before the changes will take effect.

Enabling Folder and Per-Item Permissions

The new versions of Windows SharePoint Services and SharePoint Server allow the granting of permissions to an individual object, such as a folder or document. By default, objects inherit the permissions of their parent. For example, a document library would inherit the permissions of the site, whereas a document would inherit the permissions of the document library or folder in which it was contained. To break permissions inheritance, select Manage Permissions from the drop-down menu, as shown in Figure 7-10.

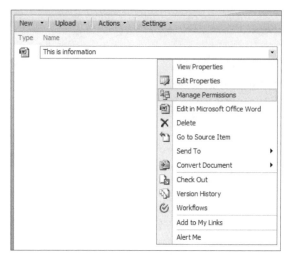

Figure 7-10   Select Manage Permissions from the drop-down menu to view object permissions.

From the following screen, you can choose to Manage Permissions Of Parent or Edit Permissions. By selecting Edit Permissions, you break the permission inheritance from the parent, copy all parent permissions to this object, and have the ability to assign permissions on the item.

If you wish to re-inherit parent permissions at a later date, you can do so from the Actions > Inherit Permissions drop-down menu. Be cautious when doing so, as all custom permissions not contained in the parent object will be lost. These changes and deletions are not sent to the Recycle Bin.

Server Farm Security

The key to a secure SharePoint installation is limiting the number of nonessential services on your servers. Be thoughtful in your server farm design and limit the external exposure of critical services, such as SQL Server connections. In addition, Windows Updates are imperative to hardening the Windows Server operating system.

Surface Area

If your server farm is Internet-facing, use caution when configuring the Windows Server system. When possible, restrict access to nonessential ports using firewalls or the Windows Server native IP Security Policies MMC snap-in. This book obviously cannot provide a comprehensive list of ports, but the following ports should be the *minimum* set that have restricted access:

- **NetBIOS ports 135, 137–139, and SMB port 445** The NetBIOS and SMB ports provide basic functionality, such as file and print sharing, but they can also be an entry point for hackers. For this reason, restrict these ports to internal use only. These ports should be blocked on externally facing firewalls or routers or restricted with the native IP Security Policies.

    Caution Much of the intra-farm communication, such as index propagation, is via NetBIOS, so never restrict NetBIOS traffic between SharePoint servers in the same farm. You should only restrict inbound NetBIOS access.

- **SQL Server ports 1433 and 1434** You should restrict access to TCP 1433 and UDP 1434 to prevent malicious hackers and code, such as the *Slammer Worm,* also known as *W32.Slammer,* from unauthorized access. Worms like this one are self-propagating and can infect an entire network within hours. Depending on the payload programmed into the worm, it can have devastating effects. You should also limit the access to your SQL Server installation to prevent authenticated, but unauthorized activity from those within your organization. If your servers exist in different, secured subnets, then consider encrypting all intra-farm traffic with IPsec. For example, if your WFEs are in a dedicated subnet, encrypting traffic to the SQL Server and SharePoint application servers further secures your installation. Optionally, you can open firewall or router ports to allow this intra-farm installation.

    For more information on selecting IPSec peer authentication, browse to http:// go.microsoft.com/fwlink/?LinkId=76093&clcid=0x409, *"Selecting IPSec Authentication Methods."*

    For information on isolating services via IP Security Policies, see http:// www.microsoft.com/technet/security/guidance/architectureanddesign/ ipsec/default.mspx.

- **Central Administration TCP Port** The port selected during installation should be protected and isolated to a single subnet when possible. Verify that your firewall or router Access Control Lists (ACLs) do not allow external access to this port. If your server farm is managed remotely, consider using Virtual Private Networks (VPNs) or Windows Terminal Services to manage your farm via Central Administration. Figure 7-11 shows an example of Central Administration and the TCP port it uses.

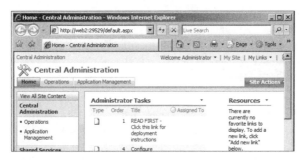

Figure 7-11 The TCP port number used by Central Administration appears after the ":" in the URL.

Tip You should *never* change the Central Administration TCP port via IIS Manager. To correctly change the TCP port, execute *Stsadm -o setadminport -port <port>*.

■ **Shared Services Provider TCP Port** The Shared Services Provider (SSP) TCP port should be restricted in much the same way as Central Administration. Exceptions should be made for the administrators of the SSP. You will probably want to delegate administration of Search, Indexing, User profiles, and similar tasks to someone other than yourself. For this reason, be careful not to exclude the IP address address or range of which the SSP administrators are a part.

Note Although you want to create a dedicated Web application to ease disaster recovery of My Sites, this practice also allows you to restrict access to SSP Administration when My Sites are not placed in the same Web application. Otherwise, the SSP Web application TCP port must be open to allow My Site access to users.

Server Placement

You can isolate and effectively protect your server farm by exclusively using Windows Server IP Security Policies, but this practice does not scale well. Using IP Security Policies in a large environment can introduce complexities with inter-server processes and client-server processes. For this reason, most medium-scale and larger implementations protect the majority of their server surface area with firewalls, routers, and proxy servers. The following is an example of securing a medium-scale server farm.

■ To properly secure a medium-scale server farm, consider placing the Web front-end (WFE) servers in a screened subnet, with the SQL Server and Application servers in a different, well-secured subnet.

For more information on screened subnets, browse to http://www.microsoft.com/technet/security/bestprac/bpent/sec3/datasec.mspx.

■ If security is paramount in your organization, you can use two screened subnets to further secure your network. In Figure 7-12, IPSec is used only intra-farm, not for all traffic. The additional firewall protects the SQL Server from vulnerabilities.

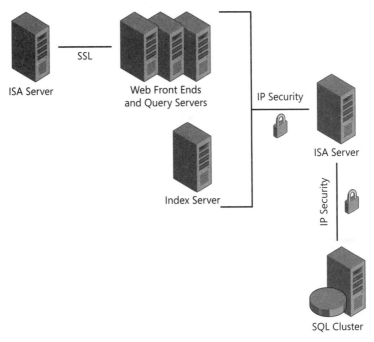

Figure 7-12   Isolate the Web front ends and SQL Server traffic to reduce the external surface area available to hackers.

Part III

Working with SharePoint Server 2007

Chapter 8

Deploying SharePoint Server Shared Services

SharePoint Server Shared Services provide a centrally managed and centrally located set of feature-rich services that can be shared among multiple Web applications in a single farm (Intra-Farm Shared Services) and multiple farms (Inter-Farm Shared Services). A Shared Services Provider (SSP) is a specialized Web application that provides a single set of enterprise services such as search and audiences, thus enabling consistency across one or multiple SharePoint Server farms.

A well-thought-out SSP design and installation are critical *before* creating site collections. For example, an SSP can be associated with multiple Web applications, but a Web application can only be associated with a single SSP. For this reason, begin your SharePoint Server installation with a single SSP and let your business requirements force you to scale. Creating multiple SSPs creates complexity and increases the overall cost of maintaining your SharePoint implementation.

In SharePoint Server 2007, SSPs have been completely detached from the Portal. This arrangement increases the flexibility of services, such as Search, user profiles, and audiences. Shared Services are only provided with SharePoint Server and are not provided with Windows SharePoint Services. The Shared Services are as follows:

- User Profiles and Properties
- My Sites, including robust personalization capabilities
- Search and Indexing
- Global Audiences
- Excel Calculation Services
- Business Data Catalog
- Session State

This chapter focuses on creating and managing a single SSP. Multiple SSPs are covered in Chapter 13, "Scaling Out to a SharePoint Technologies Server Farm." Search and Indexing is a complex topic and therefore is covered in depth in its own chapter, Chapter 12, "Configuring SharePoint Server Search and Indexing." My Sites are considered personal *portals* and are covered in Chapter 9, "Configuring SharePoint Server Portals."

Creating a Shared Services Provider

SharePoint Server 2007 requires an SSP to provide functionality to site collections, such as global audiences, Search, Indexing, Excel Calculation Services, and more. Before creating your first Web application to host site collections, always create your default SSP. At the server level, an SSP consists of a Web application, associated content database, search database, SSP configuration database, and preferably a dedicated Web application for My Sites.

Web Application Creation

To create your first (default) SSP, browse to Central Administration > Application Management > Office SharePoint Server Shared Services > Create Or Configure This Farm's Shared Services, as shown in Figure 8-1.

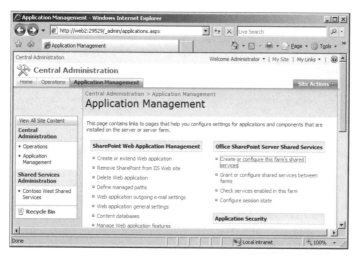

Figure 8-1   You create a Shared Services Provider in Central Administration, under Application Management.

On entering the SSP management page, you should select New SSP. The following items must be configured:

- **SSP name**   The name for your SSP should be easily recognizable and correlate to the purpose of this SSP; for example, Contoso West SSP. Although it is possible to create the IIS Web application beforehand, it is usually best to create it from

Central Administration. If you decide to use a pre-existing Web application, the application pool identity cannot be Network Service. To create a new Web application, select the hyperlink, as shown in Figure 8-2.

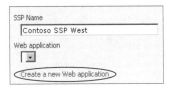

Figure 8-2   Create a new Web application in Central Administration for your Shared Services Provider.

You should follow the instructions for creating a Web application as defined in Chapter 2, "Deploying SharePoint Products and Technologies," but at a minimum, the following options should be configured:

- **IIS Web site**   Intelligently name your IIS Web site, port, and host header, as shown in Figure 8-3. Fill out the host header information, even if you plan to use assigned IP addresses. If required, the IP address and host header information can be altered in IIS Manager after creating the Web application.

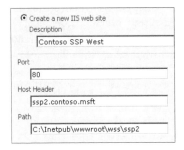

Figure 8-3   Complete the host header information, even if you plan on using assigned IP addresses.

- **Security configuration**   If you plan to provide or consume Shared Services over untrusted networks, seriously consider using SSL for this Web application. In addition, you can use Kerberos to enhance your security posture and improve performance. Remember that you must still add an SSL certificate in IIS Manager if choosing SSL. Selecting SSL here only changes the Web application scheme (https ://) in the configuration database.

  > **Tip**   You can use *stsadm -o setsspport -httpport (or -httpsport for SSL) <portnumber>* to change the TCP port number after SSP creation.

- **Load-balanced URL**   The load-balanced URL is the default internal URL for this Web application, even if you do not load balance the Web application. Verify that the automatically inserted text is correct and make any changes as required. If you plan to use a standard TCP port, you do not have to include the :<PORT> at the end of the URL.

> **Tip** If multiple administrators will access your Shared Services administration from geographically disperse locations, strongly consider using a standard port for access, such as 80 or 443. Be careful when publishing externally, however, as inadvertently publishing your SSP administration page to the Internet could be catastrophic, should a hacker gain access.

- **Application pool** *Always* create a dedicated application pool and identity for every SSP. This dedicated pool allows for isolation of the Web application and associated services, thereby improving performance and security. Note that SSP administration can now be performed by non-farm administrators, enabling the granular delegation of tasks, such as Search and Indexing. A dedicated application pool also allows for the recycling and monitoring of your SSP without affecting other Web applications in IIS. Recycling the application pool for your SSP, for example, does not affect the rest of your server farm's Web applications. You cannot use Network Service for this Web application and should always use an Active Directory account when possible.

- **Database name and authentication** It is possible to use a different database server than was specified for Central Administration and the configuration database, but only do so in large or specialized environments. The best practice is to use the same SQL Server installation for all databases. You should name the database according to the purpose of the SSP, and the name should match closely the name of the IIS Web application. Figure 8-4 shows an example of database naming for Contoso, Ltd.'s West SSP.

Figure 8-4 Carefully name your SSP content databases because they cannot be renamed.

- **My Site location** After creating the SSP Web application and content database, you must decide if you will use a dedicated Web application for hosting My Sites. Although it is easier to simply use the SSP Web application just created, doing that makes disaster recovery more difficult. If you have more than just a few My Site users, create a dedicated Web application for My Sites. This allows for application pool isolation, troubleshooting, disaster recovery, and, most important, the ability to independently load balance your My Site Web application. Use best practices when creating this Web application and databases, and use a standard URI scheme such as HTTP:// or HTTPS:// for a consistent end user experience.

Figure 8-5 is an example of the Web application settings for a dedicated My Site Web application.

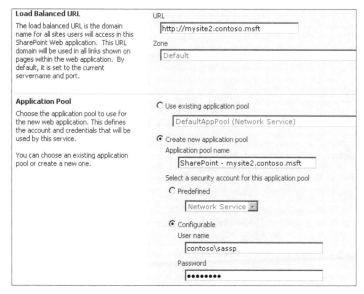

Load Balanced URL

The load balanced URL is the domain name for all sites users will access in this SharePoint Web application. This URL domain will be used in all links shown on pages within the web application. By default, it is set to the current servername and port.

URL

http://mysite2.contoso.msft

Zone

Default

Application Pool

Choose the application pool to use for the new web application. This defines the account and credentials that will be used by this service.

You can choose an existing application pool or create a new one.

○ Use existing application pool

DefaultAppPool (Network Service)

● Create new application pool

Application pool name

SharePoint - mysite2.contoso.msft

Select a security account for this application pool

○ Predefined

Network Service

● Configurable

User name

contoso\sassp

Password

••••••••

Figure 8-5   Use a standard URI scheme and naming convention to make access easy for your users.

- **SSP service credentials**   Using Farm service credentials should be sufficient for the level of security and performance found in most organizations. If you have specialized security or programmatic requirements, however, you can create a dedicated service account. If you decide to create a dedicated service account, it must be an administrator on every server in the farm.

- **SSP database**   Once again, you should use the default database server when possible. If you are hosting multiple SSPs on this database server, it is very important to name your databases intelligently. Figure 8-6 shows an example of naming when multiple SSPs are on the same server. Using Windows Authentication is the default for creating this database, but you can alternatively use SQL permissions for database creation and access.

SSP Database

Each SSP requires a database for service specific data.

Use of the default database server and database name is recommended for most cases. Refer to the Office SharePoint Server TechCenter on TechNet for advanced scenarios where specifying database information is required.

Use of Windows authentication is strongly recommended. To use SQL authentication, specify the credentials that will be used to connect to the SSP Database.

Database Server

| app3 |

Database Name

| Contoso_SSP_West |

Database authentication

⊙ Windows authentication (recommended)

○ SQL authentication

Account

| |

Password

| |

Figure 8-6   Name each SSP database so it can be identified easily for backup, restore, and management functions.

- **Search database**   The Search database hosts content, such as indexed metadata and crawl histories, and is required for Search and Indexing to function properly. Name it carefully as it cannot be changed in the future. The name should include the farm description and SSP name for ease of disaster recovery and management. Because multiple SSPs can share the same Index Server and SQL Server installations, your database name and Index Server directories should match when possible.

- **Index Server**   You must have started at least one Index Server in the farm before continuing past this configuration item. If you only have one Index Server in the farm, the option is grayed out. If you have multiple Index Servers in the farm, you will notice the limitation of only using one in the drop-down menu. If this Index Server hosts multiple indexes (multiple SSPs), renaming the Index file directory to match the SSP database name simplifies future administration. Figure 8-7 shows an example of matching SSP database names and index locations.

Search Database

In addition to the SSP database, a separate database is required for frequently changing search related data.

Use of the default database server and database name is recommended for most cases. Refer to the Office SharePoint Server TechCenter on TechNet for advanced scenarios where specifying database information is required.

Use of Windows authentication is strongly recommended. To use SQL authentication, specify the credentials that will be used to connect to the SSP Database.

Database Server

| app3 |

Database Name

| Contoso_West_Search_DB |

Database authentication

⊙ Windows authentication (recommended)

○ SQL authentication

Account

| |

Password

| |

Index Server

Select the index server which will crawl content in all Web applications associated with this SSP.

Specify the path on the index server where the indexes will be located.

Index Server

| CENTRAL |

Path for index file location

| d:\indexes\SSP_Contoso_West |

Figure 8-7   Give the Index directory a name that is similar to the SSP Search database name.

Editing a Shared Services Provider

You can edit the existing SSP Web application and services settings from Central Administration > Application Management > Office SharePoint Server Shared Services > Create Or Configure This Farm's Shared Services. To edit the Web application settings, hover the mouse and select Edit Properties in the drop-down menu. On entering the edit page, notice that many of the settings you configured during creation can be changed, whereas others cannot. A description of editable items and recommended practices follows:

- **SSP name**   You can change the name at any time, but doing so does not change all instances of the name, such as Portal Connections in Site Collections. You cannot change the Administration Site URL, as it is embedded in the code. You also cannot change the Web application that would require a fresh SSP to be created. To change the My Site Location URL, you must configure settings in SSP Administration.

    Note   You cannot delete the default SSP. You must create a new SSP, make it the default, and then delete the previously defined Default SSP. You can change the default SSP from the GUI or from the command line with *stsadm -o setdefaultssp -title <SSPName>*. Web applications do not re-associate when the default SSP is changed; only new Web applications are affected.

- **SSP service credentials**   Use caution when changing the SSP service credentials. This step should only be considered as a last resort, such as in the event of a domain re-name or account compromise. Be sure to add any new accounts to the administrators group on every server in the farm, as well as to check SQL permissions, as noted in Chapter 2.

- **SSP and Search database authentication**   Only change this feature in highly specialized environments. Changing it is not recommended for most implementations.

- **Index Server**   SharePoint Server increases your flexibility by allowing you to re-host your indexing function on any Index Server in the farm. You can select a new Index Server in the drop-down menu and/or change the Index File Location. You might want to change the Index location should your index size become quite large. You must rebuild all of your Indexes from SSP Search Administration afterward, or indexing will cease to function. Don't forget to run a full backup after a rebuild!

- **Process accounts with access to this SSP**   By default, all Web applications in this farm have access to this SSP. However, to associate this SSP with Web applications outside this farm or domain, you must enter the application pool identity for each additional Web application.

Changing Web Application Associations

You can change Web application associations after the fact, as shown in Figure 8-8.

Figure 8-8   Select the Change Associations tab to modify default Web application associations.

Changing the Web application association changes many elements, including Search, Indexing, User Profiles, Audiences, Excel Calculation Services, BDC access, and My Site defaults. Therefore, changing associations should not be done without proper consideration and testing. Figure 8-9 shows the different options available. Verify that you are modifying the correct SSP, and never choose *Select All* unless you are very sure you want to change the SSP association of all Web applications.

Central Administration > Application Management > Manage this Farm's Shared Services > Change Association between Web Applications and SSPs

Change Association between Web Applications and SSPs

The association defines which shared services are used by a Web application. A Web application may be associated to one SSP, but each SSP may have multiple Web applications associated with it.

Shared Services Provider
Select the shared services provider with which the Web applications will be associated.

SSP Name

Contoso West Shared Services (Default) ▼

Web applications
Select the Web applications which will be associated with the selected shared services provider.

Select all ☐

	Web application	Current SSP Association
☑	Contoso Portal West (2)	Contoso West Shared Services (Default)
☑	SharePoint - 37034	Contoso West Shared Services (Default)

OK   Cancel

Figure 8-9   Verify you are modifying the correct SSP before re-associating Web applications.

Configuring Shared Services

After you have installed an SSP, its configuration is performed from a dedicated, isolated administration interface. This interface can be reached from Manage This Farm's Shared Services page, as shown in Figure 8-10 or, alternatively, can be bookmarked in the browser for future administration.

Figure 8-10   Select the drop-down menu and click on Open Shared Services Admin Site to configure an SSP.

On entering SSP administration, notice that it is simply another site collection based on a highly specialized template. Although it can be modified like any other site collection, doing so is generally a bad idea and can cause issues down the road. For that reason, only modify settings, such as security, that will not be affected by future service packs and releases.

Assigning Administrators

After creating an SSP, you must assign administrators to the site collection for management. By default, farm administrators do not have access, unless defined during SSP creation. You can manage users and groups for an SSP in the same way as any other site collection. Refer to Chapter 4, "Creating Site Collections," for more information on managing users and groups.

Managing User Profiles

Managing user profiles and properties is fundamental to managing and surfacing personal information about your users. User profiles are associated with one or many Active Directory accounts and have an associated My Site if enabled. You can map profile properties to almost any authentication provider, including Active Directory objects, third-party LDAP providers, and database authentication providers. In addition, you can give users the ability to surface any information they choose. This section explains how giving users the ability to manage their profiles can assist when creating audiences for the purpose of targeting.

A user profile contains the following elements:

- Personal Site information
- Primary Active Directory account
- First name
- Last name
- Name
- Customizable fields

You can manage the customizable fields provided or add as many custom fields as required by your organization.

Defining Import Sources and Connections

Before user profiles are available for use, you must define the source for your user profile imports. Although you can create user profiles manually, most organizations have at least one default import source, which is usually the Active Directory. You can define additional import sources from any LDAP version 3 or later, Active Directory, Business Data Catalog connection, or a single OU in an Active Directory forest.

Setting the Default Import Source

Most organizations define their primary Active Directory Forest as the default source for their user profile imports. You can define the default import source from either Shared Services Administration > User Profiles And My Sites > User Profiles And Properties > Import Source, or Configure Profile Import, as shown in Figure 8-11.

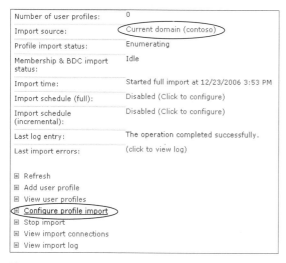

Number of user profiles:	0
Import source:	Current domain (contoso)
Profile import status:	Enumerating
Membership & BDC import status:	Idle
Import time:	Started full import at 12/23/2006 3:53 PM
Import schedule (full):	Disabled (Click to configure)
Import schedule (incremental):	Disabled (Click to configure)
Last log entry:	The operation completed successfully.
Last import errors:	(click to view log)

- ▣ Refresh
- ▣ Add user profile
- ▣ View user profiles
- ▣ Configure profile import
- ▣ Stop import
- ▣ View import connections
- ▣ View import log

Figure 8-11   You configure the default import source from Profile And Import Settings.

You can define the profile import source as a domain, forest, or custom source. In a small to medium environment, most likely you will choose between a domain or forest. If all of your users are in a single domain in a forest, then it doesn't matter which you choose. However, if you have users in multiple domains within a forest, selecting Entire Forest eases the burden of creating an import connection for every domain. Be aware that all accounts, including services and administrators, are imported and that an associated user profile is created for each one.

Configure the import source from Configure Profile Import, as shown in Figure 8-12. You can only select one import source from this interface.

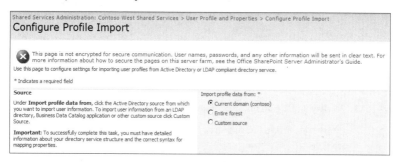

Shared Services Administration: Contoso West Shared Services > User Profile and Properties > Configure Profile Import

Configure Profile Import

This page is not encrypted for secure communication. User names, passwords, and any other information will be sent in clear text. For more information about how to secure the pages on this server farm, see the Office SharePoint Server Administrator's Guide.

Use this page to configure settings for importing user profiles from Active Directory or LDAP compliant directory service.

* Indicates a required field

Source

Under **Import profile data from**, click the Active Directory source from which you want to import user information. To import user information from an LDAP directory, Business Data Catalog application or other custom source click Custom Source.

Important: To successfully complete this task, you must have detailed information about your directory service structure and the correct syntax for mapping properties.

Import profile data from: *
- ⊙ Current domain (contoso)
- ○ Entire forest
- ○ Custom source

Figure 8-12   Select Current Domain or Entire Forest to define an import source.

The following items must be configured to successfully define the default import connection:

- **Source**   As discussed, the source can be the Current Domain, an Entire Forest, or a Custom Source.

- **Default access account**   The default access account that is used to connect to the defined LDAP and import user profile data is the default Search Content Access Account. It is recommended that you change this account and not use the default access account because it could be modified by another administrator, effectively disabling user profile imports from this source.

- **Full import schedule**   You have very granular control over how your profiles are imported. If your environment isn't changing rapidly, consider a monthly or longer Full Import Schedule. After the initial import is completed successfully, you should only need to run a full import after changing the access account or source or if you suspect the user profile index is corrupted.

- **Incremental import schedule**   Incremental imports are meant to import the delta from the last incremental or full import. Most organizations set this schedule to daily or weekly, depending on the rate at which your Active Directory changes. Keep in mind that user profile imports do more than just populate added users; properties, such as phone numbers and managers defined in Active Directory, are also updated.

Configuring Custom Import Sources

To configure custom import sources, whether they are Active Directory or other, browse to Shared Services Administration > User Profiles And My Sites > User Profiles And Properties and select View Import Connections, as shown in Figure 8-13.

Figure 8-13   To view and create import connections, select View Import Connections.

The default import connection should already be listed with the type, source, Search Base, and Active Directory throttling status (Server Side Incremental). You can edit an existing source by hovering the mouse over the drop-down menu or create a new one by selecting Create New Connection. To create a new connection other than a Business Data Catalog (BDC) connection, you must configure the following items.

- **Type**   You must specify the type of connection you are creating—Active Directory, third-party LDAP, Business Data Catalog, or Active Directory Resource. Depending on which type you select, you are presented with a different set of parameters.

  The Business Data Catalog is beyond the scope of this book. For more information on configuring the BDC user profile properties, see http://msdn2.microsoft.com/en-us/library/ms585895.aspx.

- **Connection name**   If you select LDAP or Active Directory Resource, you must input a connection name. This name enables multiple connections to individual containers/resources inside these LDAP directories. Because an Active Directory connection includes all username attributes therein, a connection name is not required.

- **Domain name**   When selecting Active Directory as the import source, you must define the domain name for the connection. You have the option to auto-discover the domain controller (preferred), or if you have a specialized installation, you may specify a domain controller. This second option may be necessary when your server farm exists in a screened subnet and you want to localize Active Directory traffic to that subnet. If you specify a domain controller, be aware that user profile imports and updating will cease if that domain controller should fail for any reason.

  > **Note**   A good situation in which to use multiple Active Directory domains is when your server farm is located in a resource forest, with no generic user authentication accounts. In this model, you set up an import connection (source) for every domain in which your authentication accounts reside. Doing so limits the visibility of your resource forest accounts.

- **Directory Service name**   If you are establishing an import connection with a third-party LDAP, you must define the server name hosting the directory. Because auto-discovery isn't enabled for third-party LDAPS, this server needs to be documented to prevent user profile import failures, should it cease to function.

- **TCP port /SSL**   You also need to define the port and select whether to use SSL. Once again, using SSL may be necessary if your server traffic will traverse public networks. The default ports work for most installations.

- **Server Side Incremental**   Choose Server Side Incremental if you plan to schedule incremental profile imports. This feature reduces the overhead of your domain controllers when performing frequent imports.

> **Caution**   If you enable Server Side Incremental in conjunction with a Windows 2000 Server Active Directory, the content access account must have the Replicate Changes permission.

- **Master forest connection settings (Active Directory resource only)**   When specifying an individual resource in an Active Directory for user profile imports, you must define the connection parameters:

    ❑   The domain name should be the Forest root domain.

    ❑   Auto-discover the domain controller when possible; otherwise specify the single domain controller to use.

    ❑   The default LDAP port is 389; the default SSL-secured LDAP port is 636.

    ❑   Specify the account with sufficient permissions to import user profiles. Use of the default account is discouraged.

- **Provider name (LDAP only)**   If you use a third-party LDAP for user profiles, you must enter the provider name.

- **Username attribute**   If you are using Active Directory, you cannot specify the username attribute because it is always *distinguishedname*. If you are importing from a third-party LDAP, however, you need to define the username attribute, which is usually *uid*.

- **Search settings**   You can auto-fill the root search base or enter one manually. If you are targeting a subtree item in the directory, you need to append the auto-filled root search base with the targeted OU, as an example. You may further limit the objects imported by selecting the user filter and scope.

    > **Tip**   You can further limit the performance impact on your domain controller(s) by specifying the page size and page time out settings. But, if these are too restrictive and you have Server Side Incremental enabled, you may get erratic import results.

- **Authentication**   By default, the access account is the account specified for content search and indexing. Using a dedicated account is recommended for stability and security. This account can be audited and limited as required.

Once you have configured custom import sources, you must use the View Import Connections interface for all future import sources. Selecting either Domain or Entire Forest deletes *all* Custom Sources you have defined.

Viewing Import Log

This version of SharePoint Server brings a robust crawl log capability. The full description of this functionality is provided under Search and Indexing administration, but it is worth noting that you can view the profile import log from Shared Services

Administration > User Profiles and Properties > View Import Log. This interface allows you to filter based on Content Sources (import connections), date, status type, and status message. If you have errors during importing, consider increasing the verbosity of the logging in Central Administration > Usage Analysis, and view the logs for import errors.

Modifying User Profiles

To view an existing user profile, browse to Shared Services Administration > User Profiles And My Sites > User Profiles And Properties. Select View User Profiles, as shown in Figure 8-14. This can only be done after performing at least one profile import.

Figure 8-14   After importing user profiles, you can view individual profile details by selecting View User Profiles.

Select the View User Profiles hyperlink to see existing user profiles. If you have several hundred or thousands of user profiles, you can filter the user list using the drop-down menu shown in Figure 8-15.

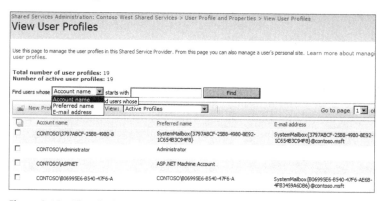

Figure 8-15   Filter the list based on criteria that best fit your environment.

To edit an account, select Edit from the profile's drop-down menu. From here, you can directly edit properties that are used in My Sites and Global Audiences (SSP Audiences). Policy restrictions, such as changing the Show To group, are limited here for any user in his or her My Site, including administrators. Notice that you can manage personal sites from here in conjunction with editing profile details.

From the same management interface, you can also create a new profile; however, the user must have an account in the directory. You can modify all available user properties. You might manually add a profile to a remote LDAP directory or when repairing user profiles in between profile imports.

Configuring User Profile Properties

User profile properties are used throughout your SharePoint Server farm for functions, such as search scopes and audiences. SharePoint Server 2007 ships with a number of profile properties, but also populates the available properties when crawling import connections (sources). You can create custom profile properties and map those properties to custom attributes in your connected LDAP directories. Profile properties are a very powerful way to expose personal information about individuals in your organization, such as skill sets and personal interests. This information can be indexed or included in audiences, thereby surfacing critical institutional knowledge. For example, you could index a profile property that collected critical skills information, such as database administration. By indexing this information, you can then search for all individuals with that skill set. By default the following sections are included:

- Details
- Contact Information
- Custom Properties

You may add additional sections to ease management of properties by selecting New Section and completing the required information.

Adding New Properties

You can create custom properties, perhaps for divisional or subsidiary information. These can be fields that are mapped and imported from an LDAP directory or specified by the user. New properties are useful when creating search scopes and creating audiences. For example, you might create a property named *Division* and map it to a correlating attribute in Active Directory. This could then allow you to create a search scope to only search documents by people in a single division. To create a new property you select Add Profile Property, as shown in Figure 8-16. You can also create a new property from User Profile Properties, as shown in Figure 8-17.

Figure 8-16   Select Add Profile Property from the User Profiles Properties interface.

Figure 8-17   Select New Property from the View Profile Properties interface.

As you select and deselect options in this interface, the page will post back. After the page refreshes, the available options change. These changes will be noted as the options are defined.

- **Name**   The name cannot be changed, so take due care when naming user properties. Your organization should define a common naming structure to make managing user properties easy. The name must meet the specifications of RFC2396; that is, it must start with a letter and cannot contain spaces or special characters, except ".", "+", or "-".

- **Display name**   The display name is for ease of identification and is not subject to the same restrictions as *Name*. The Display name should be easily identified by users and administrators for it to be useful.

- **Edit languages**   You can only have one property *Name,* but you can associate many language- specific *Display Names* with the property *Name*. This feature allows users to see the Display Name of the property in their language. To add language-specific Display Names, select Edit Languages. On opening the page, you have the ability to Add Language, edit an existing entry, or delete a current entry, as shown in Figure 8-18.

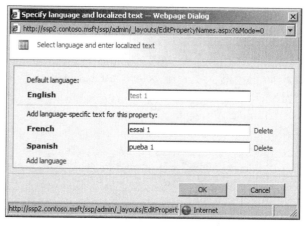

Figure 8-18   You can add, modify, or delete language-specific display names from a user-friendly interface.

- **Type**   Numerous property types are available; the following list details all options.

  ❑ *String* is the most common property type. It can be a combination of any characters, but cannot be longer than 400 characters. String is the only possible property type if you wish to allow multiple values.

  ❑ *Big Integer* allows only whole numbers, with no decimal. The length is not configurable. The field must be in the range of −9223372036854775808 to 9223372036854775808, or the user will get an error populating the field.

  ❑ *Binary* property types can only be mapped to a directory attribute. It is useful for mapping user IDs and other security IDs (SIDs). The length must be in the range of 1–7500.

  ❑ *Boolean* will show a check box that the user can select for Boolean search function.

  ❑ *Date* provides an entry for a valid date and a calendar drop-down menu for date input. It can be used for user input or mapped to a directory attribute, such as account expiration. Figure 8-19 shows an example of what the property looks like when enabled for user input.

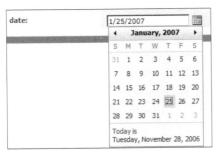

Figure 8-19   The Date property allows user input through a drop-down calendar control.

  ❑ *Date No Year* requires user input in the form of *Month ##*, for example, March 15.

  ❑ *Date Time* provides the same drop-down calendar as *Date*, but also includes drop-down controls for the hour and minute. Figure 8-20 shows an example of a Date Time property in a user profile.

Figure 8-20   The Date Time property shows the hour and minute drop-down controls.

❑ *E-mail* simply requires an @ symbol in the entry. There are no other checks in place for this property.

❑ *Float* provides a method for gathering floating point numbers. It does not accept non-numerical characters, and its length is limited to 50, which is not configurable.

❑ *HTML* allows user entry of HTML code, up to a length of 3,600 characters. It also provides a rudimentary in-screen HTML editor. Figure 8-21 shows an example of the editor included with the HTML property.

Figure 8-21   The HTML property type provides an HTML editor for user entry.

❑ *Integer* is similar to *Big Integer,* except that the acceptable range is −2147483648 to 2147483647.

❑ *Person* provides user entry requiring a match to a user in the directory. It also provides a name checker and the People Picker, as shown in Figure 8-22.

Figure 8-22   The Person property requires a valid user from the directory service to be entered.

Tip   If you see the database-link icon, as shown in Figure 8-23, the property is mapped to a directory attribute.

Figure 8-23   The database-link icon represents a mapped directory property.

❑ *Unique Identifier* should only be used to map the unique identifier associated with an account in the directory service.

❑ *URL* forces user entry in the form of *ftp://, http://, file://,* or *https://,* appended with the server host.

■ **Allow multiple values**   Multiple values can only be selected when choosing a property type of String. You must also define the value separator, either "," or ";".

- **Allow choice list** To allow a choice list, you must once again choose the property type String. After checking Allow Choice List, the screen posts back, and Choice List Settings appears further down the screen, as shown in Figure 8-24.

Figure 8-24 The Choice List Settings menu only appears after selecting Allow Choice List.

- **User description** The description can be changed any time during or after the property creation. The description annotates the property field and can be used to instruct users on the proper naming conventions or may remind users of Human Resources policies. You can have several language-defined descriptions, with users seeing the description you have defined for their language. Figure 8-25 shows a sample user description.

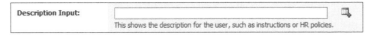

Figure 8-25 Use the user description only when necessary because it increases the size of the page.

- **Policy setting** The property privacy policy setting defines the status of the property and whether or not valid data are required for the property. If the policy setting is set to disabled, the property is not available or visible to the user. If set to Optional, then the user can choose to leave the field blank. Conversely, selecting Required forces user valid entry into the field before saving the profile.

- **Default privacy setting** Privacy settings define who can see the defined value of the property. Be careful when selecting Everyone when there is confidential information, such as home phone numbers. Information like Division, however, should probably be viewable by everyone. It is not possible to add groups of users to the default choices.

- **User override** If you do not select User Can Override, then the property privacy setting cannot be changed by the user. If you wish to allow your users to change the privacy settings for this property, select the override check box. Figure 8-26 shows the difference between a property privacy policy allowing user override and one that does not.

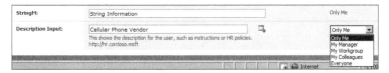

Figure 8-26   The example of a custom property, StringM, does not allow the user to change the privacy setting, but Description Input allows the change through the privacy setting drop-down.

- **Replicable**   If you wish to replicate this property as user information for all site collections, you must select Replicable. To replicate a user profile property, the policy setting must be enabled, the privacy setting must be configured for everyone, and User Can Override cannot be selected because doing so would break the replication.

    Important   If you later choose to turn off *Replicable*, be aware that previously replicated user data to site collections are not removed.

- **Edit settings**   Allowing users to edit settings allows them to change the field at any time. Although this ability is useful for some items, such as skill sets, you never want to allow the editing of properties mapped to your LDAP or Active Directory. For example, if you have defined the attributes division and manager in Active Directory and mapped those to properties in the user profile, you do not want the users overwriting this information because it will be overwritten in the next import.

- **Display settings**   To show a profile in the properties section of the user's profile page, you must select the default privacy setting of Everyone. This setting makes this option available for the users to show on their My Site. You can also choose to see the property on the edit details page, and show changes in the Colleague Tracker Web Part.

- **Choice list settings (requires Allow Choice List to be checked)**   You can define a choice list for the users or allow users to input their own field values, as shown in Figure 8-27. To add a choice list, check *Defined Choice List,* decide whether to allow users to add to the choice list, and select *Add A New Choice....* Alternatively, you can import choices from a text file with the values separated by a carriage return <Enter>.

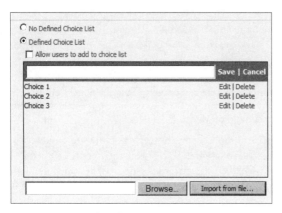

Figure 8-27   Check Defined Choice List and select Add A New Choice... to add choices.

- **Search settings**   Aliased properties are treated as equivalent to the username and user ID when searching for items authored by a user or audience targeting. You can also specify whether to index the property. Items such as home phone number may not be indexed in your organization.

- **Property import mapping**   You can create custom profile properties and map the field value to an attribute in a connected LDAP, such as Active Directory. There are 22 default values already mapped, including account name, work number, office, department, and title. You can add to these fields such values as division, language, nationality, and so forth. Map these properties back to attributes defined in your Active Directory.

> **Tip**   You can change the order in which the properties are displayed to the user by selecting the up or down arrows, as shown in Figure 8-28. If you need to move an item several spaces, it can be very time consuming.

Property Name	Change Order	Property Type
> Details	∨	Section
Id	∧ ∨	unique identifier
SID	∧ ∨	binary
Active Directory Id	∧ ∨	binary
Account name	∧ ∨	Person

New Property | New Section

Figure 8-28   To change the order of a property, select the up and down arrows.

You can edit existing properties, but many fields, such as type, policy settings, and name, are locked. You cannot change fields such as Name and Type, but you can always change the Display Name, add languages to Description and Display Name, and modify the directory mappings.

Note   You can manage all user profile property policies from a single location in Shared Services Administration > User Profiles and My Sites > Profile Services Policies.

Using Personalization Services

Although much of SharePoint Server's personalization occurs in the My Site configuration, some is configured for all users who connect to Web applications associated with an SSP. You can personalize the views of My Site horizontal navigation bar (Top Link Bar) and define Save As locations for Office applications.

Published Links to Office Client Applications

To publish links to Office applications such as Word or Excel, you must select *Published Links To Office Client Applications* in Shared Services Administration, as shown in Figure 8-29. The users will then have this location as an option in the Office application Save As menu.

Figure 8-29   To publish links to Office client applications, select the administration link.

Personalization Site Links

Personalization site links provide an easy method to provide important information to your users. You must specify a Web address, owner, and description, but be aware that the description is the Top Link Bar name. If you wish to target a specific audience, you can use Global (this SSP) audiences or Active Directory distribution and security groups. Figure 8-30 shows an example of a My Site with a Top Link Bar tab name. This is the *portal home* that can be used for instant navigation.

Figure 8-30 The description shows as the tab name on the Top Link Bar.

You can use this as a quick navigation method for internal or external sites, such as expense reports, news, human resources policies, or whatever your specific needs may be. Be aware that having too many tabs makes the screen cluttered and less user friendly. Using audiences makes the user experience much better.

Configuring Audiences

Audiences created in Shared Services Administration are also referred to as *Global Audiences*. Be aware that these are not truly global because they will only exist in a single SSP; therefore only the intra-farm Web applications that are associated with this SSP or Web applications in an inter-farm shared services arrangement will be able to find and use them. You may also *target* audiences from site collections using Global Audiences, Active Directory security and distribution lists, or SharePoint site groups.

Creating Audiences

To create an SSP audience, enter the *Audiences* management interface from Shared Services Administration. By default, there is only one audience created, and it is named All Site Users. To add new audiences, select the New Audience tab, as shown in Figure 8-31.

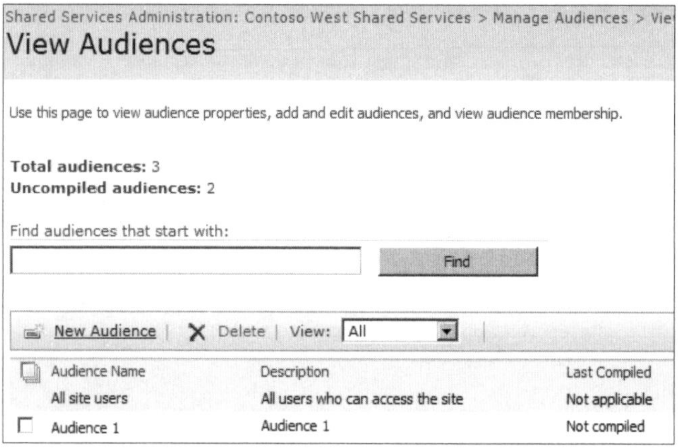

Shared Services Administration: Contoso West Shared Services > Manage Audiences > Vie

View Audiences

Use this page to view audience properties, add and edit audiences, and view audience membership.

Total audiences: 3
Uncompiled audiences: 2

Find audiences that start with:

| | Find |

☐ New Audience	✕ Delete	View:	All ▾	
☐ Audience Name	Description		Last Compiled
All site users	All users who can access the site		Not applicable
☐ Audience 1	Audience 1		Not compiled

Figure 8-31 Select the New Audience tab to create global audiences.

- **Name**   You must name your audience. Use care when creating audiences because your users will use them to target content. Changing this name after the fact can break your site collection functionality.

- **Description**   The description is optional, but is a good idea. Letting your users know what the details of the audience are, such as *Top Level Managers,* can keep the need-to-know purpose of audiences intact.

- **Owner**   You must specify the owner of this audience. This owner can change the rules, so be careful to whom you assign the role.

- **Rules**   Two choices are available.

  - *Satisfy All Of The Rules* requires that every rule defined for the audience be met before users are added. If this is too restrictive, you may not have members in your audience!

  - *Satisfy Any Of The Rules* is used more often; it allows for any combination of the rules to be met in order to insert a member into this audience. However, remember that an issue with a poorly created rule set can result in an audience that is much larger than expected.

  After choosing OK, you are taken to a screen to begin creating rules. Although you can create multiple rules for a single audience, you can only create one per screen. You have two options for the operand in a rule: User or Property. Select the *User* operand when defining distribution or security groups or possibly the management hierarchy in your organization. Selecting *Property* as your operand allows you to create audiences based on *any* of the custom properties defined in your user profiles.

- **Add rules**   You can add rules at any time. To add a rule, browse from Shared Services Administration to Manage Audiences > View Audiences > Audience Rules and select Add Rule. You may add as many rules as you like, but you should always view the membership after compiling to verify you have the correct end result.

Using Audiences

It is very important to understand that audiences are not a security authorization mechanism. They are simply a way to present applicable information to users by targeting relevant information in an interface. You can limit the viewing of almost anything in this version of SharePoint Server, including Web Parts, documents, lists, Top Link Bars, and much more. Your users can also take advantage of these audiences in lists and document libraries.

Office SharePoint Usage Reporting

Usage analysis processing is used to report how sites are used, including their files, users, bandwidth, and more. To enable usage analysis processing, you must first enable Windows SharePoint Services processing in Central Administration. Figure 8-32 shows where to enable this in Central Administration > Operations > Logging And Reporting > Usage Analysis Processing. You may also enable search query logging to run reports on search and indexing.

Figure 8-32 You must enable Usage Analysis Processing in Central Administration before you can enable SSP usage reporting.

Chapter 9

Configuring SharePoint Server Portals

If you asked ten people the definition of a portal, you might very well get ten different answers. Because no two portal implementations are alike, SharePoint Server 2007 provides a customizable and extensible foundation to make your portal unique and applicable in your environment. The ultimate goal of any portal is to create a single place for people to visit that offers a high probability that they can find what they are looking for. No matter how you design your portal, you should focus on aggregating and organizing information. Aggregated and organized information lends itself to being referenced quickly and used frequently. Information managed by a portal becomes more valuable because it can be targeted to specific audiences and therefore most likely will be used more frequently.

In SharePoint Server, portals are created by applying the Collaboration or Publishing Portal templates when creating a site collection. The Collaboration Portal template is intended for creating corporate Intranet portals. The Publishing Portal provides a robust framework for creating an Internet presence. A collaborative portal is a single location in which information is used and shared among many users. Large organizations may benefit from multiple collaborative portals that are dedicated to specific functions and are linked to a central, less collaborative portal that serves as a hub for locating information. The use of multiple portals may be indicated for different geographic regions, organizational units, or for legal or regulatory purposes.

Creating Departmental Portals

SharePoint Server gives you the ability to create many portals in a single Web application. Many organizations do not want to create portals with a lengthy URL structure, such as *http://portal.contoso.msft/sites/accounting*. To shorten the length of the URL, you can create an embedded managed path site collection. For example, you could create an accounting portal at *http://portal.contoso.msft/accounting*. However, remember that you cannot create site collections in the accounting managed path; in that path, you can only create subsites of the accounting site collection. To create an embedded managed path site collection, do the following:

1. Open Central Administration > Application Management > SharePoint Web Application Management > Define Managed Paths.

2. Select the Web application in which you wish to create the managed path.

3. In the *Add A New Path* field, enter the name you wish for the embedded managed path site collection. In the earlier example, the name is accounting.

4. You must select *Explicit Inclusion* as the Type.

5. Open Central Administration > Application Management > SharePoint Site Management > Create Site Collection. This action *must* be performed from Central Administration. You cannot create an embedded managed path site collection using self-service site management.

6. Select the correct Web application from the list.

7. Select the Explicit Inclusion you created earlier as the URL path.

8. Select the site collection type.

9. Define an administrator.

10. Click OK.

Creating Corporate Intranet Portals

Intranet portals are intended to help organizations manage their information by performing three primary functions:

■ **Aggregating**   Aggregation can include indexing, linking to, and hosting content. A corporate portal can aggregate content using hyperlinked lists or indexing services such as SharePoint Server Search and by directly hosting content, as is the case with portal document libraries. Portals can also provide access to information from sources such as SAP, Siebel, and Microsoft Office Excel spreadsheets.

■ **Organizing**   This function is accomplished through the creation of taxonomies. Taxonomies can change over time, but spending the time in the beginning to clearly define the basics will save valuable administrative resources down the road. A very common taxonomy in use today is the Dewey Decimal System used in libraries. In fact, many organizations are now using classically trained librarians to assist them with their corporate or organizational taxonomies.

■ **Presenting**   After you have completed the exercise of aggregating and organizing your data, you must research the best method to present that data, in a timely and targeted manner, to your end users. Be sure to present data that are relevant to your users; the audience capability of SharePoint Server serves this purpose nicely.

Creating a Corporate Intranet Portal

1. Browse to Central Administration.

2. Create a new Web application. Portals cannot be created as subsites and should be applied at the root of a new Web application. Chapter 4, "Creating Site Collections," describes how to create Web applications.

3. Select the Collaboration Portal from the Publishing templates, as shown in Figure 9-1.

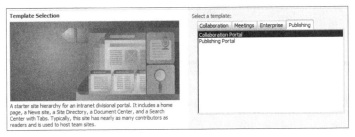

Figure 9-1   Create an Intranet Portal by applying the Collaboration Portal site template.

Customizing Portal Navigation

To enable consistent navigation throughout the portal, the SharePoint Server portal templates handle this function differently from the standard Windows SharePoint Services site methods. The standard Top Link Bar and Quick Launch are replaced with a more advanced navigational system. In addition, the tabs in the default navigation bar are subsites and not pages. These subsites, and all other subsites created beneath the portal, inherit the portal's advanced navigation. Furthermore, most of the default sites' navigation can be managed directly from the Site Actions control. For all of the portal sites, except the Document Center, you can reach the navigation configuration page by browsing to Site Actions > Site Settings > Modify Navigation, as seen in Figure 9-2. You can also modify the navigation settings from Navigation, under the Look And Feel section of Site Settings.

Figure 9-2   Use Modify Navigation to directly access a site's navigation settings.

Modifying Portal Navigation Settings

The advanced portal navigation system is configured differently from other sites. Navigation settings can be customized on a per site basis and are divided into two categories: Global and Current. Global Navigation defines which items will be displayed on the Top Link Bar. Current Navigation defines how sites will be displayed in the Quick Launch. Subsite Navigation configuration pages display a graphic, shown in Figure 9-3, that demonstrates this relationship.

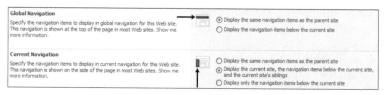

Figure 9-3   The Navigation configuration page for a subsite shows which navigation controls are affected by Global Navigation and which by Current Navigation.

Navigation elements that are shared across all portal sites are controlled from the navigation settings of the portal top-level site. Settings unique to each subsite, such as which sites are displayed in drop-down menus on the top site, are controlled from the subsite's navigation settings.

Configuring Top-Level Portal Navigation

When creating a portal, your first choice should be adding subsites and/or pages automatically to the Top Link Bar and Quick Launch. Items that are added automatically can then be hidden on an per item basis, if required. Alternatively, you may elect to add sites and pages manually to the portal's navigation controls. The order in which sites and subsites are displayed can be controlled automatically by choosing the *Sort Automatically* option on the Site Navigation Settings page. The *Navigation Editing And Sorting* control also allows headings and links to be added to the Global and Current Navigation, as shown in Figure 9-4.

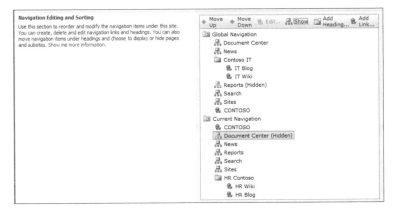

Figure 9-4   You can add headings and links to customize site navigation across your portal.

Headings added to the global navigation are displayed in the Top Link Bar and can have links displayed beneath them in a drop-down menu. Links added to the Global Navigation outside of headings are displayed directly on the Top Link Bar, as seen in Figure 9-5.

Figure 9-5   Links added beneath headings appear in a drop-down menu. (Note the relationship to Figure 9-4.)

Headings added to the Current Navigation are displayed in the Quick Launch and can have links grouped beneath them, as shown in Figure 9-6.

Figure 9-6   Links are grouped together beneath their heading in the Quick Launch. (Note the relationship to Figure 9-4.)

Configuring Portal Subsite Navigation

When configuring navigation at the subsite level, there are two options for Global Navigation:

- **Display The Same Navigation Items As The Parent Site**   By default, a subsite displays the same Global Navigation as its parent site.

- **Display The Navigation Items Below The Current Site**   Selecting *Display The Navigation Items Below The Current Site* causes navigation beneath that site to behave similarly to a portal top-level site. This option causes the Top Link Bar to display the sites beneath the current subsite. If *Show Subsites* and *Show Pages* are selected, items beneath the sites in the Top Link Bar are displayed in drop-down menus, as seen in Figure 9-7.

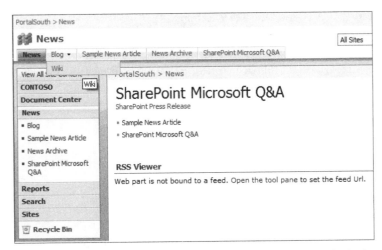

Figure 9-7   The news site's Global Navigation has been configured to display its subsites, and the Current Navigation is displaying its subsites and siblings.

There are three options for Current Navigation:

- **Display The Same Navigation Items As The Parent Site**   The Quick Launch displays the same navigation items as the parent site.

- **Display The Current Site, The Navigation Items Below The Current Site, And The Current Site's Siblings**   The site's siblings are the other sites beneath the current site's parent site. Navigation Items that have been added to the parent as links are displayed; headings and the links beneath them are not.

- **Display Only The Navigation Items Below The Current Site**   Only sites beneath the current site are displayed in the Quick Launch.

Using the Site Directory

The Site Directory is a central location for managing sites associated with the portal. Portal subsites, farm sites, and Extranet sites can all be linked to and categorized using the Site Directory. Using the Site Directory, administrators can view the portal's structure using the Site Map, view sites within the directory, approve or reject new sites, and edit or delete site links.

Creating Sites Beneath the Site Directory

Sites created beneath the Site Directory are not added automatically to the Site Directory list. To add a site to the Site Directory at creation, you must check the *List This New Site In The Site Directory* check box on the creation page, as shown in Figure 9-8.

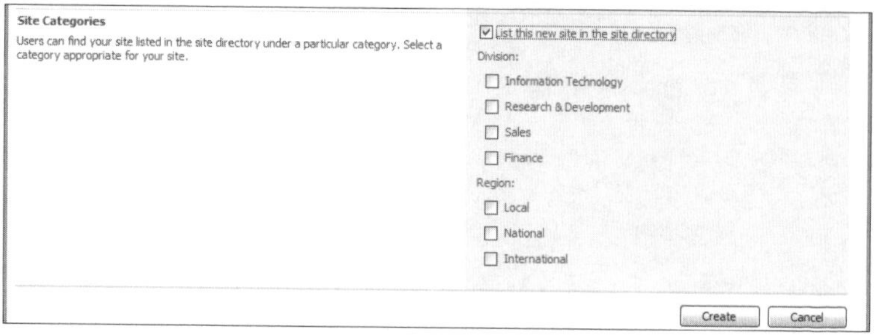

Figure 9-8   Check the List This New Site in the Site Directory check box to add a site to the Site Directory at creation.

Tip   You can also specify a Master Site Directory in Central Administration by navigating to Central Administration > Operations > Global Configuration > Master Site Directory Settings.

You must also select which Division and Region, if any, the site belongs in. A default value for both Division and Region can be defined using the List Settings options of the Sites List. To create a site beneath the Site Directory, click on the Create Site link in the top right-hand portion of the page.

Adding Links to the Site Directory

Links added to the Site Directory by users must be approved by an administrator before they become visible in the directory. Links are added automatically to the Sites List even if they are associated with a region, division, top sites, or top tasks. Checking the Top Tasks check box displays the link in the *I Need To...* Web Part on the Portal Welcome page as seen in Figure 9-9, and beneath Top Tasks under Tasks and Tools in Site Directory Categories.

Figure 9-9   Links added to the Top Tasks category are displayed in the I Need To... Web Part on the Portal Welcome page.

Managing the Site Directory Using the Sites List

The heart of the Site Directory is the Sites List because it contains the actual site entries and because it is the only place in which sites can be edited or deleted from the Site Directory. It is also where the properties for the Site Directory, such as the Division and Region categories, are defined. To access the Sites List, do the following:

1. Browse to the Site Directory.

2. Select View All Site Content.

Many of the features needed to manage the Site Directory are available through a drop-down menu in the Sites List. To access the options in the drop-down menu, place the pointer over the name of the site to be modified, and click the down arrow that appears. Doing so provides several options, as shown in Figure 9-10.

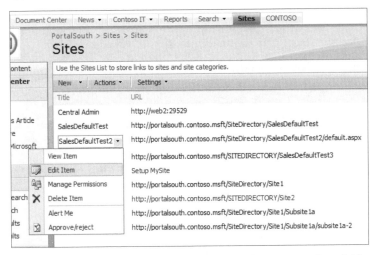

Figure 9-10   Several options for managing the Site Directory are only available from the Sites List's drop-down menu.

- **View Item**   This option displays a synopsis of the site's list items and provides a link to create a new item, edit or delete the item, manage its permission, approve or reject it, or generate an alert.

- **Edit Item**   You can alter all of the properties associated with the item from this option. Of particular importance is the Top Site check box. Selecting Top Site adds the site to the list displayed under Top Sites in the Site Directory. After a link has been added to the Site Directory, selecting this option is the only way to add it to the Top Site's list.

- **Manage Permissions**   This option allows you to define custom permissions on a per list item basis.

- **Delete Item**   To delete a site from the Site Directory, select Delete. This does not delete the site, only its entry in the Site Directory.

- **Alert Me**   This option enables an e-mail notification to be sent when changes are made to the item.

- **Approve/Reject**   By default, sites added by administrators are approved automatically. Sites added by other users must be approved by an administrator before they are added to the Site Directory.

Finding Broken Links

Sites listed in the site directory are not removed automatically from the directory when they are deleted. You can find broken links by using the Broken Link Checker at the site collection level and the Site Directory Links Scan in Central Administration. The Site Directory Links Scan regularly scans multiple site directories using a scheduled timer job.

Scanning for Broken Links at the Site Collection Level

1. In the Site Directory select *Scan For Broken Links* from Site Actions.

2. Select the types of sites you wish to scan from the View List and click OK. The View List limits the scan to items listed in the corresponding view of the Sites List.

Scanning for Broken Links from Central Administration

1. Browse to Central Administration > Operations > Site Directory Links Scan.

2. Add the URL for the site directory's Sites List to the *Site Directory View URLs* text box. Multiple entries, separated by commas, can be added. The sites will be validated before the job is created.

3. If you would like the titles and descriptions of scanned sites to be updated automatically, check the *Update Title And Description Of Links In The Site Directory Automatically* check box.

Tip   The Site Directory Broken Links Scan timer job that performs the broken links scan can be viewed and disabled by browsing to Central Administration > Operations > Timer Job Definitions.

Modifying the Sites List

Several common modifications of the Site Directory, such as changing Regions or Divisions, are accomplished by modifying the Sites List's list settings. To modify the list settings, select List Settings from the Settings drop-down menu of the Sites List, as shown in Figure 9-11.

Figure 9-11   To change several of the Site Directory settings you must alter the List Settings of the Sites List.

Changing the Options for Division and Region in the Site Directory

It is unlikely that the default division and region options will align with most organizations. To modify the division and region options you must do the following:

1. Browse to the List Settings for the Sites List.

2. Click on either *Division* or *Region* in the section labeled Columns.

3. Alter the entries listed in the text box under *Type Each Choice On A Separate Line.*

4. To require that a value be specified, select Yes from the *Require That This Column Contains Information* option buttons.

5. To set a default value, select the *Choice* option button under Default Value and enter the desired default. The default value must be one of the choices available in Step 3.

Adding a Custom Category to the Site Directory

You can create custom categories, in addition to the Division and Region categories, to better reflect the structure of your organization.

1. Browse to the List Settings for the Sites List.

2. Click on *Create Column* from the bottom of the List Settings page.

3. Enter a name for the column. This value is then displayed along with Division and Region default categories.

4. Select the *Choice (Menu To Choose From)* option button.

5. If you wish to require a value for the column, select Yes from the *Require That This Column Contains Information* option buttons.

6. Enter the desired options in the text box labeled *Type Each Choice On A Separate Line,* which contains the values: Enter Choice #1, Enter Choice #2. These values are the choices that users are presented with during site creation.

7. To allow only a single choice to be selected, choose either the drop-down menu or option buttons from *Display Choices Using.* To allow a site to be associated with multiple choices, select *Checkboxes.*

8. If you wish to give the user the option to fill in his or her own choice, select Yes from the *Allow 'Fill-In' Choices* option buttons.

9. If one of the values entered in Step 6 should be a default value, then select the *Choice* option button under Default Value and enter the name. An empty entry indicates that there is no default.

10. Check the *Add To Default View* check box to add the column to the default view. Even if the check box is not checked, the column will still be displayed on the Sites main page, as shown in Figure 9-12.

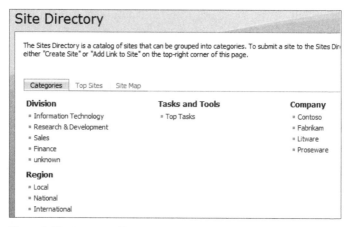

Figure 9-12 You can add custom categories, such as this one named Company, to the Category Web Part that is displayed on the Sites main page.

Viewing the portal structure with the Site Map   By default, the Site Map provides a view of the portal's subsites and the second-level subsites beneath them. It also displays items that have been created as headings in the Current, but not Global, Navigation at the top level of the portal. To view the Site Map, click on Site Map in the tool bar of the Site Directory.

Modifying the Site Map Web Part   The Site Map is generated by a Table of Contents Web Part, which can also be added to other pages. If you wish to modify the look and feel of the Web Part, it can be customized easily.

1. From the Site Map page, click on Site Actions and then select Edit Page.

2. On the Site Map Web Part's toolbar, select *Modify Shared Web Part* from the Edit drop-down menu.

In addition to the common Web Part properties, the Site Map Web Part has two property groups of particular interest: Content and Organization.

Configuring the Site Map Web Part's Content Options

1. Expand the Content group of Web Part properties.

2. Enter a location to start from in the *Start From* text box. If the *Show Content From Starting Location* check box is checked, the Web Part only displays sites and/or pages beneath the starting location.

3. Select the levels to show from the *Select Levels To Show* drop-down menu.

4. Choose to include pages, hidden sites, and hidden pages by selecting the appropriate check boxes.

Configuring the Site Map Web Part's Organization Options

1. Select *Sort Contents As They Are Sorted In Navigation* if you wish sites to be ordered as they appear in the portal top-level Current Navigation. Heading items in the Current Navigation are listed on the first level. Link items beneath heading items are not displayed.

2. Choose *Sort Contents Using the Following Settings* to order sites and pages according to their properties.

Using the Reports Center

The Reports Center allows you to consolidate information in a central location, making information visible through the use of Key Performance Indicators (KPIs) and dashboards. KPIs provide, at a glance, a visual summary of critical organizational information. KPI lists are displayed on pages using the Key Performance Indicators Web Part. For a detailed view of a KPI, use the KPI Details Web Part. Dashboards consolidate and visually summarize business intelligence information from multiple sources into a single, easily referenced page. Dashboards are made up of several business intelligence Web Parts, such as the KPI, Excel Web Access, and the Business Data List Web Part. The steps required to create a KPI list are described below.

Creating a KPI List

1. From the Reports Center, select *Site Actions, View All Site Content.*

2. Click on the Create icon located directly beneath the *All Site Content* title.

3. Click on KPI List from the Custom Lists section of the create page.

4. Give the list a meaningful name and description.

5. Selecting yes in the *Display This List On The Quick Launch* option buttons adds the list as a link beneath the Lists heading in the Current Navigation. The heading is then displayed in the Quick Launch, but the individual links are not.

Creating Key Performance Indicators

Once a KPI list has been created, you can populate it with KPIs. Four different data sources can be used to create KPIs: SharePoint lists, Excel workbooks, SQL Server 2005 Analysis Services, and manually entered data. To create a KPI, you need to navigate to the appropriate KPI list.

Creating a KPI Using Data in SharePoint List

1. Select *Indicator Using Data In SharePoint List* from the New drop-down menu.

2. Give the KPI a meaningful name and description, and enter comments to explain its use.

3. Select the list's URL by clicking on the Browse icon, or enter a value manually. To create a KPI to track items in the Sites List, enter *http(s)://[portalURL]/Site-Directory/SitesList/AllItems.aspx*.

4. Select which list view to use to populate the KPI.

5. To base the KPI on the total number of items in the list, select *Number Of List Items In The View*.

6. To base the KPI on the percentage of items that meet some acceptance criteria, select *Percentage Of List Items In The View Where*. For example, if the portal has 100 total sites in its Sites Directory and 30 of them are in the Sales division, the KPI would return a value of 30%. Be careful because calculations on columns of the type "Choice" can allow multiple selections and may return values that are misleading.

7. To base the KPI on the sum, average, maximum, or minimum of a column in a view, choose *Calculation Using All List Items In The View*.

8. Specify whether better values are higher or lower.

9. Enter values for *Display [green circle symbol] When Has Met Or Exceeded Goal* and *Display [yellow triangle symbol] When Has Met Or Exceeded Warning*.

Creating an Indicator Using Data in Excel Workbook

1. Select *Indicator Using Data In Excel Workbook* from the New drop-down menu.

2. Give the KPI a meaningful name and description, and enter comments to explain its use.

3. Use the Browse icon to locate the appropriate value for the Workbook URL, or enter the document's path. The document's URL must be relative to the current site.

4. Use the Select icon, shown in Figure 9-13, to choose a value for *Cell Address For Indicator Value,* or enter a cell manually. If the cell is entered manually, it must have the syntax *[sheet]!(cell).* For instance, for the cell G15 in a sheet named *Sales,* the appropriate value would be *Sales!G15.* You may also use a named range in place of a cell value. This has the advantage of giving the cell a meaningful name that is not dependent on the structure of the spreadsheet.

5. Specify whether better values are higher or lower.

6. Choose values for *Display [green circle symbol] When Has Met Or Exceeded Goal* and *Display [yellow triangle symbol] When Has Met Or Exceeded Warning* using the Select icon or by entering them manually.

Figure 9-13   The Select icon allows you to choose values directly from an Excel spreadsheet.

Creating an Indicator Using Data Using Manually Entered Information

1. Select *Indicator Using Data Using Manually Entered Information* from the New drop-down menu.

2. Give the KPI a meaningful name and description, and enter comments to explain its use.

3. Manually enter the Indicator Value.

4. Manually enter the values for *Display [green circle symbol] When Has Met Or Exceeded Goal* and *Display [yellow triangle symbol] When Has Met Or Exceeded Warning.*

Configuring Common KPI Properties

■ **Details Link**   The Details Page property allows you to reference a custom page to display explanatory information about the KPI. The format of the entry is validated to ensure an appropriate URL syntax, but the existence of the page is not checked.

■ **Update Rules**   All of the KPIs, except those using manually entered information, have a control option when they are updated. To update for each user the KPIs based on an Excel spreadsheet, the user in question must have permission to view the spreadsheet. If you choose to manually update the KPI, a user who cannot view the spreadsheet itself can view the last manually updated KPI value associated with it.

Creating Dashboards

Dashboards reveal organizational information contained in any structured data system, but out-of-the-box applications do work with Excel workbooks and KPIs. They provide useful mechanisms for combining information from disparate sources into a single point of reference. To create a new dashboard within a Reports Center, do the following:

1. Click on View All Site Content.

2. Click on Reports Library.

3. Select Dashboard Page from the New drop-down menu.

4. Give the dashboard a meaningful filename, title, and description. Note that the filename will appear in headings and links throughout the site.

5. Use the *Add A Link To Current Navigation Bar* option buttons to configure how, if at all, the dashboard is displayed in the Quick Launch.

6. Select the desired page layout for the dashboard.

7. In the Key Performance Indicators section, if you choose *Create A KPI List For Me Automatically,* a KPI list is created using the naming convention *[dashboard name] KPI Definitions.* Selecting *Allow Me To Select An Existing KPI List Later* allows you to configure the KPI Web Part after creation. If you choose *Do Not Add A KPI List To This Dashboard,* the dashboard page is created without a KPI Web Part.

Configuring Dashboards

Spreadsheets can be added to the page using the Excel Web Access Web Part. An appropriate workbook created with Excel 2007 in the .xlsx file format is required to use the Excel Web Access Web Part. The workbook must be published to a site included in the Trusted File Location under Excel Services Settings in the site's Shared Services Provider, and it must then be published to the site using the Excel Services option.

> **Tip** For more information on Excel Services, including Trusted File Locations, see Chapter 11, "Configuring Office SharePoint Server Excel Calculation Services."

The settings for publishing the workbook can be configured by clicking on Excel Services Options, in the publish Save As dialog box. It is possible to use the Excel Service Options to reveal only portions of a workbook, such as a chart or graph, while keeping the rest private. Finally, if portions of the workbook are to be kept private or if you want multiple views of different parts of the spreadsheet, the selected cells need to be named in Excel. You may also specify named single cells as parameters. Users are able to interact with the workbook by entering values for the parameters. The parameter values entered by users *will not* affect the workbook. To configure an Excel Web Access Web Part, do the following:

1. Select *Modify Shared Web Part* from the Web Part's Edit drop-down menu, or click on *Click Here To Open The Tool Pane* if the option is available.

2. Enter the location of the workbook in the Workbook text box, or browse to the workbook by clicking on the button marked with an ellipsis.

3. You may specify a named item in the workbook. If the named item field is left blank, the Web Part displays an item by default. By selecting a named item and clearing the Named Item drop-down menu check box in the Web Part's properties, you can ensure that only a single view of the workbook is displayed.

4. Configure the remaining options for the Web Part.

Using Online Editing in Portals

New to SharePoint Server 2007 are several publishing features. The Page Editing tool bar contains several useful tools for modifying pages, as seen in Figure 9-14. It contains tabs to modify or configure the page and workflow, in addition to several tools including spelling and checking for unpublished items.

Figure 9-14   The Page Editing tool bar allows you to interact with pages and initiate workflows.

Using the Page Drop-Down Menu

- **Save/Save and Stop Editing**   When a file is saved, but not checked in, any changes made will be lost if another user overrides the check out.

- **Check Out**   You must check out a page to alter it. When a page is checked out, other users are not able to modify it.

- **Check In**   Checking in the page through the Page drop-down menu offers several options not available through the *Check In Page To Draft* button on the toolbar.

- **Override Check Out**   When you override a page being checked out, any changes that have not been checked in will be lost.

- **Discard Check Out**   When *Discard Check Out* is used, all changes made since the last check out will be lost.

- **Page Settings**   Selecting Page Settings allows you to configure many of the page's properties, such as the title, description, audience, and page contact.

- **Delete Page**   Deleting the page moves it to the site's Recycle Bin. A page can be restored from the Recycle Bin, along with its full version history.

- **Add Web Parts**   You choose to browse, search, or import Web Parts onto the page.

- **Modify Web Parts**   Modify Web Parts displays a fly-out menu of all the Web Parts on the page. Selecting a Web Part opens the Modify Web Part interface on the left-hand side of the page.

The Workflow functionality is discussed in depth in Chapter 6, "Using Workflows and Information Management Policies."

Here are some features of the Tools drop-down menu:

- **Spelling**   Clicking on Spelling runs a spell check on the page's HTML fields. However, not all Web Parts will be checked, and the page's properties, such as Title and Description, will need to be checked from the Page Settings page.

- **Preview In New Window**   *Preview In New Window* opens a pop-up window and displays the page without any editing interface.

- **Check for Unpublished Items**   The Unpublished Items Report outlines problems on the page with a red or orange border. Items in red are broken links, whereas items in orange are links that are out of date. A detailed report can be viewed by clicking on the Full Report link in the *View The Full Report In A New Window* message.

    Note   The Unpublished Items Report only checks links within your SharePoint site.

- **Version History**   Version History displays a summary of different versions of the page. Placing the mouse over the Modified date displays a drop-down menu, as shown in Figure 9-15. From the drop-down menu you can view, restore, or unpublish a version. When a version is restored, it also needs to be published to make it visible. When a version is unpublished, the latest version is displayed to page contributors, and nothing is displayed to users with read-only permissions.

Figure 9-15   From the drop-down menu, available under Modified Date, you can view, restore, or unpublish a version.

- **Compare Text Changes**   *Compare Text Changes* displays the entire page, with differences between the previous and current versions color coded.

- **View Page Status**   *View Page Status* opens a pop-up window with a summary of information about the page.

- **View Recycle Bin**   *View Recycle Bin* opens the Recycle Bin, from which pages can be permanently deleted or restored.

Advanced Editing Using the Content Editor

The Content Editor, shown in Figure 9-16, allows pages to be customized in the browser using an interface similar to a word processor or Web page editor. With the Content Editor, you can create hyperlinks, images, lists, and table via the graphical user interface. A very useful feature is the ability to directly edit the content's HTML source code. Editing the HTML source gives you virtually unlimited control over what will be displayed on a page.

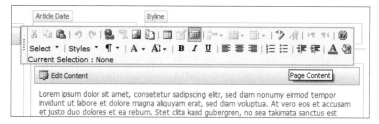

Figure 9-16   Clicking on the Edit Content link opens the Content Editor tool bar, which provides advanced editing capabilities within the browser.

Managing Content and Structure

SharePoint Server gives you the ability to view and interact with the entire portal through a hierarchical graphical user interface (GUI), as seen in Figure 9-17. Many of the actions available elsewhere can be initiated using the GUI. For instance, you can move sites and pages within portals and create new pages, sites, lists, and list items.

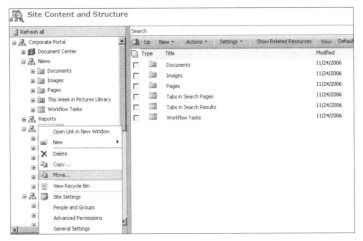

Figure 9-17 Manage Site Content And Structure allows you to copy and move between sites and to create new pages and sites.

Navigating to the Site Content And Structure Page

1. If available, select *Manage Content And Structure* from Site Actions.

2. If the link is not directly available, select *Site Settings* from Site Actions.

3. Click on *Go To Top Level Site Settings* under Site Collection Administration.

4. Click on *Content And Structure* under Site Administration.

View the Content And Structure Reports

1. Click on a site in the tree view on the left-hand side of the page.

2. In the list view on the right-hand side of the page, click on the drop-down menu labeled View and displaying the value Default View.

3. From the drop-down menu select one of the reports. The default reports are Checked Out to Me, Last Modified By Me, Pending Approval, My Tasks, All Draft Documents, Going Live Within Next Seven Days, and Expiring Within Next Seven Days.

Copying or Moving Items Using the Content And Structure Page

1. In either the tree view or the list view, rest the pointer over the name of the item that you wish to copy or move.

2. From the drop-down menu that appears next to the item's name, select Copy or Move.

3. Use the tree view in the pop-up window that appears to select a location for the item.

Deleting Items Using the Content And Structure Page

1. Rest the pointer over the name of the item you wish to delete.

2. Select delete from the dynamically generated drop-down menu.

3. Select OK from the confirmation dialog box.

Selecting Multiple Items Using the Content And Structure Page

1. In the list view on the right-hand side of the page, click the icon to the left of the Type column heading.

2. Uncheck the check boxes of any items that you do not wish to affect.

3. Select an action from the Actions drop-down menu.

Discarding Checkout Using the Content And Structure Page

If an item that requires modification is checked out, and the user who checked it out is unavailable to check it in, then the check out can be discarded. This option is only available when using the Site Content And Structure page and only to users with the appropriate permissions.

1. Find the object that is checked out using the Site Content And Structure page.

2. Select the object and choose *Discard Check Out* from the drop-down menu that appears when the pointer is held over the item's name.

Showing Related Resources Using the Content And Structure Page

The Site Content And Structure page provides a mechanism to determine what resources, if any, a page or site uses or references. Resources that are displayed include Cascading Style Sheets (CSS), links to other pages, links to the page from other pages in the site collection, and images.

1. Select an item from the tree view on the left-hand side of the Content And Structure page.

2. Select *Show Related Resources* from the list tool bar on the right-hand side of the page.

Using Internet Portals

The Publishing Portal allows you to make information visible to the broadest possible audience, the Internet. Using SharePoint's rich feature set, page editing and creation can be managed by workflows, allowing Internet content to be created by subject matter experts. Information managed for internal consumption can be filtered and re-purposed for the general public. Most Internet or Extranet access is via anonymous authentication or forms-based authentication. To create a new Internet or noncollaborative Intranet portal, you must create a Publishing site collection and enable anonymous authentication and/or forms-based authentication.

Creating an Internet Portal by Applying the Publishing Template

1. Create a new application in Central Administration.

2. Create a new site collection at the application's root, applying the Publishing Portal template.

Enabling Anonymous Access in Central Administration

1. Go to Central Administration.

2. Select the appropriate Web application from the Web application list.

3. Click on *Authentication Providers* under Application Security.

4. Select the zone on which to allow anonymous access.

5. Check the *Enable Anonymous Access* check box under Anonymous Access on the Edit Authentication page. While this can be set in IIS Manager, doing so in Central Administration writes this setting to the configuration database. If the setting is written to the configuration database, it will automatically be applied to servers as they are added to the farm.

6. Click Save.

Enabling Anonymous Access for a Site Collection

1. Verify that the site collection's web application has Anonymous Access enabled in Central Administration.

2. In publishing site collections, select *Modify All Site Settings* from the Site Actions drop-down menu.

3. Click on *Advanced Permissions* under Users and Permissions.

4. Select *Anonymous Access* from the Settings drop-down menu.

5. Select the option button labeled *Entire Web Site*. If you select the *Lists And Libraries* option button, anonymous access can be enabled for the site collection's lists and libraries. Enable only the items that require anonymous authentication; wikis and blogs are examples of standalone anonymous lists.

Enabling ASP.NET Forms-Based Authentication

Using ASP.NET pluggable authentication, SharePoint 2007 provides multiple authentication methods. Of particular interest when working with portals are ASP.NET forms and Web Single Sign-On (SSO). ASP.NET forms authentication is useful for authenticating against non-Windows authentication providers, such as SQL Server, other databases, or a Lightweight Directory Access Protocol (LDAP) provider. Forms-based authentication is also highly valuable for authenticating users via the Internet. Web Single Sign-On authentication provides a method for mapping credentials for third-party and back-end systems, for instance, line-of-business applications or databases. In addition to the default Microsoft SSO provider, Office SharePoint Server 2007 can use custom SSO providers.

Managing My Sites

When you enable My Sites, every user becomes a site collection administrator. Therefore, most My Site customization is performed by the users. The bulk of My Site personalization is done through user profiles and properties, which is a function of the associated Shared Services Provider. Please refer to Chapter 8, "Deploying SharePoint Server Shared Services," for detailed information on user profiles.

Personalizing the Top Link Bar from the Shared Services Provider

The default Top Link Bar links are to the user's My Site home page and user profile. You can add additional links to all or part of your user population. Using audiences in conjunction with personalized Top Link Bars gives you a powerful method to target such sites as Business Intelligence and such links as college alumni or news. For example, you might target a link for those who were members of an audience defined for senior management that displayed critical business metrics. Be judicious when creating Top Link Bar links; adding too many can crowd the top of the user's My Site. Add links to the Top Link Bar in My Sites by doing the following:

1. Browse to the Shared Services Provider for the My Sites.

2. Click on *Personalization Site Links* under User Profiles and My Sites.

3. Select *New Item* from the New drop-down menu.

4. Enter a URL for the site to link to.

5. Enter a description for the site. The description will be displayed in the Top Link Bar as the name of the link.

6. Specify an owner for the link.

7. Specify the audience that will see the link in their My Sites. The audience can be Global (this SSP) or Active Directory security or distribution lists.

8. Click OK.

Choosing a My Site Naming Format

By default, My Sites are simply created with the user ID of the user. For example, a user in the *contoso* Active Directory domain with a user ID of *hanm* would have a My Site named *hanm*. If you have multiple Active Directories using a My Site Web application, however, name collisions could occur. When this happens, the second user with the same user ID gets a site creation error. Although it is possible to change the behavior of My Site creation to prevent name collisions by appending the domain name before the username, like *contoso_hanm*, it is best to enable *domain_username* for all My Sites when using multiple domains.

To select a naming convention for My Sites do the following:

1. Browse to the Shared Services Provider for the My Sites.

2. Click on *My Site Settings* under User Profiles and My Sites.

3. Select either *User Name (Do Not Resolve Conflicts)*, *User Name (Resolve Conflicts By Using Domain_Username)*, or *Domain And User Name (Will Not Have Conflicts)* from the option buttons.

4. Click OK.

Chapter 10

Configuring Office SharePoint Server Enterprise Content Management

Over the last several decades, organizations have created thousands, if not millions of documents, resulting in large volumes of unstructured content. SharePoint Server 2007 includes functionality to manage this existing content and to organize future content. In addition, it can serve as an Official File Repository, known as a Records Center. This Records Center enables organizations to meet legal and regulatory needs for managing business records. Finally, SharePoint Server can be used to manage Web content, effectively allowing an organization to manage all content, whether documents or Web pages, with the same set of tools.

Understanding and Working with Content Types

Content types allow you to separate the declaration of list metadata from the list itself so you can re-use the same metadata in more than one list. List metadata are the collection of fields that are associated with each column in the list. Content types consist of site columns, which in turn are bound to fields. To understand content types in the context of document management, it is helpful to think of each document as an item in a list in which the list columns map to document properties. This is a fundamental concept—that document properties map directly to site column definitions. Windows SharePoint Services uses the site column definitions to create document properties, to copy data to and from documents as they move into and out of SharePoint document libraries, to associate information management policies and templates with documents, and to manage the state of workflow instances which may be associated with a given document. This ability to capture workflow state extends the scope of content types to include document behavior as well as static properties.

Creating Content Types

You can create a content type by completing the following steps:

1. Browse to the Site Content Type Gallery, which is located under Site Actions > Site Settings > Modify All Site Settings > Site Content Types and click the Create button.

2. You should now see the New Site Content Type page, as shown in Figure 10-1.

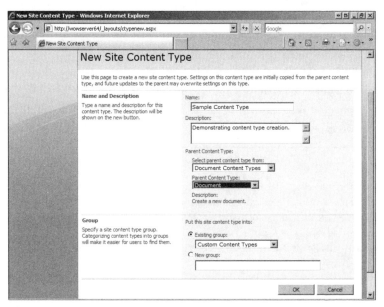

Figure 10-1 Create a new content type from Site Content Types in Site Settings.

3. Enter the desired name and description for the new content type into the appropriate fields.

4. Choose an existing content type as the parent by selecting it from the drop-down list labeled Parent Content Type. To locate the desired parent type and then to filter the list by group, use the group drop-down menu labeled Select Parent Content Type From. Every content type is derived either from the base *system* content type or from one of its children. This built-in inheritance mechanism enables one content type to extend its functionality by incorporating all of the columns declared in its parent.

5. To make it easier for users to find your new content type, select an existing group or enter the name of a new group that best describes how your content type is to be used. Press the OK button to return to the Site Content Type summary page.

Once the content type has been created, you can add the columns that best describe the metadata you want to use in your documents. Use the Add From Existing Site Columns link to select from the existing site columns, or create a new column if the existing columns do not meet your needs.

Working with Site Columns

SharePoint Server ships with a default collection of predefined site columns. These site columns are organized into groups that map loosely to the way each column is typically used. To see the available site columns, browse to the Site Column Gallery, which is found under Site Actions > Site Settings > Modify All Site Settings > Site Columns.

> **Tip**   It is possible to select or create site columns directly from the content type creation page, skipping the Site Column Gallery altogether. However, it's a good idea to browse through the gallery a few times initially to become familiar with the available columns before creating new ones, thus avoiding unnecessary duplication of columns.

From the Site Column Gallery, you can view or edit the definition of existing columns or create new columns for the site you are currently viewing. The name of the column appears as a hyperlink under the Site Column heading. If it does not appear as a hyperlink, it means that the column is declared in a parent site of the site you are viewing. To modify column definitions declared within a parent site, you must first go to the parent site and then to its Site Column Gallery. To modify an existing column definition, click its hyperlink. To create a new column definition, click the Create button. Columns created in the Site Column Gallery are available only within the current site collection. To create a site column that is available across multiple site collections, you can declare the field in an XML definition file and then deploy the field definition using a Windows SharePoint Services Feature.

From the New Site Column page, you can specify the name, data type, and group affiliation for the new column. Although every column belongs to a group, the groups are used only to organize the columns. You can change the group affiliation at any time. In actual practice, it is often necessary to use columns from many different groups when creating a new content type. Although the New Site Column page contains a *description* text box that can hold informative text about how a given field should be used, the built-in site columns do not make use of this property. It is good practice, however, to include a brief description when creating new site columns to make it easier to match a given column to its intended use.

> **Tip**   When choosing an existing site column, you should be aware that this list includes both *sealed* and *unsealed* columns that have been added by various features that have been enabled on your site. Using sealed site columns may cause problems with your content type declarations because they cannot be removed through the user interface once they have been added to a content type. This problem is exacerbated

when modifying an existing content type from which other content types have been derived. Table 10-1 lists some of the sealed columns that are added by the publishing feature. Use caution when adding them to custom content types.

Table 10-1   Sealed Site Columns Added by the Publishing Feature

Column Name	Column Group
Article Date	Publishing Columns
Contact	Publishing Columns
Contact E-mail Address	Publishing Columns
Contact Name	Publishing Columns
Contact Picture	Publishing Columns
Scheduling Start Date	Publishing Columns
Scheduling End Date	Publishing Columns
Target Audiences	Publishing Columns
Byline	Page Layout Columns
Image Caption	Page Layout Columns
Page Content	Page Layout Columns
Page Icon	Page Layout Columns
Page Image	Page Layout Columns
Rollup Image	Page Layout Columns
Summary Links	Page Layout Columns
Summary Links 2	Page Layout Columns

Creating and Using Document Information Panels

Gathering document metadata is an important part of an effective document management solution. However, most users focus on the document content and not the metadata. Consequently, important metadata are often captured inconsistently or not at all. Document Information Panels (DIPs) help avoid this problem by enabling users to enter metadata at any time during the editing process and also by enforcing the entry of data values for required fields. Document Information Panels are displayed in professional and enterprise versions of the Microsoft Office System. These client applications support integrated enterprise content management features, and automatically generate a default DIP for any document that is created or opened from within a Windows SharePoint Services document library. The data fields in the form are derived from the content type associated with the document. SharePoint Server adds the option of creating a custom DIP using Microsoft Office InfoPath 2007. Although you are limited to one custom DIP per content type, each DIP may contain multiple views.

Creating a Custom Document Information Panel

You can create a custom DIP either from the SharePoint user interface or from within the Microsoft Office InfoPath 2007 application. To create a DIP from the SharePoint user interface, perform the following steps:

1. Go to the Content Type Settings page for the content type you wish to edit. Click the *Change Document Information Panel Settings* link.

2. From the Document Information Panel Settings page, click *Create A New Custom Template* to launch InfoPath 2007.

3. When InfoPath opens, the Data Source Wizard opens automatically. Click Finish to enter edit mode.

4. InfoPath displays the auto-generated form that contains the data fields defined by the content type along with a default set of controls.

5. Edit and save the form.

6. Publish the form to update the content type.

Note   You have the option of publishing DIP templates directly to the content type resource folder or to whatever location you want. SharePoint Server updates the content type to reference the location you choose. If you publish to a location other than the content type resource folder, then additional security restrictions may be applied to the form that cause it to open in Restricted mode. In that case, the data connections between the form and SharePoint Server may not work properly. To ensure that the form opens in Full Trust mode, either digitally sign the form or create a Windows Installer that registers the form on each client machine.

Updating a Custom Document Information Panel When the Associated Content Type Changes

The ability to modify a content type independently of any documents that were derived from it means that in some situations the schema that describes the metadata associated with those documents may get out of synch with the metadata associated with the content type. By default, SharePoint Server regenerates the form template used by the DIP that is displayed in Microsoft Office client applications so that the fields declared in the associated content type match the fields that are displayed in the form. If you have created a custom DIP, then you must update the form manually.

Updating a Document Information Panel Schema from InfoPath

To update the DIP schema from within InfoPath, perform the following steps:

1. From within InfoPath 2007, select File > Open in Design Mode.

2. Go to the template form associated with the DIP and click Open.

3. Select Tools > Convert Main Data Source to open the Data Source Wizard.

4. Click Next to advance through all of the wizard screens and then click Finish on the last screen. The form schema is then re-synchronized with the content type.

5. Edit and save the form as usual.

6. Republish the form to make it available to users.

Updating a Document Information Panel Schema from SharePoint

To update the DIP schema from within SharePoint Server, perform the following steps:

1. From the Content Type Settings page, click Change Document Information Panel Settings.

2. On the Document Information Panel Settings page, click Edit This Template to launch Microsoft InfoPath 2007, which opens the Data Source Wizard automatically.

3. Click Next to advance through all of the wizard screens and then click Finish.

4. If the content type has changed since the form was last edited, you are prompted to confirm the update. Click Yes to confirm.

5. Edit and save the form.

6. Republish the form to make it available to users.

Dealing with Content Type Dependencies

Content types may be based on other content types. When changes are made to a parent content type, those changes are not reflected automatically in child content types that derive from it unless those changes are explicitly pushed down to the derived content types. Pushing down the changes from a parent content type to its children means that the schema associated with each child is overwritten with the new schema defined in the parent. Because the DIP is stored as an embedded XML document within the content type schema, pushing down the schema also overwrites any custom DIP that may be associated with the child content type. Prevent this overwriting by marking the child content type as sealed. Sealed content types are not affected by push-down operations. To mark a content type as sealed, open the Site Content Type page from the Content Type gallery and click the Advanced Settings link. From the Site Content Type Advanced Settings page, select the Yes button in the Read Only section.

Creating and Using Document Parsers

To enable support for metadata stored in custom file types, Windows SharePoint Services 3.0 provides a special framework for handling the transfer of data between any type of document and the document library in which it is stored. A document parser is a custom Common Object Model (COM) component that extracts data from a given document type and passes that data to SharePoint Server, which then promotes the data into columns of the document library. The document parser is also responsible for receiving data from SharePoint Server and demoting them into properties within the document. You configure a custom document parser by establishing an association between it and a given file type. This association is maintained in the DocParse.xml file, which is located in %systemDrive\Program Files\Common Files\Microsoft Shared\Web Server Extensions\12\CONFIG folder. The default associations are shown in Figure 10-2. To add a custom document parser, you can edit this file to include a reference to the PROGID or CLSID of the COM component that implements the document parser interface.

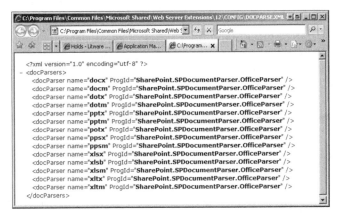

```xml
<?xml version="1.0" encoding="utf-8" ?>
<docParsers>
    <docParser name="docx" ProgId="SharePoint.SPDocumentParser.OfficeParser" />
    <docParser name="docm" ProgId="SharePoint.SPDocumentParser.OfficeParser" />
    <docParser name="dotx" ProgId="SharePoint.SPDocumentParser.OfficeParser" />
    <docParser name="dotm" ProgId="SharePoint.SPDocumentParser.OfficeParser" />
    <docParser name="pptx" ProgId="SharePoint.SPDocumentParser.OfficeParser" />
    <docParser name="pptm" ProgId="SharePoint.SPDocumentParser.OfficeParser" />
    <docParser name="potx" ProgId="SharePoint.SPDocumentParser.OfficeParser" />
    <docParser name="ppsx" ProgId="SharePoint.SPDocumentParser.OfficeParser" />
    <docParser name="ppsm" ProgId="SharePoint.SPDocumentParser.OfficeParser" />
    <docParser name="xlsx" ProgId="SharePoint.SPDocumentParser.OfficeParser" />
    <docParser name="xlsb" ProgId="SharePoint.SPDocumentParser.OfficeParser" />
    <docParser name="xlsm" ProgId="SharePoint.SPDocumentParser.OfficeParser" />
    <docParser name="xltx" ProgId="SharePoint.SPDocumentParser.OfficeParser" />
    <docParser name="xltm" ProgId="SharePoint.SPDocumentParser.OfficeParser" />
</docParsers>
```

Figure 10-2 The DocParse.xml file maps file extensions to the PROGIDs of document parsers recognized by SharePoint Server.

It is important to understand how SharePoint Server parses metadata for documents that are associated with a content type. It may be the case that the content type associated with a document does not match the content types associated with the document library to which the document is being uploaded. This can happen if a document is checked out from one document library and then is uploaded to another one. Promoting and demoting a content type are explained as follows.

- **Promoting**   Promoting a content type onto a document library means that the content type is added to the collection of content types that the document library accepts.

- **Demoting**   Demoting a content type into a document means that the columns of the content type are added as metadata fields within the document properties.

The basic rule of thumb is that SharePoint Server never promotes the content type from a document onto a document library, but instead attempts to demote the content type from the document library into the document before it is uploaded. The rules governing this process are as follows:

- If the document is not associated with any content type, then SharePoint Server demotes the default list content type into the document.

- If the document is associated with a content type, then SharePoint Server checks whether that content type is already associated with the document library. If it is, then SharePoint Server demotes the designated content type from the list into the document. If the content type definition has changed since the creation of the document, the new fields are added to the document properties.

- If the content type is not already associated with the document library, then SharePoint Server checks whether the document library allows any content type to be uploaded. If it does, then the content type is left intact within the document. If not, SharePoint Server demotes the default list content type into the document.

Managing Official Records

Because of regulatory guidelines, most organizations create the Records Center in the root of a Web application, but that isn't necessary for functionality. However, creating the Records Center in its own Web application provides you an opportunity to isolate processes when using a dedicated service account for the Web application pool identity. You create a Records Center site by using the Records Center site template. To do this, perform the following steps:

1. Either create a new site collection or go to the home page of an existing top-level site and select Create from the Site Actions menu.

2. On the New SharePoint Site page, enter the title, description, and URL of your new site.

3. In the Template Selection section, click the Enterprise tab and select the Records Center site template.

4. Click OK. You are then taken to the Records Center home page, as shown in Figure 10-3.

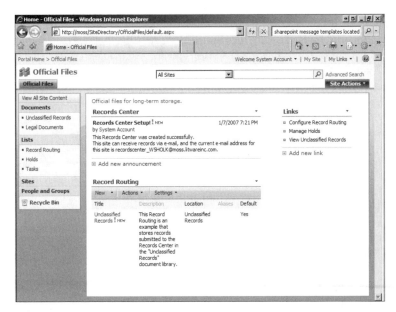

Figure 10-3   A Records Center site is created from the Records Center site template.

The Records Center site template creates the following items automatically:

- **Unclassified Records**   The document library in which incoming records that do not match any recognized content types are stored.

- **Record Routing**   The list of Record Routing types that specify how each record type should be classified.

- **Holds**   The list of holds that specify for which items record disposition should be suspended; this is typically the result of litigation associated with the record.

- **Tasks**   A standard tasks list used for workflow tracking.

Setting Up a File Plan

A file plan consists of a set of rules for managing the storage of different kinds of records. For each record type, the file plan specifies where all records of that type will be stored and the required metadata and the policies that will be applied when records are received. SharePoint Server organizes record storage rules using Record Routing Types. The first step in configuring a Records Center site is to create a Record Routing type for each type of record to be stored. Record Routing types are managed by name. This means that, when records are received, the routing type name—that is a content type in SharePoint Server—is used to determine where the record should be stored and how it should be handled. If you are using SharePoint Server or Windows SharePoint Services as the records source, it uses the content type to determine where the record should be stored. The reason you are not restricted to using content types in a Records Center is that third-party systems that do not use content types can also route records to this repository.

Creating Record Routing Types

Before you can create a Record Routing type, you must create a document library that will hold records of that type. After you create the associated document library, you can then create a Record Routing type by performing the following steps:

1. From the home page of the Records Center site, click the Configure Record Routing link or go to the Record Routing list.

2. Click New Item to create a new Record Routing item.

3. Enter the title of the Record Routing item: for example, *Contracts*. This is the name that will be associated with incoming records. If the records are sent from a Windows SharePoint Services or SharePoint Server site, it is the name of the associated content type.

4. Enter an optional description.

5. Enter the title of the document library that will contain items of this type. This title must be the name of an existing document library; otherwise the page will generate an error when you click the OK button.

6. Enter a list of aliases, delimited with a slash (/), to represent this record entry: for example, *Agreements/Legal Documents*. Aliases allow files to be submitted using a Record Routing name different from that of the associated content type.

7. Specify whether this routing item should be used for incoming records that do not match any of the defined Record Routing types. The default location for such records is the Unclassified Records routing type, which stores its items in the Unclassified Records document library.

Figure 10-4 shows the Record Routing list for a Records Center site with a custom Record Routing named Legal Documents.

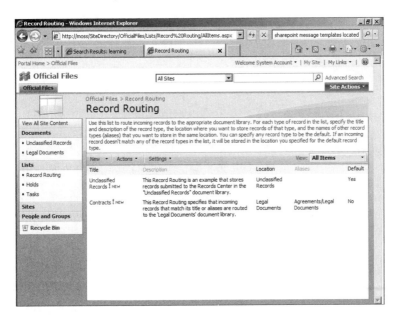

Figure 10-4   You should add custom record types, such as Legal Documents.

To complete the configuration of the file plan, edit each document library to specify the required metadata for incoming records and to set up the Information Management Policy that will govern how incoming records are handled. For example, a legal document might require a metadata field that indicates the date on which the document was filed. You can also mark certain columns as required. Figure 10-5 shows the Legal Documents document library with the Filing Date column added.

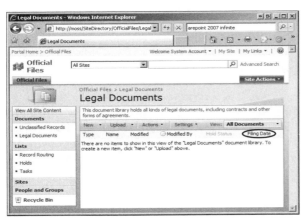

Figure 10-5   Add columns as necessary, such as Filing Date for legal documents.

To configure the Information Management Policy for a document library, select Document Library Settings from the Settings menu and then click Information Management Policy Settings from the Permissions and Management section of the Customize page. To define a policy, click the middle option button next to Define Policy... and click OK. Select the desired policy options and click Save.

Configuring the Default Send To Location

Once you have created a Records Center site, you can send official documents to the repository via e-mail by using an e-mail-enabled document library on the destination or via a Web service. You can also enable users to file official documents automatically by selecting a command from the drop-down menu of any document library in a site collection. This is a two-step process. First you must inform the SharePoint Server where the documents should be sent, and then you must set up the document library content types so that they match the record types described in the file plan of the Records Center site. If the content types do not match, then the documents are routed to the Unclassified Records document library when the user attempts to send them. To configure the SharePoint Server with the location in which to store official records, use the Central Administration Web site as follows:

1. Browse to the Central Administration Web site for the SharePoint server you wish to configure.

2. Click Application Management.

3. In the External Service Connections section, click Records Center.

4. On the Configure Connection to Records Center page, click the second option button next to Connect To A Records Center and enter the URL following the example provided. This is the URL of the Officialfile.asmx file that implements the Official File Web service. For example, *http://server/portal/_vti_bin/officialfile*.asmx.

5. Click OK.

Sending Content from a SharePoint Site

When documents are sent to a Records Center site, the name of the document's content type is passed to the record center as the Record Series parameter, which is then used to select the Record Routing type to be applied to the incoming document. Thus, the content type is the primary means for setting up an official records repository for an organization. To set up a document library for communication with a Records Center site, perform the following steps:

1. Create or select the document library you wish to use.

2. Select Document Library Settings from the Settings menu and then click the Advanced Settings link in the General Settings section.

3. Click the option button next to Yes under Allow Management Of Content Types.

4. To use the default Send To destination that was configured in the Central Administration Web site, leave the Destination Name and URL blank in the Custom Send To Destination section. Otherwise, you can override the default destination by entering a URL and friendly name.

5. Click OK to return to the Customize page.

6. In the Content Types section, in the Content Type column, click Document.

7. On the Manage Content Type page, in the General Settings section, click Name And Description.

8. Change the value of the name field to the name of your Record Routing type.

To complete the configuration of the document library, you must add any required metadata columns so that items in the library match the profile expected by the Records Center site. There are some columns, such as date and time, that will prompt for user input upon routing, but it is best to define identical columns in both the source and destination document libraries. The easiest way to do so is to use the same content type for both the document library and the Records Center site. However, you can also add the required columns manually. Once these steps are done, the configuration of the document library is complete. For any item in the library, you can select the Send To command from the context menu. The menu contains the default location of the records repository that you configured in the Central Administration Web site. Selecting that command invokes the *SubmitFile* method of the Official File Web service to submit the document, which is then routed to the location specified by the matching Record Routing type. If any required metadata columns are missing, then a dialog box appears requesting the user to supply the necessary information.

Managing Holds

A *hold* represents a suspension of the disposition and expiration processing for a document that resides in a records repository. You create a hold by adding an item to the Holds list of the Records Center site. Figure 10-6 shows a hold item being added to the Holds list.

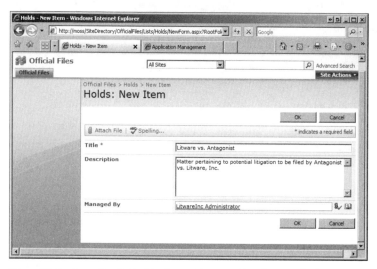

Figure 10-6 From the Holds list, choose New to add an item to the list.

To apply the hold, open the property page for the hold you wish to apply, as shown in Figure 10-7.

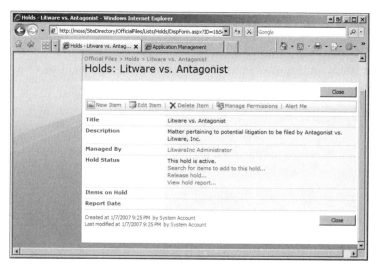

Figure 10-7 From the Holds properties page, you can search for items to add to the hold, view holds, or release holds.

In the Hold Status section, click Search For Items To Add To This Hold... From the Search For Items To Hold page, enter a search query to locate the items to which you want to apply the hold. By default, the hold you were viewing when you browsed to the search page is displayed in the drop-down list. With the query results displayed, click the Hold button.

Managing Web Content

The SharePoint Server publishing feature includes a default set of page layouts for authoring news articles. These layouts incorporate the built-in field controls, which are arranged in different configurations on the page. Each field control is in turn bound to specific metadata fields of the Article Page content type. Field controls enable page authors to enter metadata values in a WYSIWYG fashion while at the same time displaying the authored metadata values to users when the page is viewed.

Working with Master Pages and Page Layouts

You can extend the publishing framework by providing your own content types, page layouts, master pages, and field controls. Master pages typically contain navigation, logos, search box, login control, editing controls, CSS references, and other server controls. The easiest way to create a new master page is to open an existing master page using SharePoint Designer 2007 and then save it to the file system. Once you've made the desired customizations, you can then upload it to the master page gallery of a top-level site, or you can package it into a Feature for deployment to multiple sites.

Because each page layout depends on the columns that are defined in its associated content type, it is helpful while planning your extensions to consider them as a unit. This is easy to see when you examine how the Article Page content type works in conjunction with the corresponding set of page layouts. Each layout is responsible for presenting the same set of columns in different ways, but the underlying column metadata are the same.

To create a page layout, you must have a content type to base it on. In addition, the content type you select must be derived from the Page content type provided by the publishing feature. The Page content type provides the foundation set of metadata fields used by various components of the publishing framework. Although you can use any of the built-in publishing content types, such as Article Page, you typically want to create your own. You can do so easily via the SharePoint user interface as follows:

1. Browse to the Site Settings page of the top-level site in your site collection. Creating your content type in the top-level site ensures that it will be available to all publishing sites you create.

2. Click the Site Content Types link in the Galleries section. The Site Content Type Gallery page is displayed. Click the Create button at the top of the page.

3. From the New Content Type page, enter the content type name and then select Publishing Content Types from the list of parent content types you want to base

your new content type on. To reference your content type from a publishing page layout, you must base it on one of the content types in this group.

4. Click the OK button to save the content type. The new content type appears in the list on the Site Content Type Gallery page.

The next step is to add or create the columns you want to display in your publishing pages. If you want to use the standard set of field controls, such as the HTMLEdit and ImageEdit field controls, in your page layout, then you must include one or more of the publishing site columns in your content type. Depending on the parent content type you selected, some of these columns may already be included. Table 10-2 shows the primary field controls and the site columns on which they depend.

Table 10-2   Publishing Field Controls and Corresponding Field Types

Control	Site Column Field Type
RichHtmlField	HtmlField
RichImageField	ImageField
RichImageSelector	ImageField
RichLinkField	LinkField
RichLinkSelector	LinkField
SummaryLinkFieldControl	SummaryLinkField

With the content type defined, you can use SharePoint Designer 2007 to create a page layout that can be used to display document metadata.

Creating a Page Layout in SharePoint Designer 2007

1. Start the SharePoint Designer 2007 application, and open the top-level site for your site collection.

2. Browse to _catalogs\masterpage. This is the master page gallery that holds all master pages and page layouts for the site collection.

3. Right-click on the master page gallery and select New > SharePoint Content... from the context menu. A dialog box opens.

4. On the left side of the SharePoint Content tab, select SharePoint Publishing and then select Page Layout in the middle list box. The resulting dialog box is illustrated in Figure 10-8.

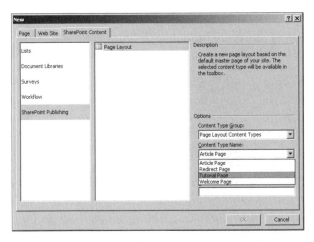

Figure 10-8   Select New > SharePoint Content > SharePoint Publishing in SharePoint Designer 2007.

5. On the right side of the dialog box, select which content type to base the new page layout on. The drop-down list only shows content types that are derived from the Page content type provided by the publishing feature. Select the content type you created above.

6. Enter the URL Name of the new page layout: for example, *tutorial_page.aspx*.

7. Enter a Title for the new page layout: for example, *Tutorial Page.*

8. Click OK to close the dialog box.

The new page layout now appears in the master page gallery of the top-level site in a pending state awaiting approval. Once it is checked in and approved for publication, it can be selected when creating a new publishing page.

Note   It is possible to create a page layout while editing a subsite. The steps are the same. However, when the page layout is saved, it does not appear in the master page gallery of the subsite. SharePoint Designer always saves the file into the master page gallery of the top-level site in which the subsite is contained. The publishing master page gallery is implemented as a standard Windows SharePoint Server document library, thereby exposing the same functionality as any other document library, including approval workflow, check-in, check-out, and versioning.

Deploying Page Layouts

Although it is convenient to use SharePoint Designer 2007 to design page layouts, it is impractical to use it to deploy them. Typically a publishing solution incorporates many layouts that are all tied to a common set of content types and master pages. It is necessary in most cases to deploy those layouts as a unit, rather than one at a time. In a typical scenario, you will want the added flexibility of being able to deploy the same set of publishing resources to multiple sites and site collections. You can deploy a set of publishing solution files using the file provisioning capabilities of the SharePoint feature framework. To deploy a page layout using this method, perform the following steps:

1. Browse to the %SystemDrive%\Program Files\Common Files\Microsoft Shared\Web Server Extensions\12\TEMPLATE\FEATURES folder on the SharePoint Server machine.

2. Create a subfolder to hold your feature definition files. The name you choose for the subfolder is the same name you use to refer to the feature in subsequent steps: for example, *MyFeature*.

3. Open SharePoint Designer 2007 and go to the _catalogs/masterpage node for the top-level site containing the page layout you wish to deploy.

4. Right-click the page layout file and then choose New From Existing Page from the context menu. A copy of the page appears in SharePoint Designer. Select File > Save As to save the file into the folder you just created. Give it the same name as the original file.

5. Open Notepad and enter the following XML code, replacing the *Id* value with a unique identifier obtained by running the GuidGen command-line utility.

```xml
<?xml version="1.0" encoding="utf-8"?>
<Feature Id="XXXXXXXX-XXXX-XXXX-XXXX-XXXXXXXXXXXX"
         Title=""Page Layout Deployment Feature"
         Description="Provisions a Page Layout"
         Version="1.0.0.0"
         Scope="Site"
         Hidden="TRUE"
         DefaultResourceFile="core"
         xmlns="http://schemas.microsoft.com/sharepoint/">
    <ElementManifests>
        <ElementManifest Location="ProvisionedFiles.xml" />
    </ElementManifests>
</Feature>
```

> **Note**   The GuidGen command-line utility is typically located in the %system-drive%\Program Files\Microsoft Visual Studio 8\Common7\Tools folder. If Visual Studio is not installed and this program is unavailable, you can use the following VB script to generate a unique ID. Copy this code to a file with a .vbs extension—for example, *makeguid.vbs*—and execute it from a command prompt using Wscript.exe.

```
guid = left(createobject("scriptlet.typelib").guid,38)
inputbox "GUID Generator",,guid
```

6. Save the file into the custom feature folder using the special name *Feature.xml*.

7. Close and reopen Notepad. Enter the following XML code, replacing the under-lined text with the appropriate text for the custom page layout file you created previously.

```
<?xml version="1.0" encoding="utf-8"?>
<Elements xmlns="http://schemas.microsoft.com/sharepoint/">
 <Module Name="TutorialLayout" Url="_catalogs/masterpage"
  Path="" RootWebOnly="TRUE">
   <File Url="tutorial_page.aspx" Type="GhostableInLibrary">
   <Property Name="Title" Value="Tutorial Layout Page"/>
   <Property Name="MasterPageDescription"
      Value="This is a description of the tutorial layout page."/>
   <Property Name="ContentType"
      Value="$Resources:cmscore,contenttype_pagelayout_name;" />
   <Property Name="PublishingAssociatedContentType"
      Value=";#Tutorial Page;
      #0x010100C568DB52D9D0A14D9B2FDCC96666E9F2007948130EC3DB0
      64584E219954237AF39003CCC5B461C57904E96DF6ACA7EBA3B38;#"/>
   </File>
 </Module>
</Elements>
```

> **Note**   The *PublishingAssociatedContentType* property is required and must be in the format given. This property is what links the page layout to its underlying con-tent type for the publishing feature. Replace the content type name (*Tutorial Page* in the above example) with the actual name of the content type you want to associate with your page layout. You must also replace the identifier with the actual content type identifier, and *be sure to include the trailing semi-colon*. To locate this value, go to the Site Content Type Gallery of the top-level site, find the content type in the list, and click its hyperlink. The content type identifier then appears in the address bar of the browser just after the *?ctype=* URL parameter.

8. Save the file using the name ProvisionedFiles.xml.

9. Open a command prompt and enter the following command, replacing MyFeature with the name of the subfolder you created in step 2.

```
stsadm -o installfeature -name MyFeature
```

When the feature is installed, the custom page layout is copied into the master page gallery, along with any additional modules and files you may wish to add to the list of module declarations in the ProvisionedFiles.xml.

Customizing the Authoring Experience

With SharePoint Server, you can customize the interfaces that your site designers will use. You can customize the Page Editing Toolbar, the HTML Editor, and the Asset Picker.

Customizing the Page Editing Toolbar

The *Page Editing Toolbar* appears at the top of a publishing page and contains a set of user interface controls that are displayed for page authors. Figure 10-9 shows the default Page Editing Toolbar for an Article Page. The Page Editing Toolbar consists of the following components:

- **Page Status Bar**   The Page Status Bar (number 1 in Figure 10-9) provides information about the current version of the page, such as whether the page is checked out and the current page status.

- **Page Editing Menu**   The Page Editing Menu (number 2 in Figure 10-9) provides a set of commands that enable an author to interact with the page. The set of actions depends on the type of page and its status. For example, if a page is pending approval and the author has approval rights, then the Page Editing Menu might provide a command to approve the page.

- **Quick Access Button Panel**   The Quick Access Button Panel (number 3 in Figure 10-9) provides shortcuts to the most popular actions.

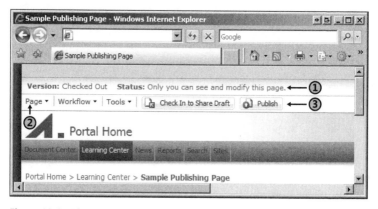

Figure 10-9   The Page Editing Toolbar.

You can customize the authoring experience by editing the XML data files used by the Page Editing Menu and the Quick Access Button Panel. Typically, you would use this approach to add buttons or quick access commands to the toolbar, but you can also remove items from the default controls by taking advantage of the order in which the XML data files are loaded.

The Page Editing Menu commands and quick access buttons are handled in the same way as the Site Actions menu that appears at the top of most SharePoint Web pages. Each control is initialized from <ConsoleNode> elements declared in an XML definition file. The Page Editing Menu commands are loaded from the EditingMenu.xml file, and the Quick Access Button Panel is loaded from the QuickAccess.xml file. Both of these files are located in the %SystemDrive%\Program Files\Common Files\Microsoft Shared\Web Server Extensions\12\TEMPLATE\LAYOUTS\EditingMenu folder.

During the loading process, the control code looks for an optional secondary XML configuration file that contains custom <ConsoleNode> elements. If that file exists, then the custom <ConsoleNode> elements are loaded into the control. Any elements in the secondary XML configuration file that have the same ID as a corresponding node in the primary configuration file take precedence over the element that was read previously. In this manner, you can hide or change the default commands to suit specific requirements.

The secondary XML configuration files have specific names: CustomEditingMenu.xml and CustomQuickAccess.xml, respectively. Thus, to customize the Page Editing Menu, make a copy of the EditingMenu.xml file and rename it CustomEditingMenu.xml. Similarly, to customize the Quick Access Button Panel, make a copy of the QuickAccess.xml file and rename it CustomQuickAccess.xml.

Customizing the HTML Editor Field Control

The HTML Editor field control is one of the most important tools for authoring Web pages, and is the one control found on most page layouts. Authors use this control to enter content directly into publishing pages in WYSIWYG fashion. Depending on how the control is configured, authors can edit the HTML source and browse for reusable content fragments from a centralized repository.

Using Constraints   Table 10-3 lists the attributes you can use to control the behavior of the HTML Editor field control. These attributes must be set individually for each instance of the control you wish to configure. This means that you must first locate the associated markup within each page layout file and then add or remove the appropriate attributes

Table 10-3   HTML Editing Constraint Attributes

Attribute	Description
AllowExternalUrls	If false, then only URLs internal to the current site collection are allowed to be referenced in a link or an image
AllowFonts	Determines whether content may contain <Font> tags
AllowReusableContent	Determines whether content may contain reusable content fragments stored in a centralized list
AllowHeadings	Determines whether content may contain HTML heading tags
AllowHyperlinks	Determines whether content may contain links to other URLs
AllowImages	Determines whether content may contain images
AllowLists	Determines whether content may contain ordered or unordered lists
AllowTables	Determines whether content may contain table-related tags such as <table>, <th>, <tr>, and <td>
AllowTextMarkup	Determines whether content may contain bold, italic, and underlined text
AllowHTMLSourceEditing	If false, then the HTML editor does not switch to HTML source editing mode
DisableBasicFormattingButtons	If true, then the basic formatting buttons are disabled

Using Custom Styles   You can use custom CSS stylesheets to control the presentation of content on publishing pages. You do this by configuring each individual instance of the HTML Editor field control to look for a specific set of custom styles in the stylesheets associated with the page layout. When the HTML Editor field control is configured in this way, content authors can select from the list of predefined custom styles and apply them to content without typing HTML and CSS code.

If the HTML Editor detects new CSS classes whose names have the special prefix ms-rteCustom-XXXX, where XXXX is the display name of the custom classes, it displays the custom classes instead of the default classes installed with the system. In addition, each custom style can be defined specifically for certain types of content. The HTML

Editor displays the custom classes to the user only if the specified type of content is selected. For example, to define a custom CSS class for bulleted lists, you can add code similar to the following to the CSS stylesheet associated with the page layout:

```
UL.ms-rteCustom-ArialSmallCapsList {
font-family:Arial; font-size:8pt; text-transform:small-caps;
}
```

Because the same CSS stylesheet is shared among all instances of the HTML Editor, you can configure each instance to look for a specific subset of styles. You do this by using the PrefixStyleSheet attribute. The default prefix is *ms-rte*. Using the PrefixStyleSheet attribute you can specify your own custom prefix. For example, the following declaration sets the prefix to MyCustomPrefix:

```
<PublishingWebControls:RichHtmlField id="Content"
FieldName="PublishingPageContent" runat="server"
PrefixStyleSheet="MyCustomPrefix"/>
```

This instance of the HTML Editor now finds and displays the following styles whenever the user selects a bulleted list:

```
UL.MyCustomPrefix-ArialMaroonList { font-family:Arial; color:maroon; }
UL.MyCustomPrefix-VerdanaBlueList { font-family:Verdana; color:blue; }
```

The styles are displayed as *ArialMaroonList* and *VerdanaBlueList.*

Customizing the Asset Picker

The Asset Picker is a popup HTML dialog box that allows authors to locate references to list items in the current site collection. It is used most often when the author of a Web page needs to insert the URL of an image contained in a picture library or of a separate page contained in a document library. Without the Asset Picker tool, the author would have to browse from the page he or she is working on to copy and paste the required URL reference. In addition to the inconvenience of copying and pasting, the author might be more likely to make a mistake while copying the link or may reference a file located in an untrusted location, thereby causing potential authentication problems for users who view the resulting page. Figure 10-10 shows an example of the Asset Picker that is used by several of the publishing field controls for selecting images and documents. The Look In pane on the left side of the picker window provides shortcuts to a predefined set of SharePoint libraries in the current site collection. You can extend this set of shortcuts to include one additional location within your site collection for individual field controls in separate page layout files. This feature might be useful if your page authors frequently reference resources that are located somewhere other than the default locations.

Figure 10-10   The Asset Picker is used by several of the publishing field controls for selecting images and documents.

Note that there are several limitations to using this approach: (1) You must directly edit the markup for existing page layouts. This means that your customizations might be overwritten if those layouts are updated. (2) You can only specify one additional location for images and one location for documents. (3) You must repeat the customization for every field control in which you wish to display the additional location. (4) You must use the same relative location in every site collection in your SharePoint Server Farm.

There are eight page layouts included as part of the Web Content Management (WCM) feature set provided with SharePoint Server. They are located in the %SystemDrive%\Program Files\Common Files\Microsoft Shared\Web Server Extensions\12\TEMPLATE\FEATURES\PublishingLayouts\PageLayouts folder on the file system and are displayed in the master page gallery for the site. You can add a custom picker shortcut for any of the RichHtmlField or RichImageField controls found in any of these files by performing the following steps:

1. Open the site in SharePoint Designer, browse to the _catalogs/masterpage folder, select a page layout, and open the file for editing.

2. Locate the control you wish to extend. The publishing field controls are indicated by <Publishing WebControls:RichHtmlField> or <PublishingWebControls:RichImageField> tags.

3. Add a DefaultAssetLocation attribute to define the URL for the custom shortcut in a URL picker.

4. Add a DefaultAssetImageLocation attribute to define the URL for the custom shortcut in an image picker.

5. Save and close the .aspx file.

The URL references you use must be relative to the same site collection. For example, if you have a picture library in your site collection called Company Pictures, you might customize the image picker for an Article Page layout as follows:

```
<PublishingWebControls:RichImageField
id="ImageField" FieldName="PublishingPageImage"
runat="server"
DefaultAssetImageLocation="/Company Pictures"/>
```

> **Note**   If the specified URL reference cannot be resolved, then the Asset Picker inserts a shortcut that displays all of the top-level folders in the current site collection. If the URL refers to any location external to the current site collection, then the additional shortcut is ignored.

Converting Documents into Web Pages

The Web Content Management features of SharePoint Server allow you to convert documents of any type into Web pages that can be published to SharePoint sites and then updated automatically when the source document is modified. This is a powerful feature because it lets users write content using the applications they are familiar with instead of having to learn how to edit HTML files. SharePoint Server includes built-in converters for the following file types associated with the 2007 Office System: DOCX to HTML, DOCM to HTML, XSN to HTML, and XML to HTML. The XML converter enables you to supply a custom XSLT stylesheet that can convert your custom XML file into HTML. There is no PowerPoint converter.

To use the document-to-page conversion framework, you start by enabling document conversions at the Web application level. You do this from the Central Administration Web site.

Enabling Document Conversions for a Web Application

To enable document conversions for a web application, follow these steps:

1. From the Central Administration Web site, go to the Operations tab and click the Services on Server link and verify that the Document Conversions Load Balancer Service and the Document Conversions Launcher Service are running.

2. From the Application Management tab, click the Document Conversions link in the External Service Connections section.

After enabling the document conversions, you can start a conversion manually, or you can set up an asynchronous timer job that invokes the conversion on a schedule that you specify.

Configuring a Document Converter

Document converters are configured using converter definition files, which are XML files based on the Document Converter Definition schema. You add a custom converter to the SharePoint configuration database by packaging the XML definition in a feature. When the feature is activated, the converter is available on each site and document library in the Web application. The following example shows the converter definition file for a custom document converter that converts Office Excel (.xls) files to Office Word (.doc) files.

```
<?xml version="1.0" encoding="utf-8" ?>
<Elements xmlns="http://schemas.microsoft.com/sharepoint/">
  <DocumentConverter ID="{3f8ae556-93ec-46de-bcb3-0a89616a20b3}"
    Name="Excel to Word"
    App="XL2WORD.exe"
    From="xls"
    To="doc"
    ConverterUIPage="XL2WORD.aspx"
    ConverterSpecificSettingsUI="XL2WORDConfig.aspx"
    ConverterSettingsForContentType="XL2WORDConfig.ascx"
  />
</Elements>
```

When the document conversion process is started, SharePoint Server passes the document to be converted along with an XML file containing converter-specific settings to the Document Conversions Load Balancer Service. This service determines how and where the specified document converter should be launched, depending on the current server farm configuration. The Load Balancer Service then calls the Document Conversion Launcher Service to invoke the specified document converter. You can control which settings are available for a given document converter by supplying a custom configuration settings page that is used to gather conversion settings from the user. To specify a custom settings page, set the ConverterSpecificSettingsUI attribute to the file name of the custom .aspx file you want to use. You can also use the default page (DocTrans.aspx), but then substitute your own custom control to retrieve converter-specific settings by setting the ConverterSettingsForContentType attribute to the file name of a custom .ascx file.

Managing Electronic Forms

InfoPath Forms Services provides an integrated platform for publishing form templates that can be either opened in Microsoft Office InfoPath 2007 or rendered in a Web browser. Deploying form templates to the server enables organizations to streamline business processes, thereby increasing data accuracy by applying standardized policies and business rules to the data-gathering process.

Creating Browser-Compatible InfoPath Forms

InfoPath forms that you want to display in a browser must be compatible with InfoPath Forms Services. When developing new forms, you can use the compatibility settings of InfoPath 2007 to disable features that are incompatible with InfoPath Forms services.

When upgrading existing forms, you can use the Design Checker task pane to high-light potential problems with items already present in the form.

To open the Design Checker task pane, select Design Checker from the Tools menu. The contents of the Design Checker task pane depend on the current compatibility set-tings. Figure 10-11 shows the Design Checker task pane with browser compatibility errors and warnings displayed. Clicking on items in the Browser Compatibility list causes the problem item to be selected in the user interface so you can make the nec-essary changes.

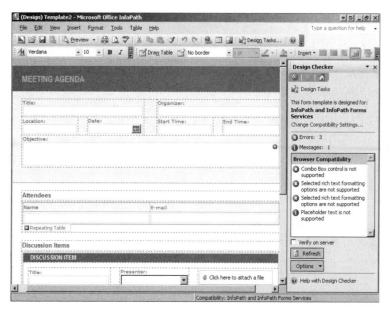

Figure 10-11   The Design Checker task pane shows compatibility errors and warnings.

Deploying Forms That Do Not Require Full Trust

InfoPath forms that do not contain code can be deployed directly to a SharePoint site using the Publishing Wizard. To enable the form to be rendered in a browser, perform the following steps:

1. Start the InfoPath 2007 client application and load the form template you wish to publish.

2. Select the File > Publish command to start the Publishing Wizard.

3. Leave the option button next to *To A SharePoint Server With Or Without InfoPath Forms Services* selected and click Next.

4. Enter the URL of the SharePoint server to which you want to upload the form. Click Next.

5. Ensure that *Enable This Form To Be Filled Out Using A Browser* is checked.

6. Select the option button next to Document Library.

7. Click OK.

Deploying Forms That Require Full Trust

InfoPath forms that have been designed to run managed code must be trusted before they can be accessed by users. Forms that are intended to be run only on client machines can be digitally signed and then uploaded to a form library. When users click on a form, the associated template is downloaded to the user's machine and then loaded into InfoPath. Alternatively, a Windows Installer can be provided to end users who can run it locally to "register" the form on their machine.

The process is different for forms that are intended to be opened from within a browser. In this case, some additional steps are required to ensure that the forms do not contain malicious code and can be run safely on the server machine. First, the form template must be modified so that it contains references to the server on which it will be deployed. Then, the form template is uploaded to the server by a farm administrator. Finally, the template is activated in one or more site collections to make it available to users.

Preparing a Form Template for Deployment

To prepare a form template for deployment to a server, perform the following steps:

1. Start the InfoPath 2007 client application and load the form template you wish to publish.

2. Select the Tools > Form Options... command. The Form Options dialog box appears.

3. Under Compatibility/Browser compatibility, ensure that the check box next to *Design A Form Template That Can Be Opened In A Browser Or InfoPath* is checked.

> **Note**   With this option checked, you may receive compatibility warnings if the form template uses features that are not compatible with InfoPath Forms Services. You should resolve these issues before attempting to deploy the form.

4. Select the File > Publish command. The Publishing Wizard dialog box then appears.

5. Select the option button next to *To A SharePoint Server With Or Without InfoPath Forms Services,* and then click Next.

6. Enter the URL of the server to which the template will be deployed. Click Next. InfoPath retrieves information about the server farm.

7. Ensure that the check box next to *Enable This Form To Be Filled Out By Using A Browser* is checked, and then select the option button next to *Administrator-Approved Form Template (Advanced)*. Click Next.

8. Enter a location for saving the modified .xsn file. Click Next.

9. Select the form fields that you want to promote to columns in the document library using the Add... button.

> **Note**   InfoPath retrieves the available site column groups from the Share-Point server you specified in step 6. If you choose a column whose name matches one of the existing columns, InfoPath automatically selects the site column group to which it belongs. If the column you select does not match an available site column, then InfoPath automatically selects *None: Create New Column In This Library*. To map a field to a different column, you can override this setting by first selecting the field and then changing the site column group to one that contains the column to which you want to map the field. Select the target column from the Column Name drop-down list.

10. When you have added all of the columns you want to promote, click Next and then click Publish to save the updated template file.

11. Click Close to close the dialog box.

Uploading a Prepared Form Template to an InfoPath Forms Services Server

1. Open the SharePoint Services Central Administration Web site.

2. From the Application Management page, click the Manage Form Templates link in the InfoPath Forms Services section.

3. Click the Upload Form Template link.

4. Enter the location of the previously published form template.

5. Optionally click the Verify button to check the template for errors.

6. If the browser contains a previous version of the same form template, specify whether to upgrade the existing template.

7. Click Upload to complete the operation.

Activating a Form Template to a Site Collection from Central Administration

1. Open the SharePoint Services Central Administration Web site.

2. From the Application Management page, click the Manage Form Templates link in the InfoPath Forms Services section.

3. Locate the form template you wish to activate. Select Activate To A Site Collection from the drop-down menu.

4. In the Activation Location section, click the drop-down menu and select Change Site Collection.

5. On the Select Site Collection dialog box, select Change Web Application from the Web Application drop-down menu.

6. Click the name of the desired site collection and then click OK.

7. Click OK on the Activate Form Template page to activate the form.

Activating a Form Template to a Site Collection from Site Settings

1. Browse to the top-level site of the site collection you wish to activate.

2. Select Modify All Site Settings from the Site Settings link of the Site Actions menu.

3. Click the Site Collection Features link in the Site Collection Administration section.

4. Locate the form template you wish to activate and click the Activate button.

Configuring Office SharePoint Server Excel Calculation Services

Excel Calculation Services is part of Microsoft's business intelligence (BI) platform provided by Microsoft Office SharePoint Server 2007 Enterprise Edition. Excel Calculation Services supports the server-side loading, recalculation, and rendering of Office Excel 2007 workbooks in a browser-based version. It addresses a problem faced by many organizations in which users work with large Excel workbooks that contain complex formulas to generate data values. When the files are stored on a file server, these workbooks can take a long time to load and recalculate on a workstation. With Excel Calculation Services, the workbook file is stored in a SharePoint Server document library, thereby allowing Excel Calculation Services to calculate the results on the server. Excel Calculation Services then renders the results in a Web browser by generating an HTML version of the spreadsheets and charts in the workbook. This functionality allows users who do not have Office Excel 2007 installed on their workstation to view the information. In addition, Excel Calculation Services can provide a single location where users work with spreadsheets, preventing the need and desire to share spreadsheets via e-mail. This functionality assists some organizations with regulatory compliancy and presents a single version of the truth.

Getting Started with Excel Calculation Services

Excel Calculation Services is part of a set of components known as Excel Services that allow server-side access to Office Excel 2007 workbooks. These components include Excel Web Access for rendering and displaying workbook contents, Excel Calculation Services for recalculating formulas in workbooks and executing server-side queries to external data, Excel Calculation Services Proxy for managing load balancing of service calls in a multiserver environment, and Excel Web Services for providing programmatic access to workbook data from remote clients. This section reviews some of the key planning issues related to implementing Excel Services.

Key Planning Concepts

Excel Services requires that you install the Enterprise Edition of SharePoint Server or upgrade to this edition from the Standard Edition. Planning an Excel Calculation Services implementation begins with assessing the total number and size of workbooks to be served by Excel Services and the resource requirements of processing these workbooks. Each workbook that is accessed uses RAM and processor resources for calculating and rendering the workbook, as well as RAM and disk space for caching its output. Adding more resources to the server and load balancing Excel Services across multiple servers can improve scalability and performance.

Office Excel 2007 workbooks can be stored either in SharePoint Server document libraries, in shared folders on file servers, or on any standard Web server that provides access to the workbook through a URL. Storing workbooks in document libraries is the most secure option, whereas using file shares connected to Excel Calculation Services will require the least retraining of your users.

Implementation Checklist

The key steps involved in planning the implementation of Excel Calculation Services are summarized in this section. Each is covered in more detail later in the chapter.

- **Enable Excel Calculation Services in your farm**   Before working with Excel Calculation Services you must configure the service to run on one or more servers in your SharePoint Server farm. Your options are as follows:

    1. **Single-server or small farm:** This model is appropriate for relatively small workbooks that are accessed infrequently.

    2. **Dedicated server:** This scenario works well for larger, complex workbooks or those that are accessed frequently throughout the day. This is the most common configuration for businesses that are implementing Excel Services.

    3. **Load-balanced servers:** Having multiple Excel Services servers is ideal for organizations that need fault-tolerance in their Excel Services environment or that are accessing workbooks programmatically through Excel Web Services.

- **Determine storage locations** Excel 2007 workbooks can be stored in any document library in a SharePoint site or can be stored in a file share or on a standard Web site. SharePoint document libraries offer the greatest security and flexibility, whereas file share storage gives you the convenience of not having to move existing workbooks off their current server.

- **Define trusted file locations** Excel Calculation Services only loads and processes workbooks stored in document libraries or non-SharePoint sources that are specifically configured as trusted locations. Keep the number of these trusted locations to a minimum.

- **Configure security on document libraries** Most users require only View Items access to files in document libraries in order to view the output from Excel Calculation Services. Other users require Add and Edit access to publish and modify files through Office Excel 2007.

- **Publish Excel 2007 workbooks** Using the Publish feature in Office Excel 2007, users can upload workbooks with specific options that control which parts of the workbook are displayed in the browser. Consider which sheets or named ranges within workbooks should be displayed and whether users will be allowed to input values for recalculating results.

- **Configure a SharePoint Server to display workbook content** Using dashboards and Excel Web View Web Parts, you can configure sites to display targeted portions of workbook content to users and decision makers. Design your dashboards around specific business goals, and display data that give decision makers a snapshot view of performance or progress toward those goals.

Configuring Excel Servers in the Farm

To configure Excel Calculation Services on a server, you need to install the server with the Complete option. The next step is to start Excel Calculation Services in the Services On Server page in Central Administration. Because Excel Calculation Services is hosted in a Shared Services Provider (SSP) in SharePoint Server, you need to create at least one SSP before you can use Excel Calculation Services.

Enabling Excel Calculation Services

1. Open Central Administration from the Start menu.

2. Click the Operations tab.

3. Click Services On Server.

4. If the Status Of Excel Calculation Services is Stopped, click the Start link to the right.

Single-Server and Small Farm Deployment

To configure Excel Calculation Services (ECS) in a single-server or in a small farm deployment, simply enable it on the same server as the Web application services, as shown in Figure 11-1. In this configuration, the server that renders Web pages to the user is the same one that performs the ECS processing on the workbooks. The benefit of consolidating services is that all processing and caching are done on one server, thereby eliminating traffic delays between servers. The disadvantage of this model is that more services are competing for resources on the server and the responsiveness of the server to the user may degrade. This configuration is optimal in scenarios in which the demand for ECS is relatively light.

User   Web Application   SQL Server
           + Excel Calculation Services

Figure 11-1 Excel Calculation Services in a small farm deployment.

Dedicated Excel Server Deployment

ECS runs as a separate service within the SharePoint Server architecture and can be run on a separate server from the Web application service. For organizations looking for a more scalable solution, a dedicated application server running ECS, as shown in Figure 11-2, is cost effective.

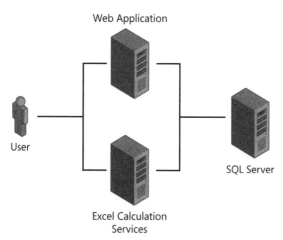

Web Application

User

SQL Server

Excel Calculation
Services

Figure 11-2 Excel Calculation Services in a dedicated server deployment.

Configuring a Dedicated Excel Calculation Server

1. Install SharePoint Server on the dedicated server and join it to the farm. See Chapter 2, "Deploying SharePoint Products and Technologies," for more information.

2. Open Central Administration from the Start menu.

3. Click the Operations tab.

4. Click Services On Server.

5. Next to Excel Calculation Services, click the Start link to the right. Do not start any other services on the server.

Load-Balanced Excel Server Deployment

When a single dedicated Excel Calculation server does not provide adequate performance or fault-tolerance, it may be necessary to scale out the capacity to multiple servers. Excel Calculation Services architecture supports automatic load balancing of requests across multiple application servers configured with Excel Calculation Services, as shown in Figure 11-3. To configure a farm in this model, perform the steps above for a dedicated server deployment on each of the Excel Calculation servers, and then select the Load Balancing Scheme in Excel Services Settings. See the section, "Configuring Excel Services Settings," later in this chapter for details about setting the Load Balancing Scheme. In addition, you must install any custom assemblies or user-defined function files required by Excel Calculation Services on each load-balanced server.

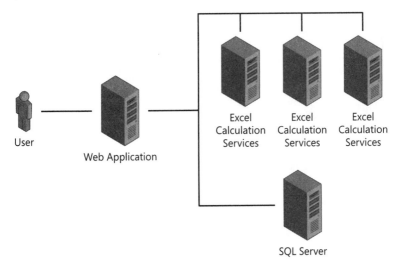

Figure 11-3   Excel Calculation Services in a load-balanced deployment.

Note Although front-end Web server applications in the farm require an external load-balancing device or software, such as Microsoft Network Load Balancing service, ECS does not. Load balancing is managed by the Proxy component.

In addition to increasing performance of ECS in the farm, adding multiple application servers provides redundancy and ensures continuous service if one of the Excel Calculation Servers fails. Scaling out ECS is covered in Chapter 13, "Scaling Out to a SharePoint Technologies Server Farm."

Configuring Trusted File Locations

ECS is designed with control and security in mind. Therefore, to allow workbooks to be processed by ECS, you must explicitly designate which document libraries or external locations are allowed. Doing so minimizes the impact of workbook processing on your servers and avoids inadvertently exposing information that should not be published through Excel Web Services. A Trusted File Location can be either a SharePoint 2007 Server document library, a shared folder on a file server, or a Web site on a standard web server. The Report Center site template is designed to provide a single site for deploying consolidated pages displaying figures, charts, graphs, and performance indicators that can help analysts and decision makers perform their jobs. The Report Center includes a Report Library list, which includes pre-configured content types and for Office Excel 2007 files (Reports) and Web Part pages (Dashboards) for displaying data from Excel Calculation Services.

Creating a Trusted File Location

The settings defined on the Trusted File Location control the security, caching, and data access behavior for each location. Use the steps below to configure a Trusted File Location for each document library that will be used to store workbooks accessible through Excel Calculation Services. You can also allow access to workbooks stored in file shares and non-SharePoint Web sites by configuring Trusted File Locations for these locations as well.

1. Open Central Administration from the Start menu.

2. In the Shared Services Administration section on the left, click your Shared Services Provider.

3. In the Excel Services Settings section, click Trusted File Locations.

4. Click Add Trusted File Location.

5. On the Add Trusted File Location page, type the URL or UNC of the file location and select other options as described below.

6. Click OK to add the Trusted File Location.

Trusted Location Settings

This section describes each of the settings that are shown on the Add Trusted File Location page indicated in the previous set of steps.

Location

- **Address and Location Type**   The value you enter in the Address field depends on the option selected for Location Type.

  - ❏ **Windows SharePoint Services:** Designates a specific document library in a site as the trusted location: for example, *http://spserver/records/ excellibrary.*

  - ❏ **UNC:** Enters the Universal Naming Convention (UNC) path to a shared folder on a file server: for example, *\\fileserver\excelfiles.*

  - ❏ **HTTP:** Provides the URL to a Web site that hosts Office Excel 2007 workbooks: for example, *http://webserver/directory.*

- **Trust Children**   Check this box to allow Excel Calculation Services to trust subdirectories and child folders in the trusted location.

- **Description**   Use this field to document the functional purpose of the trusted location and the reason it is being trusted. The description is not displayed elsewhere.

Session Management

- **Session Timeout**   This is the length of time that a session can sit idle without any user interaction before it is closed down by the browser. Each open session counts toward the Maximum Sessions Per User limit defined globally for Excel Calculation Services (see the section "Configuring Excel Services Settings" later in this chapter).

- **Short Session Timeout**   If a user opens a site, but does not take any action with the workbook or chart displayed in the browser, then the session is considered a Short Session and will time out according to this value.

- **Maximum Request Duration**   This is the maximum number of seconds that Excel Calculation Services will use in attempting to process and display data from an Excel 2007 workbook. The default of 300 seconds (5 minutes) is designed to prevent Excel Calculation Services from being tied up processing overly large workbooks. To correct timeout errors, either increase the value of this setting or provide more processing power on the server.

Workbook Properties

- **Maximum Workbook Size**   This value represents the largest size for a workbook that Excel Calculation Services will process. Users are able to upload workbooks that exceed this size to the trusted location, but cannot display the workbook data in the Web View.

- **Maximum Chart Size**   This value represents the largest size for a chart that Excel Calculation Services will process.

Calculation Behavior

- **Volatile Function Cache Lifetime**   This value defines for how long a dynamic function's results are cached. Many functions within workbooks change infrequently. Enter **-1** to have the value calculated once when the workbook loads, **0** to force it to be re-calculated every time the function is called, or a value in seconds from 1 through 2,073,600 (24 days) to set a specific cache duration.

- **Workbook Calculation Mode**   The calculation mode determines the mechanism that Excel Calculation Services uses to trigger data recalculations in workbooks. These settings, except for the File setting, override the workbook settings. The options are File, Manual, Automatic, and Automatic Except Data Tables.

External Data

- **Allow External Data**   This setting controls what type of Office Data Connection (ODC) sources are permitted in workbooks by Excel Calculation Services. The setting of None prohibits all ODCs; the other settings permit either all ODCs or only those stored in Trusted Data Connection Libraries.

- **Warn On Refresh**   Check this box to warn users before refreshing Office Data Connections.

- **Stop When Refresh On Open Fails**   Check this box to stop the loading and display of a workbook if the Office Data Connection cannot be refreshed.

- **External Data Cache Lifetime**   This setting determines the lifetime of data derived from an Office Data Connection when the connection is refreshed either automatically or manually. The default setting is 300 seconds (5 minutes) for each type of connection.

- **Maximum Concurrent Queries Per Session**   This setting limits the number of Office Data Connection queries that a single workbook session can contain.

User-Defined Functions

■ **Allow User-Defined Functions**   Check this box to allow workbooks to reference installed dynamic-link libraries (DLLs) that provide User-Defined Functions.

Workbook Security

One of the challenges faced when controlling access to Excel workbooks is allowing users to view specific parts of a workbook while restricting them from viewing or editing the entire workbook. If a user is a member of the default site Visitors group, then they have the rights to view and download workbooks from any document library on the site. Users with these rights could view the entire content of the workbook if it is not otherwise protected. The recommended approach in SharePoint Server is to give users restricted rights on the document libraries that are set up as trusted locations for Excel Calculation Services. Two SharePoint Server permissions control this behavior at the site level: Open Items, which allows users to open a file in its client application such as Office Excel 2007, and View Items, which allows a user only to view the content of a workbook through Excel Web View but not to open or download the file. To implement this configuration, create a new security permission level for the site by copying the Read permission level and removing the Open Items permission. Then assign this permission level to a group that will hold all the users who should not have the right to open workbooks on this site. For more details on configuring site permission levels and groups, see Chapter 7, "Implementing Security for SharePoint Products."

Note   Information Rights Management using Rights Management Server is not supported for workbooks that are accessed through Excel Calculation Services.

Publishing Office Excel 2007 Workbooks

Office Excel 2007 integrates with SharePoint Server to provide a new publishing feature that sets Excel Services options that define how the workbook will function in Excel Calculation Services. Uploading an Office Excel 2007 workbook directly to a trusted location document library makes it accessible, but you can only set the Excel Services options through the Publish command.

Publishing a Workbook to Excel Calculation Services

1. Open and edit the file in Office Excel 2007.

2. From the File menu, point to Publish and select Excel Services, as shown in Figure 11-4.

Figure 11-4 Publishing a workbook to Excel Calculation Services.

3. For the Save As Type, select either Excel Workbook (.xlsx) or Excel Binary Workbook (.xlsb). A binary workbook can be useful in instances where there are compatibility or performance issues because the data are stored in binary format instead of XML.

4. In the File Name box, type the full URL path to the document library along with the file name of the document: for example, *http://spserver/records/excellibrary/portfolio analysis.xlsx.*

5. Click the Excel Options button in the lower right corner of the dialog box.

6. On the Show tab of the Excel Services Options dialog box, shown in Figure 11-5, click the drop-down list and select either Sheets or Items in Workbook and check which objects should be visible to users. See the next section for more details.

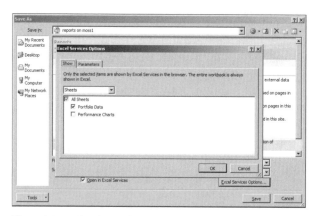

Figure 11-5 The Show tab in the Excel Services Options dialog box.

7. On the Parameters tab, click Add. The Add Parameters dialog box, shown in Figure 11-6, then appears.

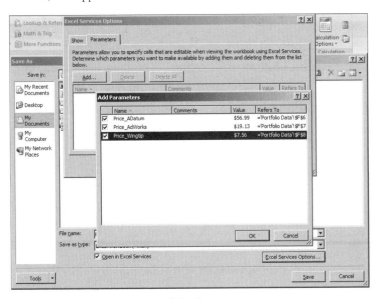

Figure 11-6   The Add Parameters dialog box.

8. Check the box next to the parameter that users can use to input values. See the next section for more details.

> **Important**   Only cells that are given Defined Names in Office Excel 2007 appear in the Add Parameters dialog box.

9. Click OK.

10. Click Save to save your workbook to the document library.

Configuring Excel Calculation Services Publishing Options

You are given several choices when publishing from Office Excel 2007.

Restricting Visibility

By default, when you publish a workbook to Excel Services, the entire workbook is processed and rendered to users who view it in a Web browser. A powerful feature of Office Excel 2007 is the ability to restrict which sheets or objects within the workbook can be seen by users. Restricting access to parts of the workbook in the Web browser affects all users, including the workbook author. On the Show tab of the Excel Services Options dialog box, shown in Figure 11-5, you can select the following options:

- **Entire Workbook**   This option does not restrict workbook visibility.

- **Sheets**   This option allows only specific sheets to be seen. Use this option to hide sheets with supporting data or calculations that you do not want to expose while displaying only the sheet(s) showing the results.

- **Items In The Workbook**   This option allows you to select specific named ranges, charts, tables, pivot tables, and pivot charts in the workbook to display. Only objects with Defined Names appear in the list.

Defining Parameters

When you publish a workbook to Excel Calculation Services, users who view the workbook in the browser are not able to edit the data in the cells. To allow users to input data for calculations in the workbook, you need to expose input parameters. A parameter is a named cell in the workbook that is exposed through a data entry screen in Excel Web Access. Users enter values in the input screen to update the calculations in the workbook. Users can update parameter values even if the cell is on a sheet that is hidden from view. The parameter values input are temporary and apply only to a specific user's session.

Opening Excel Workbooks in the Browser

When a document library is registered as a Trusted File Location with Excel Calculation Services, users can either open the workbook directly in Excel or they can view the workbook content directly in the browser. Opening a workbook in the browser provides a read-only view that still allows users to scroll, navigate between tabs, and sort and filter data. While viewing a workbook in the browser, data and results on a sheet are displayed but users cannot see the formulas or link to references that produced the results. If you have enabled parameter options, then users can enter values for those parameters and see the calculated results.

Viewing a Workbook in the Browser

1. Browse to the document library that contains the workbook.

2. From the document context menu select View In Web Browser.

Configure the Default Click Action to Open in a Browser

1. From the document library toolbar, click Settings and then click Document Library Settings.

2. Under General Settings, click Advanced settings.

3. In the browser-enabled Documents section, select Display As A Web Page.

The Excel Web Access Web Part

Excel Web Access is the component of SharePoint Server that renders Office Excel 2007 workbook content in HTML format in a Web browser. One of the innovations of Excel Web Access is that all of the conversion is done on the server so that no Active X controls or other binary objects are delivered to the browser. Excel Web Access allows users to open an entire workbook in their Web browser and, through the Excel Web Access Web Part, to display selected objects from workbooks on a dashboard page.

Adding an Excel Web Access Web Part to a Dashboard

1. Open the dashboard and select Edit Page from the Site Actions menu.

2. In the zone where you want the chart or sheet to appear, click Add A Web Part.

3. Scroll down the list to the Excel Web Access Web Part, select the check box next to it, and then click Add.

4. On the dashboard, click on Click Here To Open The Tool Pane link.

5. Next to the Workbook text box, shown in Figure 11-7, click the ellipsis button (...) and browse to the workbook that you want to display.

6. In the Named Item text box, type the name of the range of cells or chart objects to display in the Web Part.

7. Click OK.

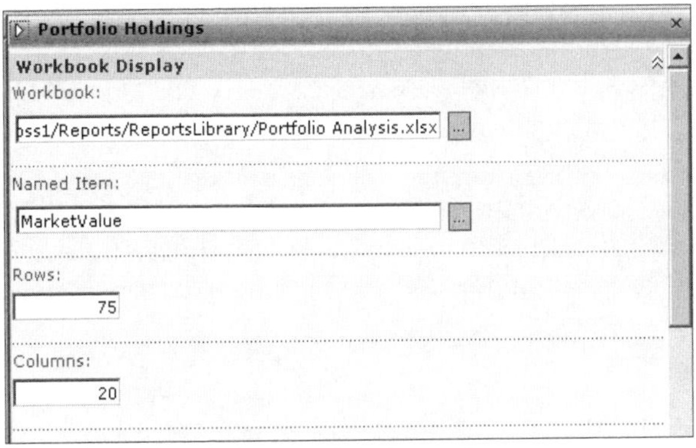

Figure 11-7   Excel Web Access Web Part properties.

Configuring Excel Services Settings

This section explains the settings found on the Excel Services Settings page in Shared Services. These settings control the global behavior of Excel Services in the farm.

Modifying Excel Services Settings

1. Open Central Administration from the Start menu.

2. In the Shared Services Administration section on the left, click on your Shared Services Provider.

3. In the Excel Services Settings section, click Edit Excel Services Settings.

4. Modify the settings as needed.

5. Click OK.

Security

Excel Calculation Services supports two authentication modes defined in the Excel Calculation Services Settings in the Shared Service Provider: Impersonation and Process Account. Using Impersonation, Excel Calculation Services loads a workbook using the Windows credentials of the user logged into the browser. The Impersonation option restricts access to a workbook based on the permissions of the domain user account used to connect to the SharePoint site. If any trusted locations point to a workbook located outside of SharePoint, then additional configuration steps are required to enable Kerberos Delegation and define a Service Principal Name.

For more information on configuring Kerberos authentication, see the Microsoft Knowledge Base article at http://support.microsoft.com/?id=832769.

With the Process Account option enabled, the application pool identity account for the Web application is used to access the workbook. Because the application pool identity account is used to access all workbooks, it is only necessary to ensure that the account has at least Read permissions on all trusted locations outside of SharePoint document libraries.

File Access Method

This setting specifies the type of account that is used to open and read workbooks stored in trusted locations. There are two options:

- **Impersonation**   Allows Excel Calculation Services to open the workbook as the user who is accessing the file through the browser.

- **Process Account**   Allows Excel Calculation Services to use the Excel Calculation Services service process to open the workbook.

Connection Encryption

For greater security within your network you can set Excel Calculation Services to allow only those connections that use an encryption protocol, such as Internet Protocol security (IPsec) or Secure Sockets Layer (SSL). With this option enabled, Excel Calculation Services rejects any attempt to view a workbook unless it is done through an encrypted connection.

Note   To configure Security settings from the command line use the *set-ecssecurity* operation of Stsadm.exe. For example, the following command sets the File Access Method to use Impersonation:

```
stsadm.exe -o set-ecssecurity -ssp sharedservices1
-fileaccessmethod useimpersonation
```

Load Balancing

The settings described in this section control how Excel Services automatically distributes and manages the requests among multiple servers with Excel Calculation Services enabled.

Load-Balancing Scheme

When you have deployed more than one dedicated Excel Calculations Services application server, then workbook calculation jobs are directed to one of the servers based on one of these three redirection methods:

- **Workbook URL**   This is the default method. Workbook processing is assigned to an application server based on the pattern of the URL. This ensures that a workbook is always recalculated on the same server, thereby taking advantage of caching on that server.

- **Round-Robin**   As requests for workbook processing are received, they are passed to each of the application servers in sequential order. This setting yields a more even distribution of requests, but may not take advantage of caching on the application server.

- **Local**   This setting is equivalent to Round-Robin, but does not defer to using Excel Calculation Services on the front-end Web server if it is enabled. This option is the most efficient for small workbooks or those requiring little calculation.

Note   Excel Calculation Services creates a hash value from the workbook URL and uses it to determine to which Excel Calculation Server to direct the request. The redirection depends on the pattern of hash values and may not result in an even distribution of load across multiple Excel Calculation Servers.

Retry Interval

The Retry Interval is the maximum number of seconds that the Web front-end server will wait before attempting to connect to Excel Calculation Services again following a failed connection. The default value is 30 seconds and can range from 5 seconds up to 2,073,600 or 24 days. To reduce overall load on your Excel Calculation Server, increase this interval.

> **Note**   To configure load-balancing settings from the command line use the *set-ecsloadbalancing* operation of Stsadm.exe. For example, the following command sets the Load Balancing Scheme to Round-Robin:

```
stsadm.exe -o set-ecsloadbalancing -ssp sharedservices1
-scheme roundrobin
```

Session Management

A user generates a session whenever he or she views a workbook in the browser or views a portion of a workbook in an Excel Web View Web Part. Each session will remain active for the lifetime set in the Session Management settings defined for a Trusted Location. The default Maximum Sessions Per User is 25.

> **Note**   To configure Session Management settings from the command line use the *set-ecssecurity* operation of Stsadm.exe. For example, the following command sets the Maximum Sessions Per User to 50:

```
stsadm.exe -o set-ecssessionmanagement -ssp sharedservices1
-maxsessionsperuser 50
```

Memory Utilization

Memory utilization can be managed by configuring the following settings:

- **Maximum Private Bytes**   Private bytes represent the total private virtual memory (in megabytes) allocated to an Excel Calculation Services process. The default value of -1 sets the limit to be 50% of the physical memory on the server. Setting the Maximum Private Bytes to less than 100 MB may result in Excel Calculation Services being unable to process and display workbooks.

- **Memory Cache Threshold**   This setting governs how much memory is reserved for caching previously processed workbooks. When the threshold is exceeded, older cache is flushed to free up memory. To maximize the reuse of cached workbooks, the default value is set to 90% of the Maximum Private Bytes. Reduce this value to lower the memory footprint of cached workbooks.

- **Maximum Unused Object Age**   Workbook elements that are not currently loaded in a user session may take up unnecessary memory. This setting controls the lifetime of these objects, in minutes, from the last time they are accessed. The default setting of -1 prevents these objects from being purged from memory automatically.

Note   To configure Memory Utilization settings from the command line use the *set-ecsmemoryutilization* operation of Stsadm.exe. For example, the following command sets the Maximum Private Bytes to 1000 MB:

```
stsadm.exe -o set-ecsmemoryutilization -ssp sharedservices1
-maxprivatebytes 1000
```

Workbook Cache Location

The Workbook Cache Location is used as a temporary store for workbook elements after they have been processed by Excel Calculation Services. The default location is the folder defined by your TEMP environment variable and can be changed to any local folder to which the application pool has Write permissions. The upper limit of this setting is the amount of free disk space on the drive.

Note   To configure Workbook Cache settings from the command line use the *set-ecsworkbookcache* operation of Stsadm.exe. For example, the following command sets the Workbook Cache Location to E:\ecscache:

```
stsadm.exe -o set-ecsworkbookcache -ssp sharedservices1
-location e:\ecscache
```

External Data

There are two options for managing external data:

- **Connection Lifetime**   This is the duration in seconds that an Office Data Connection will remain active before timing out. The default value is 1800 seconds or 30 minutes.

- **Unattended Service Account**   This account is used to authenticate to an Office Data Connection data source if the workbook is configured to use Integrated Windows Authentication for the data connection.

Note   To configure External Data settings from the command line, use the *set-ecsexternaldata* operation of Stsadm.exe. For example, the following command sets the Connection Lifetime to 1000 seconds:

```
stsadm.exe -o set-ecsexternaldata -ssp sharedservices1
-connectionlifetime 1000
```

Configuring Trusted Data Connection Libraries

An Office Data Connection (ODC) is a persistent set of data connection settings that can be stored in an Office Excel 2007 workbook or in SharePoint Server for use in multiple workbooks. ODCs allow users to create their own queries into databases in the organization and to extract data and display it in their Office Excel 2007 workbooks. Although it is possible to query any database table and display the results in a workbook using an ODC, dynamic tables derived from standard databases are not supported by Excel Calculation Services. Excel Calculation Services can only refresh and display data derived from an Analysis Services query.

Because access to organizational data should be protected at all times, it is recommended that those ODCs that are approved for use by users be stored in a Data Connection Library. A Data Connection Library is a list that can store ODC files and can be referenced by users who need to use those ODCs to access data. The advantage of using a centralized library for ODC files is that, if any of the connection information related to the data source changes, then only one file needs to be updated. As a security control over ODC files, you must explicitly trust a Data Connection Library for Excel Calculation Services to be able to refresh the connection.

Configuring a Data Connection Library as Trusted

1. Open Central Administration from the Start menu.

2. Click the link for the Shared Services Provider.

3. Under Excel Services Settings, click Trusted Data Connection Libraries.

4. Click Add Trusted Data Connection Library.

5. Type in the URL address of the Data Connection Library you want to add and, optionally, add a description.

Configuring Trusted Data Providers

Office Data Connections can connect to virtually any data source for which a data driver is configured on the machine making the query. In the case of ODC files stored in Data Connection Libraries, these drivers must be installed and configured on the Excel Calculation Server. In addition, Excel Calculation Services must be configured to explicitly trust the driver by entering it into the list of Trusted Data Providers. Excel Calculation Services is configured to trust a set of data providers that includes SQL Server 2000, SQL Server 2005, Oracle 9.2, and IBM DB2. If your organization uses any database systems not on this list and you want to access them through Excel Calculation Services then you need to configure the drivers as trusted. Once the drivers have been installed on the server and trusted, they should be available through any ODC that has authenticated access to the data. To configure a Trusted Data Provider, first install the driver for the data source and then take the following steps.

Adding a Trusted Data Provider

1. Open Central Administration from the Start menu.

2. Click the link for the Shared Services Provider.

3. Under Excel Services Settings, click Trusted Data Providers.

4. Click Add Trusted Data Provider.

5. In the Provider ID section, as shown in Figure 11-8, type the identifier of the driver you want to add as a Trusted Data Provider.

6. Select one of the following provider types:

   ❑ OLE DB: Use for most Microsoft and many third-party drivers that have been written to use the current OLE DB interface.

   ❑ ODBC: Use for drivers that confirm to the Open Database Connectivity standard used by most database manufacturers.

   ❑ ODBC DSN: Use to identify a reference to a Data Source Name on the local server that contains connection string information for an ODBC driver.

7. Click OK.

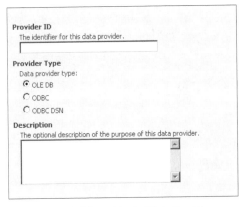

Figure 11-8   Adding a Trusted Data Provider.

Configuring User-Defined Function Assemblies

As part of the focus on security built into SharePoint Server, ECS has been designed to prevent users from executing potentially malicious code inside Office Excel 2007 workbooks. As a result, many of the automation features used in workbooks on the desktops will not run on the server. Such features as Active X controls, VBA macros, links to other spreadsheets, workbooks with add-in references, and DDE links will generate an error in Excel Calculation Services. In place of code embedded in the workbook, Excel Calculation Services supports custom code libraries installed on the server and configured as trusted libraries. A User-Defined Function is a code module compiled as managed code under the Microsoft .NET Framework version 2.0. User-defined functions written to run in the Office Excel 2007 client cannot be used directly by Excel Calculation Services. A library that is configured to run under Excel Calculation Services is known as a User-Defined Function Assembly. These assemblies can be installed into a folder on the server, into a network share accessible by the server, or into the Global Assembly Cache (GAC) on the server. Once the assembly is installed on the server, it must be trusted within Excel Calculation Services.

Configuring a User-Defined Function Assembly

1. Open Central Administration from the Start menu.

2. Click on the link for the Shared Services Provider.

3. Under Excel Services Settings, click User-Defined Function Assemblies.

4. Click Add User-Defined Function (UDF) Assembly.

5. Under the Assembly field, as shown in Figure 11-9, enter the unique identifier for the UDF file.

6. For a local file, type the full path: for example, D:\ExcelUDFs\ CustomFunctions.dll or \\ExcelServer\ExcelUDFs\CustomFunctions.dll.

7. For an assembly in the GAC, type the Strong Name: for example, *CustomFunctions, Version=1.1.0.0, Culture=Neutral, PublicKeyToken=d7012336c6ae8fd27.*

8. Select the Assembly Location option that corresponds with the path—either GAC or Local File.

9. Click OK.

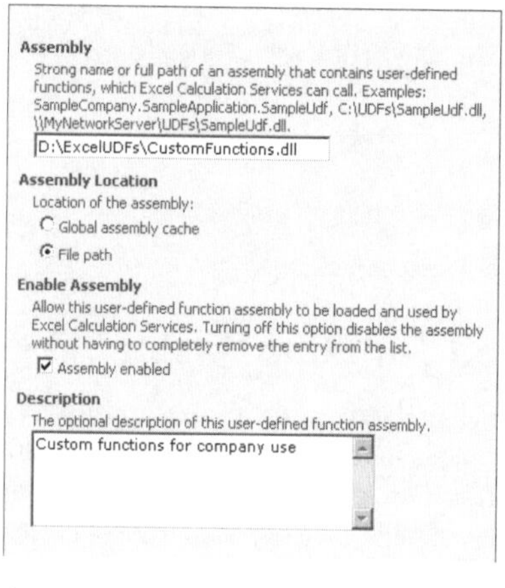

Figure 11-9   Adding the User-Defined Function Assembly.

Configuring SharePoint Server Search and Indexing

Aggregated search and indexing is one of the most important features of Microsoft Office SharePoint Server 2007. This chapter shows you how to use the various features of Search.

At the heart of the search engine is the crawler. The crawler goes out and gathers from the content source the content that needs to be placed in the index. After the index is built, users execute a query against the index to receive a result set. The crawler does only what it is instructed to do. Hence, when it crawls content, it only crawls the content that you have instructed it to crawl, and the crawl actions occur within the security rule and timing rules that you create manually.

For those who ran previous versions of SharePoint Server, the crawler was encapsulated inside the Gatherer service. The Gatherer service is now called the crawler. The crawler works by connecting to the content source and extracting the data. However, it can only connect to the content source if the appropriate protocol handler is installed. The protocol handler is used by the crawler to connect to the content source. Once connected, the crawler opens the files (read permission is all that is required for this action) and extracts the contents of the file without copying down the entire file. The crawler can only extract content if the correct iFilter (Index Filter) is installed on the indexing server. The iFilter instructs the crawler as to what type and kind of documents it will be reading once it arrives at the content source. For example, if you need to crawl the contents of a file server, then the crawler will load the "File" protocol handler, which will allow the crawler to use Server Message Blocks (SMB) and Remote Procedure Calls (RPC) to connect to the content source. The crawler will also load various file-type iFilters, such as Word, Excel, and text, so that, once connected, the crawler can open the files on the file server and read its content.

After the crawler has connected to the content source and has cracked open the documents, it streams the content from the content source to the index server. When the content arrives at the index server, the Indexer chunks the stream into 64-KB chunks, performs word breaking and stemming on the words, removes the noise words (words that you have specified not to appear in the index), and then sends the content itself to the index (Content Store) and the metadata to the SQL search databases for the Shared Services Provider, also known as the Property Store.

Creating and Managing Content Sources and Crawl Settings

Creating content sources is the first administrative task in building an aggregated search and indexing topology. This work is accomplished inside the Shared Services Provider interface.

Content Source Types

In SharePoint Server 2007, content sources can have multiple start addresses. A start address is the URL location at which you wish the crawler to start the crawl process. The crawl settings instruct the crawler as to how deep and wide the crawl process should take place.

The content source types include the following:

- SharePoint sites
- Web sites
- File shares
- Exchange public folders
- Business Data Catalog (BDC)

Crawl Settings

The crawl settings are contextualized to the content source type so that the settings that appear are appropriate for the content source type that is selected. For example, if you select the File Share content source type, you do not see the Crawl Everything Under The Hostname For This Start Address crawl setting because that setting doesn't apply to a file share start address.

To create a new content source, open the Home page for your Shared Services Provider (SSP), and click on the Search Settings link, as shown in Figure 12-1.

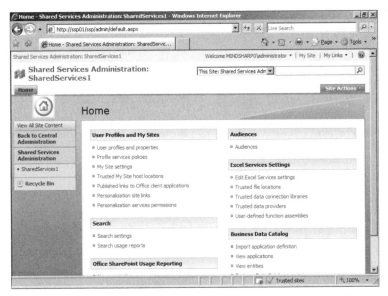

Figure 12-1   The Search Settings link in the Shared Services Provider interface.

To create a new content source, click on the Search Settings link and then follow these steps:

1. Click on the Content Source And Crawl Schedule link. The Manage Content Sources page then appears.

2. Click on the New Content Source button. The Add Content Source page then appears.

3. Enter a name for the content source.

4. Select the content source type.

5. Enter the start address(es). Note that you can enter multiple start addresses, but each needs to match the content source type selection for the content source to work properly.

6. Select the crawl settings.

7. Select the crawl schedule(s).

8. Select whether you want to crawl the content immediately.

9. Click OK.

Crawl Rules

Formerly known as site path rules, crawl rules instruct the crawler on additional configurations for crawling a particular content source. Because these rules can be either specific to an individual content source or global to general settings, such as *http:// *.com,* they cannot always be applied at the content source level.

Crawl rules allow you to configure include/exclude rules, specific security contexts for crawling that are different from the default content access account, and the actual path to which you want the rule to apply. Figure 12-2 illustrates the default interface with a common global rule configured. Because many Web sites use complex URLs, you might want to consider implementing a global rule that instructs the crawler to crawl any complex URL that it encounters.

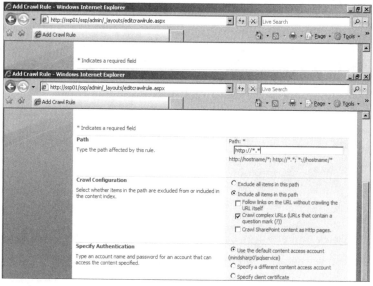

Figure 12-2   The Crawl Rule interface.

To create a new crawl rule, follow these steps:

1. In the Shared Services Provider, click on the Search Settings link. This brings you to the Configure Search Settings page.

2. Click the Crawl Rules link. The Manage Crawl Rules page then appears.

3. Click the New Crawl Rule button. The Add Crawl Rules page then appears.

4. Enter a path URL in the Path input box.

5. Configure the Crawl Rule settings as needed.

6. Specify if you need a unique security context to support the crawl rule or if you can leave the rule using the default content access account.

7. Click OK. Your new crawl rule should now appear on the Manage Crawl Rules page.

Managing File Types

From a global perspective, you can instruct the crawler as to what type of file is available for crawling by using the file types feature. If the file type extension doesn't appear on the Manage File Types screen, shown in Figure 12-3, then the crawler will not crawl that file type. To state this another way, the crawler only crawls the file types that appear on the Manage File Types screen.

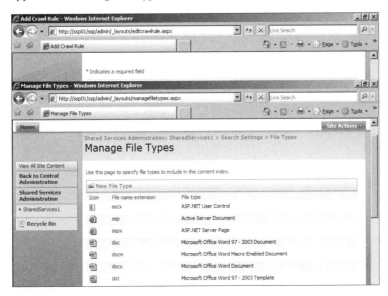

Figure 12-3   The Manage File Types screen.

It's easy enough to add a new file type. All you need to do is follow these steps:

1. From your Shared Services Provider's Home page, click on the Search Settings link. This presents you with the Configure Search Settings page.

2. Click on the File Types link. The Manage File Types page then appears.

3. Click the New File Type link. The Add File Type page then appears.

4. Enter the file's extension in the file extension input box, as seen in Figure 12-4.

5. Click OK.

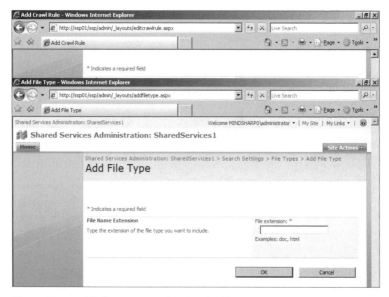

Figure 12-4   Add File Type page showing the file extension input box.

Now, what the interface does not tell you is that entering the file type really accomplishes nothing. You also need to ensure that you have installed an iFilter for that file type on your SharePoint server(s). Because there is no interface to tell you which file types have been installed on your servers, you need to rely on your deployment documentation to inform you whether the correct iFilter for that file type has already been installed. There is no interface within SharePoint Server to install a new iFilter. Instead, rely on the setup instructions from the iFilter's manufacturer to install and use the iFilter.

Crawl Logs

The crawl logs enable users to view the successes and errors that have been experienced in the crawl efforts. By default, the log displays successes, warnings, and errors, as seen in Figure 12-5.

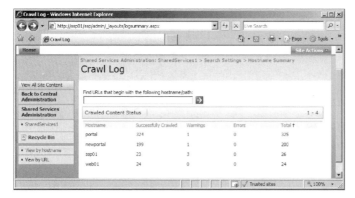

Figure 12-5   The default crawl log screen showing successes, warnings, and errors from completed crawls of content sources.

To view the Crawl Logs page, follow these steps:

1. From your Shared Services Provider's Home page, click on the Search Settings link. This presents you with the Configure Search Settings page.

2. Click the Crawl Log link. The Crawl Log page then appears.

You can view messages related to a specific content source, as shown in Figure 12-6. These messages tell you about the experience of the crawler and allow you to learn rich troubleshooting information for unsuccessful crawl efforts.

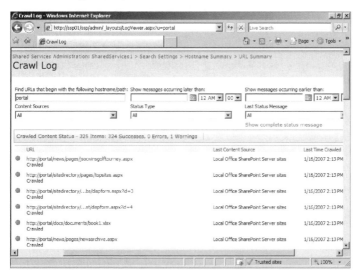

Figure 12-6   The Crawl Log page reveals crawl history messages related to a specific content source.

To view specific messages related to a specific content source, follow these steps:

1. From the Crawl Log page, click on the link for the content source you wish to investigate. This presents you with a page similar to what is shown in Figure 12-6.

2. Referring to Figure 12-6, note that you can sort and filter the list based on the following elements. The filter button is not shown in Figure 12-6, but it is present on the right portion of the screen that is not illustrated:

   ❑ Content source

   ❑ Hostname/path

   ❑ Status type

   ❑ Date/time

Metadata Property Mappings

Metadata fields are added to the crawled properties by the Archival plug-in. This plug-in looks at the metadata as it is being crawled and whenever a new metadata type is found, that type is added automatically to the crawled properties list. To access the crawled properties list, follow these steps:

1. From the Shared Services Provider Home page, click on Search Settings. This presents you with the Configure Search Settings page.

2. Click on the Metadata Property Mappings link. The Metadata Property Mappings page then appears, as illustrated in Figure 12-7. The mappings column details the metadata property's formal name along with the data type for that property.

3. From the Metadata Property Mappings page, click on the Crawled Properties link in the left pane. The Crawled Properties View of the Metadata Property Mappings page then appears, as shown in Figure 12-8.

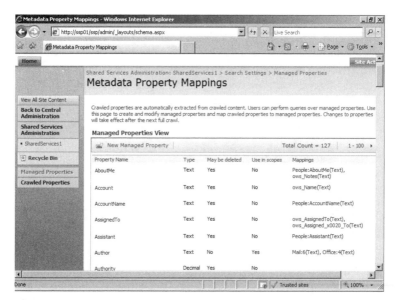

Figure 12-7   The Metadata Property Mappings page.

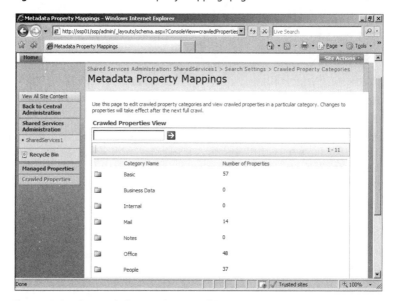

Figure 12-8   The Crawled Properties View of the Metadata Property Mappings page.

From here, you can drill down into the folders, view the metadata that have been added to the Shared Services Provider, and then open the individual metadata property and view its properties.

Within each property, you can configure managed property assignments as well as select the check box to allow that property's values to be indexed. These two configuration options are illustrated in Figure 12-9.

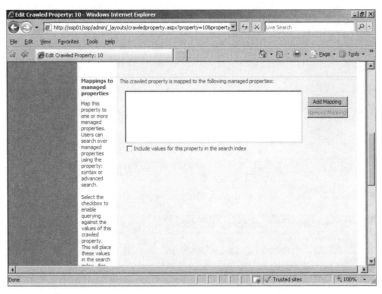

Figure 12-9   The configuration options for a crawled property.

The value in mapping crawled properties to managed properties is that it groups metadata into usable units. The metadata (crawled properties) are grouped together into a logical, single unit (managed properties). Managed properties can then be used to create search scopes and enable your users to search for metadata values without return false-positives from out-of-scope metadata values. Managed properties can also be included in the Advanced Search Web Part interface for surgical query of specific crawled properties.

> **Real World**   Grouping crawled properties into managed properties is one of the valuable new features in SharePoint Server 2007. For example, let's say that you have three document types: (a) document type A that lists the Author in the Author metadata field; (b) document type B that lists the Author in the Creator metadata field; and (c) document type C that lists the Author in the Originator metadata field. In this scenario, you have (essentially) the same metadata for three different document types residing in three different metadata fields. When these documents are crawled, each metadata field is entered into the Property Store as a separate Crawled Properties. However, you can group these three crawled properties into a single Managed Property so that you can use them as a single unit when querying for author names across these three different document types.

By default, 127 managed properties are created automatically when the SSP is created. You can create a new managed property by following the following steps:

1. From the Home page of the Shared Services Provider, click on the Search Settings link. This presents you with the Configure Search Settings page.

2. Click on the Metadata Property Settings link. The Metadata Property Mappings page then appears.

3. Click on the New Managed Property link. The New Managed Property page, as illustrated in Figure 12-10, then appears.

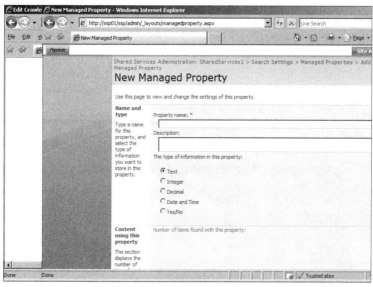

Figure 12-10   The New Managed Property page.

4. Enter a name and description for the new managed property.

5. Select the type of information this property will represent.

6. Enter at least one crawled property that will be grouped by this managed property.

7. Select the check box to allow the property to be used in a search scope.

8. Click OK.

To use a managed property within a search scope, follow these steps:

1. From the Home page of the Shared Services Provider, click on the Search Settings link. This presents you with the Configure Search Settings page.

2. Click on the View Scopes link. The View Scopes page, as shown in Figure 12-11, then appears.

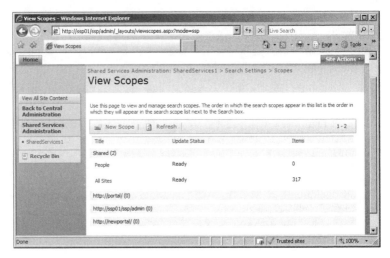

Figure 12-11 The View Scopes page.

3. Click on the New Scope link. The Create Scope page, as illustrated in Figure 12-12, then appears.

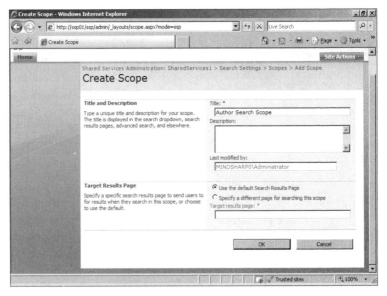

Figure 12-12 The Create Scope page.

4. For purposes of this exercise, enter a title and then click OK. This action takes you back to the View Scopes page, and your new scope appears on this page, as shown in Figure 12-13.

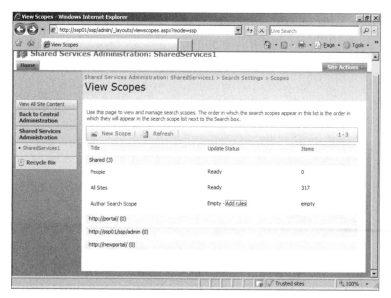

Figure 12-13   The View Scopes page with the new scope added.

5. Click the Add Rules link. The Add Scope Rule page, as shown in Figure 12-14, then appears.

6. In the Scope Rule Type section, select the Property Query option button. The screen then changes to look like the one shown in Figure 12-14. Notice that you can then select the managed property you wish to build the scope off of, as well as entering the value for that property that will help define the scope. Note that only those properties that are enabled to be used in search scopes appear in the drop-down list.

7. Click OK. You have now defined a search scope using a managed property.

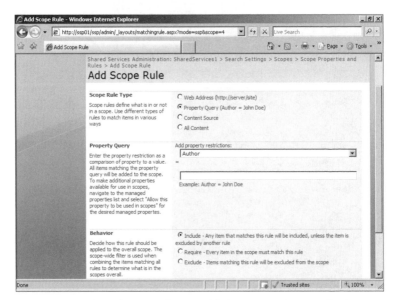

Figure 12-14   The Add Scope Rule page with the Property Query option button selected.

To add a managed property to the advanced search Web Part, you need to work with the page that displays the result set for the end user. To do this, follow these steps:

1. Go to the result page and click Edit Page on the Site Actions menu.

2. Open the Edit menu for the search Web Part and select Modify Shared Web Part. This opens the Web Part properties pane.

3. Expand the Miscellaneous section in the properties pane and look for the property called *properties*. There you will find an XML string that allows you to define which properties will be displayed in the advanced search. Your best option here is to copy the string to Notepad for editing.

4. Edit the XML string and save it back into the property. You can save the XML in the following format, which is copied directly from the Web Part. For the XML to hold any real value, there needs to be a profile property in the schema.

```
<Properties>
<Property Name="Department" ManagedName="Department"
ProfileURI=
"urn:schemas-microsoft-com:sharepoint:portal:profile:Department"/>
<Property Name="JobTitle" ManagedName="JobTitle"
ProfileURI=
"urn:schemas-microsoft-com:sharepoint:portal:profile:Title"/>
<Property Name="Responsibility" ManagedName="Responsibility"
```

```
ProfileURI=
"urn:schemas-microsoft-com:sharepoint:portal:profile:SPS-Responsibility"/>
<Property Name="Skills" ManagedName="Skills"
ProfileURI=
"urn:schemas-microsoft-com:sharepoint:portal:profile:SPS-Skills"/>
<Property Name="QuickLinks" ManagedName="QuickLinks"
ProfileURI=
"urn:schemas-microsoft-com:sharepoint:portal:profile:QuickLinks"/>
</Properties>
```

You need to pay attention to the following elements:

- Property name
- Managed property name
- Profile URI (Universal Resource Identifier)

If you look at the URN (Universal Resource Name) string carefully, you will notice that the profile name is being pulled out of the profile URN. This is why there needs to be a profile property in the schema before this XML has any real effect.

Server Name Mappings

Server name mappings allow you to hide the server's real name in the links for the result set by instructing SharePoint Server to replace the server's name with the alias you enter in the server name mappings area. For example, if your server name is something like FS01MSPNorth (File Server 01 in Minneapolis at the North Office), it might be better to give the user "Server01" in the result set. The alias hides your server-naming convention from the user and also spares the user from receiving a complicated or convoluted server name.

To create a new server name mapping, follow these steps:

1. Click on the Server Name Mapping link from the Configure Search Settings page.
2. Click the New Mapping link.
3. Enter the name of the server in the Address In Index input box
4. Enter the alias name you want to appear in the result set in Address In Search Results input box.

Search Results Removal

This feature is new to SharePoint Server 2007. It allows you to immediately remove content from the index by entering the URLs for the content you want to remove in the index. This can be helpful if objectionable material has accidentally appeared in the index.

The URLs To Remove input box is shown in Figure 12-15. After entering the URLs you wish to remove, click the Remove button.

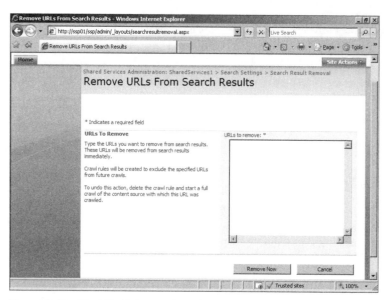

Figure 12-15   The URLs To Remove input box allows you to instantly remove content from the index.

Creating and Managing Search Scopes

In the previous section on managed properties, we described how to create a search scope. In this section, we discuss some of the additional administrative actions that you can perform regarding search scopes.

First, you can create search scopes and associate one or more rules within the scope to help define its focus or breadth. To create a new scope, refer to the section on Metadata Property Mappings.

Second, search scopes that you create at the SSP level are considered shared scopes. This means that these scopes are shared across all of the Web application's site collections that are associated with the SSP. Site collection owners then have the choice whether to use the scope within their site collection.

To select whether the shared scope is used in the site collection, follow these steps:

1. From the Site Collection Administration menu in the root site, click the Search Scopes link. If this link doesn't appear, be sure to activate the features for the search center or install the search center Web site into your site collection. You are then presented with the View Scopes page, shown in Figure 12-16.

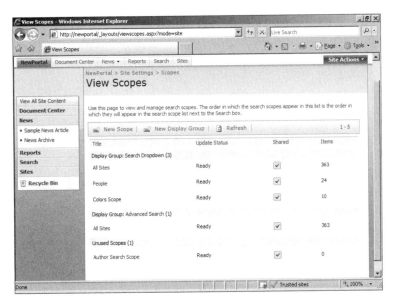

Figure 12-16   The View Scopes page.

2. Click on the display group link to which you wish to add the shared scope; for example, Search Dropdown. You are then presented with the Edit Scope Display Group page, shown in Figure 12-17.

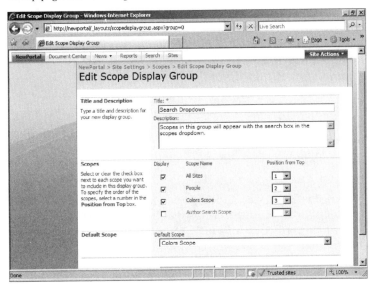

Figure 12-17   The Edit Scope Display Group page.

3. Select the scope you wish to be the default scope for the display group.

4. Click OK.

To enable the display group to appear in the drop-down list of the search Web Part in the Search page, perform the following steps:

1. From the Search Center page, click on Site Settings.

2. Click Edit Page. The default.aspx page for the search center moves into edit mode, and the Web Part zones appear on the page.

3. In the top Web Part zone, click the Edit drop-down list for the Search Web Part and select Modify Shared Web Part.

4. Within the Web Part's properties pane, expand the Scopes Dropdown section and select Show Scopes Dropdown, seen in Figure 12-18.

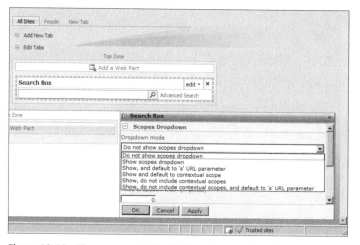

Figure 12-18 The scopes selection list from the search Web Part's properties.

5. Click OK.

6. Click Publish.

7. The Scopes Dropdown list should now appear in the search Web Part. If you selected a different scope to be the default scope, then that scope appears as the default. You can select the default scope for a scopes display group from the default scopes drop-down list in the Edit Scope Display Group page, as shown in Figure 12-19.

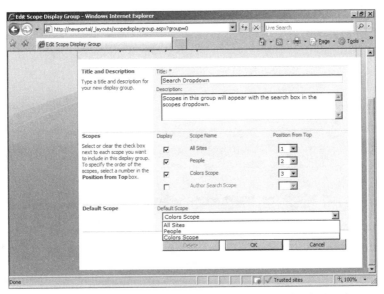

Figure 12-19   Selecting the Colors scope as the default scope for the Search Dropdown Scopes display group.

Configuring Crawler Impact Rules

Crawler impact rules can be used to calibrate the aggressiveness of your crawl efforts. The default settings ask for eight documents in a single request and then wait 0 seconds before asking for another eight documents after the first set of documents has been received. You can change both the number of documents in a single request (up to 64 documents) and insert a wait period between requests, configured in seconds.

You may need to calibrate how quickly and aggressively SharePoint Server crawls a content source to ease the burden on the target server. In addition, you may also need to configure one or more rules to help ease the burden of the crawl procedures on the Web front-end servers in your farm. This is because all of the crawl processes are actually passed to the Web front-end server, which then connects to the content source server on behalf of the index server and executes the crawl procedures. The index server does not connect directly to the target content source server. Instead, all of the crawl requests are proxied through your Web front-end servers. Therefore, as a side note, when monitoring the performance of the index server to assess the load placed on it by the crawl action, be sure to simultaneously monitor the Web front-end server to gain a full picture of how the crawl procedures are affecting the servers in your farm.

To create new crawler impact rules, perform these steps:

1. From the Applications tab in Central Administration, click the Search Service link. You are then presented with the Manage Search Service page.

2. Click the Crawler Impact Rules link. The Crawler Impact Rules page then appears.

3. Click the Add Rule link. The Add Crawler Impact Rule page, as shown in Figure 12-20, then appears.

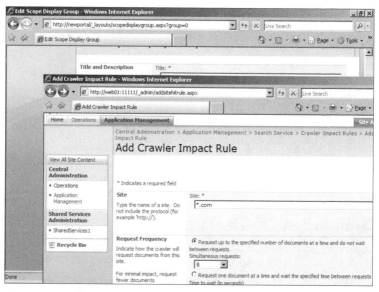

Figure 12-20 The Add Crawler Impact Rule page.

4. Enter the site URL (wildcards are allowed on this page; refer to Figure 12-20).

5. Configure the request frequency in terms of both seconds and number of documents requested.

> **Note** Because there are option buttons, you cannot configure both settings at the same time. If you want to change the number of documents requested and configure a wait time between requests, first make your document selection and then configure the wait time. The document selection configuration will persist when the wait time configuration option button is selected.

Configuring Relevance Settings Through Authoritative Pages

Relevance settings can be managed through the authoritative pages in the SSP. The relationship of individual documents or content items to authoritative pages is defined in terms of click distance. If all other ranking elements are equal, then the more clicks that are required to traverse from the authoritative page to the content item, the less relevant that item is for a given query.

Ask yourself this question when setting authoritative pages: Where do my users go most often to find their information or to start browsing for their information? The answer or answers to that question will be the URLs that you should enter into the authoritative pages input boxes. Figure 12-21 illustrates the authoritative pages input boxes.

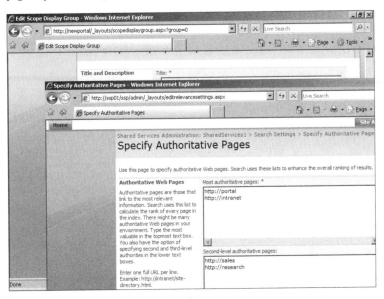

Figure 12-21   The Specify Authoritative Pages input boxes.

You can achieve a level of granularity by entering primary, secondary, and tertiary URLs, thereby formulating an overall hierarchical relevance topology for your SSP. You can also set some sites to be the lowest on the relevance scale by placing their URLs in the Sites To Demote input box.

URLs within the same input box are grouped equally, meaning that there is no hierarchical order implied by the URL list. In addition, wildcards, such as *http:foo/**, are not accepted in these boxes. To set relevance settings, perform the following steps:

1. Open the Home page for your SSP. Click on the Search Settings link. You are then presented with the Configure Search Settings page.

2. Click on the Specify Authoritative Pages link. The Specify Authoritative Pages page then appears.

3. Input the URLs in the appropriate boxes to configure relevance settings for your environment.

4. Click the Refresh Now check box if you want to have the relevance settings recomputed immediately.

5. Click OK.

Configuring the Thesaurus and Noise Word Files

There are several ways to configure the result set that your end users will receive. The thesaurus and noise word file are the two features most commonly used to configure the result set. In this section we discuss the more common ways to configure these elements.

Configuring the Thesaurus

The thesaurus is a method to manually force the expansion or replacement of query terms as the query is executed against the index. It allows you to create expansion or replacement sets, as well as weighting and/or stemming the terms within the expansion or replacement sets.

The thesaurus is configured via an XML file, which is located by default in the *drive:*\Program Files\Office SharePoint Server\Data\ directory and has the format of TS<*XXX*>.XML, where *XXX* is the standard three-letter code for a specific language. For English, the file name is Tsenu.xml.

The default code for the file is as follows:

```
<XML ID="Microsoft Search Thesaurus">
<!--  Commented out
    <thesaurus xmlns="x-schema:tsSchema.xml">
    <diacritics_sensitive>0</diacritics_sensitive>
        <expansion>
            <sub>Internet Explorer</sub>
            <sub>IE</sub>
            <sub>IE5</sub>
        </expansion>
        <replacement>
            <pat>NT5</pat>
            <pat>W2K</pat>
```

```
        <sub>Windows 2000</sub>
    </replacement>
    <expansion>
        <sub>run</sub>
        <sub>jog</sub>
    </expansion>
</thesaurus>
-->
</XML>
```

To create new expansion sets, perform the following steps:

1. Open My Computer and go to the location of the thesaurus XML file.

2. Open the XML file using Notepad or some other text editor.

3. Enter your expansion terms within the tags using well-formed XML, as illustrated here:

```
<expansion>
    <sub>term1</sub>
    <sub>term2</sub>
    <sub>term3</sub>
</expansion>
```

4. Save the file.

5. Restart the Mssearch.exe service.

To create new replacement sets, perform the following steps:

1. Open My Computer and go to the location of the thesaurus XML file.

2. Open the XML file using Notepad or some other text editor.

3. Enter your replacement terms within the tags using well-formed XML. Note that the terms being replaced are in the <sub> extensions, and the term to replace them is in the <pat> extension. This is illustrated here:

```
<replacement>
    <sub>term1</sub>
    <sub>term2</sub>
    <pat>term3</pat>
</replacement>
```

4. Be sure to save the thesaurus files.

Configuring the Noise Word File

The noise word file is a text file that contains all of the words that you don't want to appear in the index. When a word is placed in the noise word file, the indexer removes that word during the indexing process so that the word itself doesn't appear in the index. Words that you would place in this file are those that have little or no discriminatory value in a search query in your environment. Such words often include the following:

- Pronouns
- Adverbs
- Adjectives
- Conjunctions
- Prepositions
- Articles
- Single letters
- Single numbers
- Your organization's name

The noise word files are located in the same directory as the thesaurus. All you need to do is open the file using Notepad and enter the words that you do not want to appear in the index. To configure the noise word file, perform the following steps:

1. Go to the noise word file and open it using Notepad or some other text editor.

2. Enter the words you do not want to appear in the index.

3. Save the file.

4. Run full index builds to effect your changes in the index.

Working with Query Reporting

Within the SSP, you can view query activities to help you understand the words and phrases for which the users are searching. These reports help you know what sites and keywords to configure as Best Bets, which are predetermined content items that will appear in the Best Bet Web Part on the search results page based on the keywords in the query. In addition, you may be able to discover how to better train your users in using the search features by learning about their past behavior.

To find the query reports, follow these steps:

1. From the Home page in your Shared Services Provider, click the Site Usage Reports link. You are then presented with the Search Queries Report page, shown in Figure 12-22.

2. Scroll through the page to view the reports you want to view.

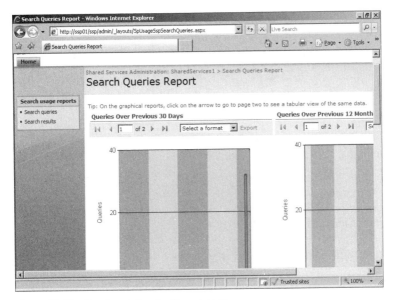

Figure 12-22   The Search Queries Report page.

Understanding Query Reporting

There are actually two types of reports in the SSP: the Search Queries and the Search Results reports. The Search Query report contains these reporting elements:

- *Queries over the previous 30 days:* Use this report to understand the raw queries that have occurred in the last 30 days.

- *Queries over the previous 12 months:* Use this report to understand the raw queries that have occurred in the previous 12 months.

- *Top query origin site collection over the previous 30 days:* Use this report to understand which users (based on site collection membership) have been executing the least and most queries in the previous 30 days.

- *Queries per scope over the previous 30 days:* Use this report to understand which scopes are most and least often used for searching in the previous 30 days.

- *Top queries over the previous 30 days:* Use this report to understand what the top queries have been over the last 30 days; it should help you build a better keyword and Best Bet topology.

The Search Results report contains at least the following information:

- *Search results top destination pages:* Use this report to learn what the most popular destinations are so that you can properly include those sites in your relevance settings.

- *Queries with zero results:* Use this report to learn about how to educate your users on executing better queries and how to build out your content source topology should your users be consistently looking for information in the index that isn't there.

- *Most clicked Best Bets:* Use this report to see what the most popular Best Bets are and ensure that those sites are included in your relevance settings.

- *Queries with zero Best Bets:* If there are many queries for a given term that don't have Best Bets, use this report to help build some Best Bets that will help users find what they are looking for faster.

Working with Keywords and Best Bets

Keywords are query terms to which we tether Best Bet locations so that when a keyword is used in a query term, the Best Bet location appears in the Best Bet Web Part on the search results page. The purpose of Best Bets is to direct users to items the business has identified as most appropriate. For example, if a user enters "human resources" as a query phrase, a Best Bet pointing to the Human Resources policy manual might be a good idea, because it is a strong possibility that this person might be looking for policy information from the Human Resources department. Another Best Bet for this query would be the location of the Human Resource department's Intranet site. The Best Bets offer the user an alternative to the normal search query results.

Keywords and Best Bets are configured at the site collection level by the site collection administrator. They are not configured as part of the SSP nor are they transferable between site collections. To create new keywords and Best Bets, perform the following steps:

1. From the root site in a site collection, click Site Actions, point to Site Settings, and select Modify All Site Settings.

2. From the Site Collection administration menu, click the Search Keywords link. You are then presented with the Manage Keywords page, as shown in Figure 12-23.

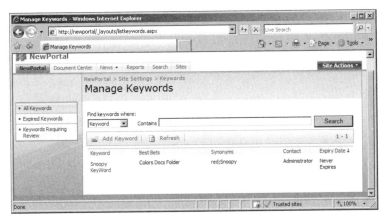

Figure 12-23   The Manage Keywords page.

3. Click the Add Keyword link. The Add Keyword page, as seen in Figure 12-24, then appears.

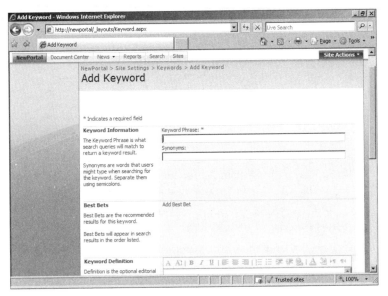

Figure 12-24   The Add Keyword page.

4. Enter a single keyword or a keyword phrase in the Keyword Phrase input box. What you enter here is what is matched to the query terms by SharePoint Server, and it is also the title of the keyword entry on the Manage Keywords page.

5. Enter any synonyms that you might want to include. The synonyms need not appear in the index, but additions or deletions to the synonyms are not realized in the result set until after the next full crawl of your content sources.

6. Click the Add Best Bet link. You are then presented with the Add Best Bet—Web Page Dialog box shown in Figure 12-25.

Figure 12-25   The Add Best Bet—Web Page Dialog box.

7. Enter a keyword definition that will help explain the keyword result in the result set.

8. Enter contact and publishing information and then click OK. You are then taken to the Manage Keyword page where you will see your new keyword entry.

9. Run a full crawl of all your content indexes so that they are made aware of your new keyword entry.

10. After your full crawls have been completed, go to the Search Center and execute a query using either the keyword that was entered in the Keyword Phrase or one of the synonyms. You should see a result set similar to that of Figure 12-26, where the Best Bet appears (by default) in the upper right-hand portion of the search result page.

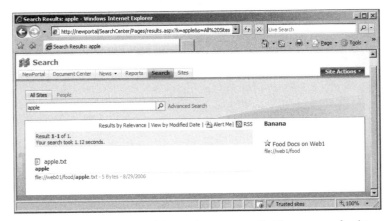

Figure 12-26   An illustration of the Apple query term that is a synonym for the Banana Best Bet.

Part IV
SharePoint Performance and Operations

Chapter 13

Scaling Out to a SharePoint Technologies Server Farm

The two primary reasons for scaling out a server farm are to achieve high availability and performance. For example, those looking for high availability need at least two Web front-end (WFE) servers, two application servers, and a clustered SQL Server back end. If performance is strictly the goal, you may have only a single four CPU SQL Server server with one very fast WFE server and one application server. Whatever your goal, it is important to note that the new versions of Windows SharePoint Services and Microsoft Office SharePoint Server do not have as many limitations regarding scaling and topology choices as earlier versions. But this increased flexibility in server farm design may make it difficult for some administrators to design an appropriate physical and logical farm topology. If you are not sure how to design your specific server farm architecture, begin with a topology discussed in this chapter and simply change it to meet your needs. This chapter presents four examples of farm topologies: small, medium, large, and enterprise. Due to search limitations, Enterprise farms are covered only as SharePoint Server farms in this chapter.

Remember that these topologies are not concrete rules on which to build your specific implementation; they are simply real-world suggestions about where to begin. Most medium-scale and larger organizations would do well to begin with at least two WFE servers, an application server, and a clustered SQL Server implementation.

Preparing for Scaling Out to a Server Farm

If you plan to scale out to a farm, be sure to install SharePoint products first on the server that is destined to host the Central Administration Web application. This server could also host other applications such as Document Conversion or content indexing. You should also plan your network infrastructure in advance to provide the best level of service possible. A Gigabit Ethernet (Gig-E) network infrastructure should be considered the minimum in most enterprise farm scenarios, but 100 Base-T network speeds are sufficient in smaller farms. In addition, having multiple switches and using Network Interface Card (NIC) teaming, when possible, can add fault-tolerance to your solution.

When planning for a farm, be sure to include the SQL Server installation in the planning process because it will be the foundation for your new farm. If you have database administrators (DBAs) on staff, include them in the planning from the beginning. A poorly designed and implemented SQL Server installation can easily be the bottleneck in a SharePoint products server farm.

Windows SharePoint Services Farm Topology Examples

There are fewer limitations on scaling a Windows SharePoint Services 3.0 server farm than existed in SharePoint Services 2.0. This latest version gives you the ability to add servers in single-server increments and in many different configurations. Most implementations function quite nicely when one of the following farm topologies is used. Choosing another topology is quite possible, but give close attention to scaling out limitations of such services as search servers or Windows SharePoint Services Web application servers.

Small Farm

A small server farm consists of a WFE server that hosts all applications except SQL Server. This is one step up from a Basic or Standalone installation and usually adds performance because the SQL Server utilization is moved to a dedicated server. It also provides the foundation for scaling out at a later date. Depending on the number of processors, processor speed, the amount of memory in the server, and how many Web applications are running on the server, you should be able to service several hundred to several thousand users with a small farm topology. The minimum hardware for a small farm Web server or SQL Server is a dual 2.5-GHz processor, but dual 3.0-GHz processors are recommended. The WFE server should have at least 1 GB of memory, but this amount of memory only supports one or a very few Web applications. If you require multiple Web applications, 2 GB is the minimum amount of memory needed. Likewise, your SQL Server hardware should have at least 2 GB of memory, with 4 GB recommended. Figure 13-1 shows an example of a small farm.

User Requests   Web Front-End Server   Dedicated SQL Server
Application Server
Central Administration

Figure 13-1 A small farm consists of a single server hosting all applications, except SQL Server.

Medium Farm

In a medium farm topology, you may scale out further by adding additional WFE servers by installing an additional physical server into the farm and starting the Windows SharePoint Services Web application service from Central Administration > Operations > Services On Server. Be aware that simply adding another WFE server to the farm usually does not increase fault-tolerance. To increase fault-tolerance, you must implement load balancing using the Windows Server 2003 Network Load Balancing (NLB) service or install a hardware load-balancing solution. Scaling WFE servers is covered later in this chapter. In addition to adding WFE servers to a medium farm, you can also add multiple search servers to a farm. Figure 13-2 shows an example of a medium farm.

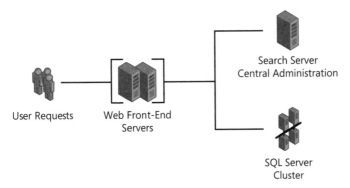

Search Server
Central Administration

User Requests   Web Front-End
Servers

SQL Server
Cluster

Figure 13-2   A medium farm has multiple WFE servers.

Large Farm

A large Windows SharePoint Services farm usually has multiple search servers and two SQL Server instances, as shown in Figure 13-3. Large server farms can service well over 100,000 users and complex collaborative implementations. Be careful when creating Windows SharePoint Service farms, however, because there are no automated publishing or content deployment features. In addition, there is no centralized search capability, and this search limitation in conjunction with the lack of content management and deployment functionality often forces organizations to upgrade to SharePoint Server 2007.

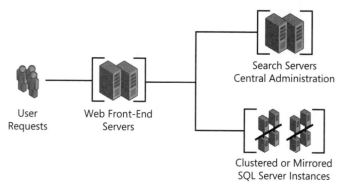

Figure 13-3   A large farm could have multiple SQL Server installations for performance.

SharePoint Server Farm Topology Examples

When purchasing SharePoint Server you gain several additional application services, also called server roles, such as Excel Calculation Services, Document Conversions, and separated Indexing and Query services. With this added functionality and flexibility, however, you can create a topology that functions poorly or not at all. Therefore, it is a wise idea to start with one of the following tested server farm topologies and modify as necessary.

Small Farm

A small SharePoint Server farm is identical to a small Windows SharePoint Services farm, except that additional service demand could be placed on the hardware, as is the case with Excel Calculation Services or Document Conversions. For environments other than development and testing, you should consider a medium farm or larger if you require such services as Excel Calculation Services or Document Conversions. A small SharePoint Server farm can be a good starting place for departments or small organizations. Remember, only use the services you need, and only scale out with additional servers when necessary.

Medium Farm

A medium farm should be considered the minimum configuration for those desiring a highly available solution. A medium farm provides at least two WFE servers, one application server hosting any combination of SharePoint Server applications, and a dedicated SQL Server. If you require high availability for your applications servers as well, you should have an additional application server hosting Excel Calculation Services, Document Conversions, and Indexing. In a medium farm, you might dedicate one server to a specific SharePoint Server role, such as Excel Calculation Services. If possible, clustering your SQL Server installation is also advisable when building a medium server farm topology. Figure 13-4 shows an example of a beginning medium farm server topology when using two WFE servers.

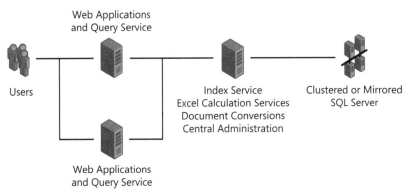

Figure 13-4   Placing the Query service on both WFE servers provides redundancy for searching should the Index server fail.

As seen in Figure 13-4, the Query role is enabled on both WFE servers. Although scaling out Search and Indexing is covered in more detail later in this chapter, an important design feature is that the Index server copies the indexes to the Query servers. The Query servers, and not the Index server, actually answer user requests for searches. Therefore, the Index server could fail in this example, yet user searches would continue to function. Note that if you did not replace or repair the Index server, user searches results would eventually become inaccurate. In addition, you might have to move the Central Administration service in this example if Indexing or another application service impedes your ability to manage your server farm. This is often the case when Indexing CPU usage slows the Central Administration Web application to the point that Central Administration is unusable.

Large Farm

If you require dedicated servers for application services, such as Document Conversions, Indexing, Query, or Excel Calculation Services, you will need to implement some variation of a large SharePoint Server farm. There are many options available when scaling out, but be sure to test in a lab environment, rather than merely depending on your design in production. Figure 13-5 shows an example of a large server farm with dedicated Excel Calculation Services servers.

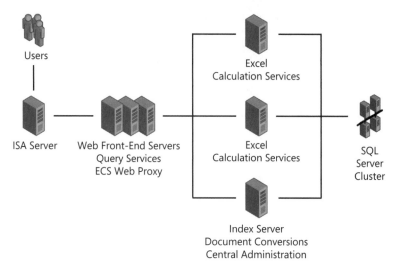

Figure 13-5   When moving Excel Calculation Services from the WFE servers, the WFE servers automatically proxy requests to the application servers.

You could also reverse the Query Services and Excel Calculation Services server roles in Figure 13-5 if you require dedicated Query Services. If you were to do this, then the search proxy service would send requests from the WFE servers to the Query servers. In addition, you cannot host Query Services on an Index server if you have more than one server hosting the Query Services role.

Enterprise Farm

The maximum ratio of WFE servers to SQL Server cluster is 8:1. Although it is possible to scale out beyond this point, doing so is neither recommended nor supported by product support services. This essentially limits you to eight WFE servers per Web application. However, you are not limited to eight WFE servers in a farm because you can have multiple SQL Server installations, each with a set of eight WFE servers. When you require throughput greater than that possible with eight WFE servers, you can add additional SQL Server clusters as required. But don't forget: only one SQL Server cluster can host your configuration database. The SQL Server cluster that hosts the configuration database should be monitored constantly for failure.

To add additional SQL Server clusters to your server farm, simply select a different SQL Server when creating a new content database. However, include a second SQL Server cluster only when absolutely necessary. Having more than one SQL Server clusters creates complexity in your server farm performance, disaster recovery, and troubleshooting. Figure 13-6 shows an example of a large server farm using two SQL Server clusters, with extreme scaling of all SharePoint Server services.

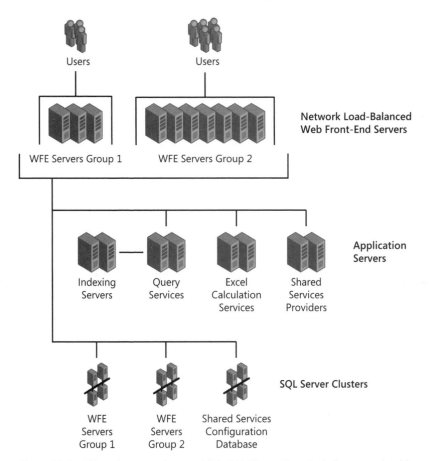

Figure 13-6   Although you can have multiple SQL Clusters in a single farm, you should only do so when absolutely necessary.

In the previous example, all WFE servers proxy Excel Calculation Services requests and search queries. In addition, there is a dedicated SQL Server cluster for Shared Services and the configuration database.

Scaling Out Windows SharePoint Services

There are far fewer concrete rules when creating a server farm topology than there were in Windows SharePoint Services 2.0 or SharePoint Portal Server 2003. As you progress through the next few sections, make design notes on the nuances of each individual service and how those will affect your design.

Adding Web Front-End Servers

When creating a Web application, you are actually creating an entry in the configuration database with Internet Information Services (IIS) information, a corresponding IIS virtual server, and a content database that will host the site collections within that Web application. However, assigned IP addresses, Secure Sockets Layer (SSL) certificates, and multiple host header entries are not created in the configuration database. In fact, you cannot add multiple host headers from Central Administration.

To scale out from a single WFE server that already hosts Web applications, you need to install Windows SharePoint Services on another server in the same domain. Preferably, you should scale to a server that is on the same IP subnet and that does not host any other applications. To add another WFE server, you must do the following:

1. Install Windows SharePoint Services using the installation binaries.

2. Choose to run the SharePoint Products and Technologies Configuration Wizard.

3. Select *Yes, I Want To Connect To An Existing Server Farm*.

4. Enter the SQL Server instance in which the server farm's configuration database exists.

5. Select the correct configuration database from the drop-down menu if multiple SharePoint products are installed into this SQL Server instance.

6. Click Finish after the wizard completes.

After adding a server to a farm, you will notice in IIS Manager that all IIS sites are created or are in the process of being created. If all Web applications in this server farm are not immediately present, wait until they have been created before continuing. If you are using host headers, then your Web applications are created automatically and can be used independently or can be added to a load-balancing solution. Remember, until you have made a DNS entry for your new servers or added them to a load-balanced solution, the new server will not be used for Web applications. If you did not select a load-balanced URL during the Web application creation, you must also create an Alternate Access Mapping for your newly created load-balanced URL. To ready the WFE servers for load balancing, do the following:

1. Open Central Administration > Operations > Alternate Access Mappings in a browser.

2. Select Add Internal URLs to create another mapped URL to the Default zone, or Edit Public URLs to create a new zone.

3. Choose the Alternate Access Mapping Collection (existing Web application) to which you wish to add an URL mapping.

4. Enter the URL, protocol, host, and port: for example, *http://portal.contoso.msft.*

5. Select a zone.

6. You should now see multiple mappings for a single Web application. Windows SharePoint Services Web applications do not return data to a client request without an Access Mapping matching the requesting URL.

It is important to understand that, by default, every Web application exists on every server in the farm. If you wish to serve Web applications on isolated hardware, simply exclude the specific Web application you do not wish to serve from this server in DNS or load-balancing solutions. For example, if you had three Web applications in a farm named *http://portal, http://mysite,* and *http://corporate,* but you wished to serve the first two from an internal set of servers and the *http://corporate* site from dedicated, Internet-facing hardware, your solution might look like that shown in Figure 13-7.

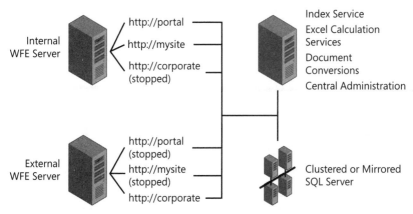

Figure 13-7   Simply turn off the server in IIS Manager and do not include it in DNS or load- balancing solutions when you wish not to serve specific Web applications on a server.

In the previous example, we would stop the unused Web applications in IIS Manager on servers, which would reduce the amount of memory used on those servers in addition to verifying IP traffic flow. When using this topology, understand that if this server is restored or if you stop, start, or restart the Windows SharePoint Services Web application service from Central Administration, all servers in the farm will start all Web applications in IIS. This feature must be planned for, should there be a need to modify Web applications from Central Administration.

Web Parts and Custom Code

If you install additional applications, such as Antivirus or custom Web Parts, be sure to install them on all of the necessary servers in the farm. Forgetting to install a custom Web Part on a WFE server, for example, could result in an inconsistent user experience in which it works for users on one WFE server, but not for the users on another. Here is a short list of items that are often forgotten when adding servers to a server farm:

- Custom Web Parts

- Web.config modifications

- Language packs

- SharePoint Technologies Antivirus program

- iFilters for indexing and crawling, which must exist on all WFE servers in the farm, by default

- Icons for non-native documents, such as Adobe Acrobat PDF documents

- SSL certificates

- Client certificates for crawling certificate-based SSL content sources, which must exist on all WFE servers in the farm

- Third-party backup and restore software

Real World   When scaling to multiple WFE servers, it is useful to use Solutions to deploy custom Web Parts, Web.config modifications, and other customized content. Solutions allow custom code to be deployed and synchronized on all the servers in the farm. The solution (.wsp) file is CAB based and contains all of the information necessary to install the custom code and to register it as a safe control. The first step in deploying a solution is adding the solution to the single, central repository for your farm's solutions—the Solution Store. To see a list of all solutions in the Solution Store, use the command *stsadm.exe -o enumsolutions.* To add a file to the Solution Store, use the command *stsadm -o addsolution -filename <filename path>.* When you replace or add a WFE server to the farm, you can now re-deploy your solutions manually, or automatically using a timer job. To deploy solutions from the command line, execute *stsadm.exe -o deploysolution.* They may also be deployed by navigating to Central Administration > Operations > Global Configuration > Solution Management. You can also retract solutions using the command *stsadm.exe -o retractsolution.*

Additional information is available at http://msdn2.microsoft.com/en-us/library/aa544500.aspx *and* http://msdn2.microsoft.com/en-us/library/aa981325.aspx.

Internet Information Services

As a general rule, it is best to perform any IIS metabase maintenance from the Central Administration console when possible. Changes that can be made from Central Administration persist throughout the farm because they are written to the configuration database and are present on all new or replaced servers in the farm. However, there are situations that require direct IIS management, such as installing SSL certificates or implementations requiring load balancing using assigned IP addresses to accomplish IP traffic management. Using assigned IP addresses makes it easier to use hardware load balancing and use dedicated NICs for Web applications. For example, if you had two Web applications in your Windows SharePoint Services farm, you could assign each Web application a different IP address, with each IP address assigned to a dedicated NIC. Figure 13-8 shows the logical flow of such a setup.

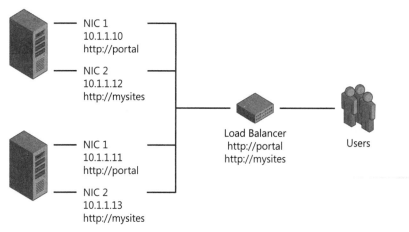

Figure 13-8   Assign an IP address to each NIC and the corresponding IP to each Web application in IIS Manager.

Configuring Multiple Windows SharePoint Services Search Servers

You can enable the Windows SharePoint Services Search service on multiple servers in your server farm. This allows you to scale your search architecture and improve search performance on large server farms. Simply add a server to the farm and enable the Windows SharePoint Services Search service on new servers. Be aware that Windows SharePoint Services Search is enabled on a per-content database basis, not per Web application. Figure 13-9 shows an example of adding multiple search servers to a server farm.

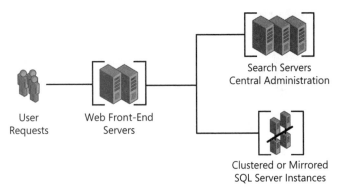

Figure 13-9   You can add Search servers to increase search and indexing performance in large Windows SharePoint Services farms.

To add additional Windows SharePoint Services search servers to a farm, simply start the Search service on another server in the farm. By default, existing content databases will not use the newly added search server. You must change the Windows SharePoint Services search server association from Central Administration > Application Management > Content Databases > Manage Content Database Settings. Select the new search server in the drop-down menu.

Scaling Out SharePoint Server

A SharePoint Server farm is defined by a common configuration database. When installing an additional server into a SharePoint Server farm, you must do the following:

1. Run the SharePoint Server installation binaries.

2. Choose an Advanced install.

3. Choose Complete—Install All Components. You can add servers to form a SharePoint farm.

4. Select Install Now.

5. When asked, check the box to run the SharePoint Products and Technologies Installation Wizard and choose Next.

6. When asked, select *Yes I Want To Connect To An Existing Farm.*

7. Enter the SQL Server instance hosting the farm's configuration database.

8. From the drop-down menu, select the correct configuration database.

9. Do not select Advanced unless you wish to move the Central Administration Web application to the server currently being configured. If you choose this option, Central Administration will no longer be available on the first server in the farm.

10. Choose Finish when the wizard is completed.

Adding Web Front-End Servers

When using SharePoint Server WFE servers, you have the ability to assign additional server roles to the system. Many medium and larger farm topologies include the Query service on your WFE servers. This is a good practice, unless the Query service demands more processing capability than your WFE server hardware can sustain. SharePoint Server is very flexible, however, so you may always add an additional server to the farm to offload application services if performance declines as a result of the shared hardware.

> **Tip**   If you want to assign IP addresses to an IIS Web application without using host headers, you must make additional configuration changes in IIS Manager, as noted in the following support article: *http://support.microsoft.com/kb/927376*. This is also the case when using SSL certificates in Extranet or Internet scenarios.

Deploying Multiple SharePoint Server Query Servers

If you plan to implement more than one WFE server, it is a good idea in medium to large farm topologies to move the Query server role to at least two WFE servers. If you are using load balancing, you should try to have identical server roles on each WFE in the load-balanced cluster. The Query service would then be started on each WFE server in that cluster.

> **Important**   If you have more than one Query Server, the Index server cannot simultaneously serve Query and Index services.

If multiple Index servers are being served by their respective multiple Shared Services Providers, then the content indexes from all Index servers are copied to all Query servers in the farm. Because Query servers contain a copy of all indexes in the farm, you must prepare for the required file system space by calculating the total space of all of the indexes in your farm, with at least 50% extra room for growth or index rebuilds. The Query server role is a subset of Search server and is an option when starting the Search service from Central Administration. To enable the Query role on a server, you must take the following steps.

1. Install all binaries and complete an Advanced installation with the Complete option.

2. Successfully complete the SharePoint Products and Technologies Wizard.

3. Open Central Administration. From the bottom of the Home screen, select the newly added server in the Farm Topology Web Part.

4. On opening the Farm Topology configuration screen, select the Office Share-Point Server Search hyperlink under Service, or select the Start hyperlink.

5. Select *Use This Server For Serving Search Queries*. Do not select *Use This Server For Indexing Content*.

6. You can change the Farm Search Service Account, but using the same account (default and pre-populated) that was used for Indexing is recommended.

7. Specify the index file location. This location must be shared, via NetBIOS, so the indexes can be propagated from the Index server(s). If you have very large indexes, seriously consider moving this location to a drive other than the system drive. Figure 13-10 shows an example of the interface.

8. Next, you must enter credentials to create a network share to this directory.

9. Click OK.

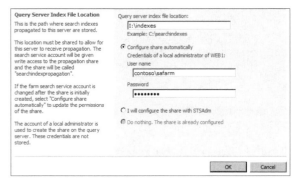

Figure 13-10   You should change the index file location to suit your specific requirements.

Although it is usually unnecessary, you may create the directory and share before con-figuring the Query service. If you decide to do so, the NTFS permissions must allow the Index service account and the server farm account, which should be the same in most farm configurations, to have everything but Full Control assigned. If you are unsure, the farm account is defined as the Central Administration Web application pool identity, and the Log On account for the Windows Server 2003 Service account Office SharePoint Server Search is the Index service account. You must also share the directory with Change permissions to the same two accounts. If neither Indexing nor Query server roles have been enabled for this server, you cannot use the *stsadm -o osearch* command.

> **Tip**   To change the index or propagation directories from the command line:
>
> ```
> stsadm -o osearch -role Query -farmcontactemail <email>
> -farmserviceaccount <DOMAIN\username>
> -farmservicepassword <password> -propagationlocation <directory>
> ```

Deploying Multiple SharePoint Server Index Servers

If you have a single Shared Services Provider (SSP), adding an additional Index server to the farm is pointless; an SSP can only use one Index server. The purpose of creating additional Index servers in a farm is to dedicate indexing resources for multiple SSPs. Conversely, you do not need additional Index servers to serve additional intra-farm SSPs. Multiple intra-farm SSPs can use a single Index server. Consider the following points when adding additional Index servers:

- The index on an Index server is managed by a Shared Services Provider.

- One hundred million documents is the maximum recommended limit for a single content index.

- There is one index per Shared Services Provider; thus a Shared Services Provider cannot make use of multiple Index servers.

- Two separate SharePoint Server farms cannot use the same Index server because an Index server cannot be connected to two separate configuration databases.

- To increase Indexing capability, you must add additional processors, memory, network interface cards, or a combination thereof. Otherwise, you must create an additional SSP. Doing so creates a considerable amount of complexity in your design because you now have multiple user profiles, search databases, audiences, Business Data Catalogs, and a complex My Sites configuration.

- Multiple intra-farm Shared Services Providers can share a single Index server. Therefore, the only reason to create multiple Index servers is for isolated security, inter-farm SSPs, or intra-farm SSP indexing performance.

See the section "Creating Multiple Shared Services Providers" at the end of this chapter for more information on intra-farm and inter-farm SSPs.

Create an additional Index server only when absolutely required. If you decide to add an Index server, you must do the following:

1. Successfully run an Advanced and Complete installation from the SharePoint Server binaries.

2. On opening Central Administration, select the new Index server in the Farm Topology Web Part.

3. In the Service list, select the Office SharePoint Server Search hyperlink, or choose Start.

4. Do not select *Use This Server For Serving Search Queries.*

5. Do select *Use This Server For Indexing Content.*

6. Enter the Farm Search Service account and password. This is preferably the server farm account, which is the application pool identity for the Central Administration Web application.

7. You cannot change the default index file location. That is defined by each individual Shared Services Provider.

8. You must select the Indexer Performance. If no other services are to be served on this hardware, consider selecting Maximum. One caveat to selecting Maximum is the possibility of overwhelming content sources if you intend to build a large content index.

9. Decide whether to use all WFE servers for crawling or to dedicate crawling to a single server. Only dedicate crawling to a single WFE server in small farm topology or in highly specialized implementations.

10. Click OK.

After adding an Index server to the farm, you must configure a new or existing Shared Services Provider to use this Index server. Be aware that changing the Index server for a given SSP does not move the Indexes to the new server. You must re-crawl all of the content sources defined in the SSP before restoring full search functionality. To associate an existing SSP with your new Index server you must follow these steps:

1. Open Central Administration.

2. Browse to Central Administration > Application Management > Manage This Farm's Shared Services.

3. Hover the mouse cursor over the Shared Services Provider you wish to modify, as shown in Figure 13-11.

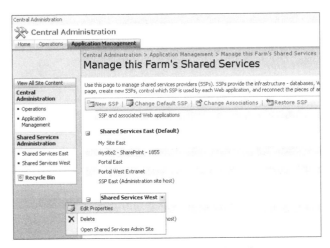

Figure 13-11   Select Edit Properties from the drop-down menu.

4. Select Edit Properties from the drop-down menu.

5. Scroll down to the Index Server section.

6. From the drop-down menu, select the new Index server from the list, as shown in Figure 13-12.

Figure 13-12   Choose the new Index server in the drop-down menu.

7. Change the default path for the index file location. This should match the name of the Shared Services Provider, as shown in Figure 13-12.

8. Click OK.

9. From Central Administration > Application Management > Manage This Farm's Shared Services, select the Shared Services Provider using the new Index server.

10. From Shared Services Administration, select Search Settings.

11. In Search Settings, select Content sources and crawl schedules.

12. Click on Start All Crawls, as shown in Figure 13-13.

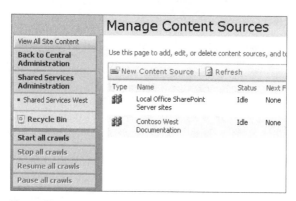

Figure 13-13   You can start crawls individually, or select Start All Crawls to build the index.

Scaling SharePoint Server Excel Calculation Services

For the most part, scaling out Excel Calculation Services is an easy process. Simply add another server to the farm, or choose an existing low-use system and enable Excel Calculation Services.

Be aware that a highly used Excel Calculation Services server can consume 100% of a system's CPU and network bandwidth. For this reason, it is important to monitor the usage of any multirole server that is serving Excel Calculation Services. For example, if you ran this service on your WFE servers, they would function normally until the Excel Calculation Service consumed enough CPU to slow Web content rendering. If this happens, you need to add another server to the farm to host Excel Calculation Services.

WFE servers, by default, proxy all Excel Calculation Services requests to Excel Calculation Services servers. The Web proxy service performs the load balancing in the Excel Calculation Services architecture. The Web proxy uses a proprietary load-balancing technique to identify the correct server to process the requests and to direct requests to cached information. This allows frequently requested workbooks to be served from the Excel Calculation Services server that last answered an identical request. The Web proxy can load balance multiple, separate workbook calculations across multiple Excel Calculation Services servers, but it cannot load balance a single calculation.

Figure 13-14 shows the logical architecture of Excel Calculation Services when co-hosted on a server servicing the Index role.

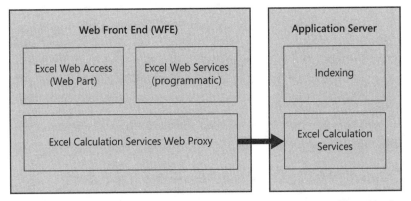

Figure 13-14   The Excel Calculation Services Web Proxy communicates with and load balances Excel Calculation Services.

To add an Excel Calculation Services server to the farm, you must do the following:

1. Successfully run an Advanced and Complete installation from the SharePoint Server binaries.

2. On opening Central Administration, select the new server to host Excel Calculation Services in the Farm Topology Web Part.

3. In the Service list, select Start next to the Excel Calculation Services hyperlink.

For more information on Excel Calculation Services architecture, visit http://msdn2.microsoft.com/en-us/library/ aa972194.aspx#Office2007ExcelServicesOverview_ArchitectureDeployment.

Adding and Load Balancing Document Converter Services

If your organization will use Document Conversion extensively, you should consider adding servers to your farm to process the additional load. To load balance the Document Converter process, you must enable two services:

- **Document Conversion Launcher Service**   The launcher service communicates with the WFE server and initiates the conversion request to the load-balancer service, if it is started. If the load-balancer service is not started, the document conversion is handled on the first Document Conversion Launcher service in the farm. The Document Conversion Launcher service can co-exist with any other server role in the farm.

■ **Document Conversion Load Balancer Service**   The load-balancer service maintains the state of document converters in the farm and routes the conversion request appropriately. This communication is via http and is in the form of a URI (uniform resource identifier), very much like a URL (uniform resource locator).

To enable Document Conversion load balancing, start the Document Conversion Load Balancer Service from Central Administration on a lightly used application server in the farm. You may then enable the Document Conversion Launcher service on any server in the farm. If needed, you may install additional servers into the farm for the specific purpose of document conversion.

Creating Multiple Shared Services Providers

Much like Active Directory forests, you should only add a second Shared Services Provider (SSP) when absolutely necessary. Adding another SSP greatly increases the complexity of your overall design. For example, adding a second SSP infers the creation of another user profile database, Search services, My Sites host, and much more. However, there are a few reasons to create multiple SSPs:

■ Legal, regulatory, or government regulation

■ Geographic dispersal: you cannot use intra-farm Shared Services over a Wide Area Network (WAN) link with a delay greater than 80 ms.

■ Indexing limitations, such as geographic, size, or WAN latency

■ Extranet or Internet needs, such as an Extranet portal or Internet publishing site

■ SharePoint hosting solutions

Although many of the limitations of creating multiple SSPs can be overcome, doing so is usually not worth the administrative effort or financial expenditure. If you require additional SharePoint Server farms you should consider inter-farm shared services, covered later in this chapter. If you choose to create multiple SSPs, consider the following items:

■ **User profiles and properties**   Creating a second SSP gives you a second set of user profiles. If the second SSP is in the same server farm, you can import the same user profiles again, if needed. Obviously, this increases the processor and disk usage of both the directory controller and SSP Web application.

■ **My Sites**   By default, creating a second SSP creates another set of My Sites. You should plan for using a single My Site Web application even if using multiple SSPs. Creating multiple My Site providers is covered at the end of this chapter.

■ **Indexing**   Creating another SSP also creates a second index. Although this index can exist on the same Index server as the first SSP, a single index cannot be shared between SSPs. For this reason, you must crawl all content twice if you wish it to exist in both SSPs. Creating a second content index can dramatically increase the complexity of your SharePoint Server implementation and should be avoided.

- **Search scopes**   All of the search scopes you created in your first SSP will not be visible in the second SSP. There is no way to synchronize or copy these search scopes. If the same scopes need to exist in the second SSP, they must be re-created.

- **Audiences**   Like search scopes, audiences cannot be shared between SSPs.

- **Excel Calculation Services**   Excel Calculation Services can only be shared intra-farm. When creating a second server farm, you must enable Excel Calculation Services locally on that farm if required.

Intra-Farm Shared Services

By default, all Shared Services within a SharePoint Server farm are considered to be intra-farm. Any Web application within that server farm can be associated with that SSP and therefore consume services. If multiple Shared Services Providers and the associated Web applications share a common configuration database (configDB), they are also referred to as Intra-farm Shared Services. Multiple Intra-farm Shared Services do not provide absolute process isolation, but can be useful when creating a second index server or isolating user profiles and audiences. Generally speaking, creating multiple Intra-farm Shared Services Providers does not add performance to a SharePoint Server farm. A few reasons for creating multiple Intra-farm SSPs are as follows:

- Regulatory or legal requirements, such as HIPAA, Sarbanes-Oxley, or legal case isolation. For example, many Records Centers use a second Intra-farm SSP to search and index official files and official file status.

- Specialized indexing requirements, as is the case with ISPs.

- Intranet and Extranet separations. For example, you might have one SSP to service indexing, audiences, and profiles for your internal users while having a second SSP to serve only indexing to your external users. This is useful when you do not wish to expose your internal content via search to external users.

Inter-Farm Shared Services

Inter-farm Shared Services are necessary when a second farm is required. If possible, you should consume Shared Services from a centrally located SSP. This simplifies your implementation by having a single place for user profiles and properties, one set of audiences and search scopes, and a single content index. However, there is one service that cannot be shared: Excel Calculation Services. When consuming Shared Services from another SharePoint Server farm, you are prompted to choose the local Intra-farm

Shared Services Provider to use for Excel Calculation Services. For this reason, there must be a default Shared Services Provider in every SharePoint Server farm, even when consuming Shared Services from another farm. A few reasons for implementing Inter-farm Shared Services are as follows:

■ Absolute security and process isolation

■ Implementing Portable SharePoint Server farms: for example, a SharePoint Server farm might move geographically inside a large insurance company that services customers affected by natural disasters.

■ Geographic: Intra-farm Shared Services must be at LAN speeds.

Caution   Inter-farm Shared Services should not exceed 80-ms network delays. Longer delays might work, but are not recommended or supported.

Configuring Multiple My Site Providers

By default, you have a single My Site Web provider per SSP. Remember that a dedicated Web application is recommended; *http://mysite.contoso.com,* for example. A common reason for creating multiple My Site Web applications might be to enable regional access to a often used My Site Web application while retaining the best practice of a single Shared Services Provider. This is called Global My Site deployments in SharePoint Server 2007 and allows a single My Site per user, but the My Site Web application can be shared by multiple SSPs. If you have multiple My Site providers associated with a single SSP, you must use audiences to direct the users. A My Site provider is a Web application that is managed by an SSP. A single SSP can direct users, based on audiences, to multiple My Site Providers. Because a My Site provider must be managed by an SSP, you must have SharePoint Server 2007 installed on the destination farm to host a My Site provider. To enable multiple My Site Web applications (providers), do the following:

1. Create the My Site Web application in the desired SharePoint Server farm.

2. Apply the My Site Host site collection template, preferably in the root of a dedicated Web application to host My Sites.

3. On the server farm you wish to configure for multiple My Site trusted hosts, go to SSP Administration > My Site Settings.

4. Under the Multiple Deployments section, select Enable My Site to support global deployment.

5. From the same SSP Administration home page, browse to Trusted My Site Host Locations.

6. From the New drop-down menu, select New Item.

7. You must enter in an URL; the description is optional.

8. Most likely, you will want to enter a target audience. This can be an Active Directory Security or Distribution list, or a SSP Global Audience.

If a user is in more than one My Site Trusted Location audience, he or she is directed to the first one in the list. Select Change Order from the Actions drop-down menu to change the order. In addition, a user in multiple My Site audiences is directed to the next available My Site provider upon creation, should the first one in the list be unavailable.

Chapter 14

Backup and Restore of SharePoint Products and Technologies

The new versions of Windows SharePoint Services and SharePoint Server include improved tools for backing up and restoring content. Most notably, they give you the ability to back up and restore the entire farm from the command line. This allows for the automated scripting and scheduling in Windows Server 2003 for enterprise-level SharePoint Products backups. Yet, to complete successfully a backup of your Share-Point Products Web applications and associated content, you are still required to use additional tools, such as the Internet Information Services (IIS) configuration backup and restore tool. The backup and restore features of SharePoint Products does both content recovery and disaster recovery as follows:

- Content recovery
    - ❑ Document Versioning
    - ❑ Recycle Bin
    - ❑ *Stsadm.exe -o [import | export]* (site migration tool)
- Disaster recovery
    - ❑ Central Administration Graphical User Interface (GUI) Backup And Restore
    - ❑ *Stsadm.exe -o [backup | restore]* (site collection backup and restore)
    - ❑ *Stsadm.exe -o [backup | restore] -directory* (catastrophic backup and restore)

Many organizations require a combination of these backup methods to ensure a fully restored and functional server farm in the event of a disaster. The following items must be backed up and are discussed within this chapter:

- Complete operating system backups of all servers in the farm

- Individual IIS Metabase backups

- All InetPub folders when modifying IIS directories, as is the case with the Web.config file

- Indexes and associated Shared Services Provider Search database

- Web application configuration not stored in the configuration database (SSL certificates, assigned IP addresses, multiple host headers)

Content Recovery

Always use a content recovery method before using a disaster recovery method because it lessens the impact on other users. For example, using a site collection restore method for a single user's deleted file would overwrite everyone else's content as well, because you must overwrite the entire site collection when restoring. Start with the simplest method and progress as required to restore content. Depending on the severity of the file loss, corruption, or deletion, there are three native tools available to restore content to a usable state: document versioning, using the Recycle Bin, and using the migration tool.

Document Versioning

An often overlooked method of restoring content is the native document versioning. When a user calls you or your Helpdesk about a corrupted file, always check the document library and try to restore the last version if possible. For this reason, always store at least a few Major Versions of a document. To enable Major Versioning for a document library, do the following:

1. From the Document Library Settings menu, select Document Library Settings.

2. Under the General Settings column, select Versioning Settings.

3. At a minimum, select Create Major Versions, as shown in Figure 14-1. If disk space is of concern, limit the number of Major Versions to be retained. Selecting at least two Major Versions will give you some comfort room should a file corruption occur.

4. Click OK.

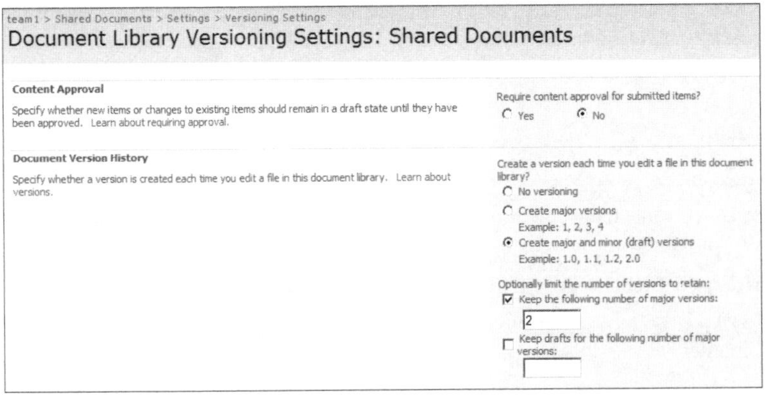

Figure 14-1   You should select at least two Major Versions for every document library if you want to use versioning as a content recovery method.

Configuring the Recycle Bin

One of the most useful and anticipated features of both Windows SharePoint Services and SharePoint Server is the Recycle Bin. Although most small to medium organizations can function quite nicely with the out-of-the-box settings, larger organizations will want to finely tune the Recycle Bin to prevent problems. Before configuring your Recycle Bin settings, it is important to understand that the Recycle Bin retention policies are set in Central Administration on a per-Web application basis. The actual management of deleted content, however, is performed on a per-site collection basis. This feature allows site collection administrators to manage deleted content, but does not give them the ability to modify retention settings.

In its default state, the Recycle Bin has two stages: First Stage (user deleted) and Second Stage (administrator/system deleted). The settings for these are not as straightforward as they appear and can have a wide-ranging system impact if not thought out and configured carefully.

Configuring the Recycle Bin Global Settings

Configure the Recycle Bin from Central Administration > Application Management > Web Application General Settings. Figure 14-2 shows an example of the Recycle Bin settings in Central Administration.

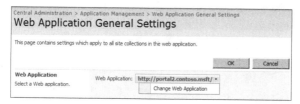

Figure 14-2   Verify that you are in the correct Web application before changing Recycle Bin settings.

Modifying the Global Recycle Bin Settings for a Web Application

1. From Web Application General Settings, select the Web application you want to modify.

2. At the bottom of the Web Application General Settings interface, verify that the Recycle Bin Status is set to On.

3. Select the number of days that items should remain in the Recycle Bin before they are deleted.

4. Optionally, turn off time-based deletion. If this is selected, then items are only moved from the first stage when a user manually empties his or her Recycle Bin, and items are only automatically emptied from the second stage if a Site Quota is used and % Of Quota is defined. Changing the Recycle Bin expiration policy to Never does not turn off the first stage of the Recycle Bin. In fact, the first stage is not configurable.

It is important to note that contents deleted to the first stage of the Recycle Bin count against the site quota and individual quota. If you do not set a site quota, there is no maximum size limitation on the first-stage Recycle Bin. It is only constrained by the number of days you set.

> **Caution**   If you turn the Recycle Bin off for a Web application and click OK, all Recycle Bins in that Web application, in both the first and second stage, are emptied. Although this action is useful for resolving an immediate low disk space situation, it should generally be avoided.

Configuring the Second Stage of the Recycle Bin

When a user deletes an item, that item is moved into the second stage of the Recycle Bin. The second stage does not count against the site quota or individual quota. However, its size is limited to a percentage of site quota size or is unlimited if you do not use a site quota. The second stage uses the "first in, first out" methodology for deleting files. That is, once the maximum size for the second stage of the Recycle Bin is reached, the oldest file in the stage is deleted to make room for newly deleted content.

Configuring the Second Stage of the Recycle Bin

1. Open Central Administration > Application Management > Web Application General Settings.

2. Select and verify the Web application you want to modify.

3. At the bottom of the interface are shown the Recycle Bin settings.

4. Change the percentage of the live site quota for second-stage items. The default is 50%, but a better starting point for most organizations is about 20% of live site quota. Depending on the amount of activity in your site collections, you may need to adjust this number to meet your needs. Figure 14-3 shows an example of both the global and second-stage settings of the Recycle Bin.

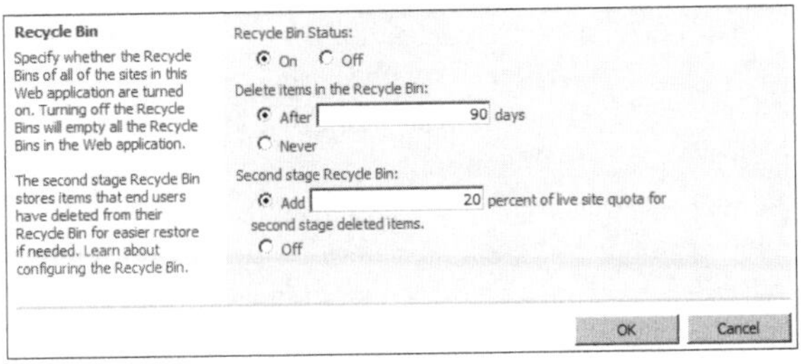

Figure 14-3   Consider 20% of live site quota for a second-stage starting point.

Optionally, you may turn off the second stage of the Recycle Bin. If you select this option, items removed in the first stage (user stage) of the Recycle Bin are deleted permanently. This option removes the ability for a site collection administrator to restore content that users have deleted from their Recycle Bin.

Important   Remember that you are *adding* the percentage of live site quota for a Web application when modifying the second stage. This means if you have designed your site quotas for 100-GB content databases, they can now grow to 150 GB to include the second stage.

Managing the Recycle Bin in a Site Collection

Site collection administrators manage content in both stages of the Recycle Bin from Site Actions > Site Settings > Site Collection Administration > Recycle Bin. In the Quick Launch, you can select which stage to manage. Checking an item in either stage and restoring that item will restore a full fidelity copy to its original location. This copy will include all versions and will be restored with the last user modified date, not the deleted or restored date. Figure 14-4 shows an example of both stages of the Recycle Bin management in a site collection.

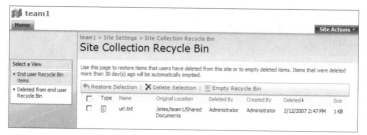

Figure 14-4   Click on a stage to manage deleted content for users.

Using the Migration Tool

The tool Smigrate.exe found in Windows SharePoint Services 2.0 and SharePoint Portal Server 2003 has been replaced and enhanced with the *stsadm.exe -o [import | export]* command-line options. The Stsadm.exe command is located in the C:\Program Files\Common Files\Microsoft Shared\Web Server Extensions\12\bin directory and is available in both Windows SharePoint Services and SharePoint Server. Both products support the creation of Content Migration Packages, which are XML files that allow sites and site collections to be imported and exported along with their dependencies, such as security features, user roles, workflows, and metadata. One major enhancement is the ability to migrate content including user permissions. This feature allows you to back up and restore single lists or items from a site collection or subsite and to include the associated user permissions. The following are examples of exporting and importing a site collection using Stsadm.exe:

```
stsadm.exe -o export -url
http://portal.contoso.msft/sites/team1
-filename c:\backups\team1.bak
-includeusersecurity -versions 3
```

```
stsadm.exe -o import -url
http://portal.contoso.msft/sites/team1
-filename c:\backups\team1.bak
-includeusersecurity -updateversions 1
```

In this example, the imported versions of objects were added to the existing objects, instead of overwriting them. In addition, all file permissions were retained. The SharePoint Products team does not recommend using command-line migration for bulk backup and restore because doing so is CPU intensive. Instead, use command-line migration to move content between farms, as when recovering content using an alternate server farm. Alternatively, some organizations script this command to back up high-profile sites and site collections.

> **Tip**   You can import and export subsites when using Stsadm.exe with the *-import* and *-export* parameters.. Doing so is not possible with Stsadm.exe using the *-o backup* and *-o restore* options.

When using *stsadm.exe -o export,* you can define the following parameters:

- **-url**   The *-url* parameter specifies the site collection to be exported; for instance, *http://portal.contoso.msft.*

- **-filename**   The export file is created with the name Filename.cmp, or you can specify a filename extension, such as .bak.

- **-overwrite**   This optional overwrite parameter causes previous export attempts to be overwritten. If the overwrite parameter is not used, both the .export.log file and the .cmp file from previous attempts must be deleted or the process will fail.

- **-includeusersecurity**   The optional *-includeusersecurity* parameter causes groups and group membership information to be included, as well as preserving timestamps, security information, and users.

- **-haltonwarning**   The optional *-haltonwarning* parameter stops execution when a warning is encountered.

- **-haltonfatalerror**   The optional parameter *-haltonfatalerror* stops execution when a fatal error occurs.

- **-nologfile**   The optional *-nologfile* parameter prevents the creation of a log file.

- **-versions**   The optional *-versions* parameter defines which versions of files and list items will be exported. There are four versioning options.

  1—Option 1 exports only the last major version for files and list items. This is the default setting.

  2—Option 2 exports the most current version, either major or minor.

  3—Option 3 exports both the last major and last minor versions.

  4—Option 4 exports all versions for file and list items.

- **-cabsize**   The *-cabsize* parameter specifies the maximum file size, in megabytes, for the Content Migration Package (.cmp) file. The default file size is 25 MB, and the maximum size is 1024 MB.

  Tip   To export content larger than the default 1024 MB limit, use Stsadm.exe to increase the default template size in bytes:

  ```
  stsadm -o setproperty -pn max-template-document-size -pv
  30000000
  ```

- **-nofilecompression**   In addition to not compressing the file, the optional *-nofilecompression* parameter causes a directory with the appropriate XML files to be created instead of a .cmp file.

> **Important**   You cannot import from an NTFS directory created with the nofilecompression option.

- **-quiet**   The optional -*quiet* parameter suppresses output to the console, except for a notification on completion.

When using *stsadm.exe -o import,* you can define the following parameters:

- **-url**   The URL parameter specifies where to import the Content Migration Package (.cmp) file to; for example, *http://portal.contoso.msft.*

- **-filename**   The filename parameter specifies the name of the file to import from.

- **-includeusersecurity**   The optional -*includeusersecurity* parameter causes groups, timestamps, security information, and user information to be imported.

- **-haltonwarning**   The optional -*haltonwarning* parameter stops execution when a warning is encountered.

- **-haltonfatalerror**   The optional -*haltonfatalerror* stops execution when a fatal error occurs.

- **-nologfile**   The optional -*nologfile* parameter suppresses the creation of a log file.

- **-updateversions**   The -*updateversion* parameter specifies how versions will be merged on import and has three options:

  1—Option 1, the default, adds new versions to those that already exist in the .cmp file.

  2—Option 2 overwrites the file and all its versions, keeping only those already in the destination.

  3—Option 3 causes files that already exist in the destination to be ignored.

- **-quiet**   The optional -*quiet* parameter suppresses output to the console except for a notification on completion.

Disaster Recovery

When content level recovery methods do not work or when you have a complete farm failure, disaster recovery methods should be used to restore content. Be aware that disaster recovery methods may cause a loss of data. For example, if you restore a content database from a previous night's backup, all content written to that database since that backup occurred will be lost. For this reason, always attempt a restore using a content recovery method first.

> **Note**   All native SharePoint Products tools must be backed up to a disk drive. You must use an additional backup program, such as Windows Server 2003 Backup or Restore, to move that content to tape.

Using Central Administration Backup and Restore

The new backup and restore tool for Windows SharePoint Services 3.0 and SharePoint Server 2007 is greatly improved over the last version. You now have the ability to restore entire farms, including the configuration database. The backup and restore tool even allows restoration to an alternate SQL Server instance to permit alternate server farm restoration and testing. Unfortunately, you still do not have the ability to back up to tape or schedule backups from the GUI. You access the GUI Backup interface from Central Administration > Operations > Backup And Restore > Perform A Backup, as shown in Figure 14-5. On opening the Perform A Backup Web page, you are presented with all of the available components that can be backed up.

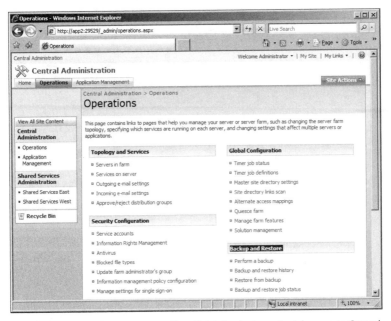

Figure 14-5 To back up or restore SharePoint Products content, browse to Central Administration > Operations > Backup And Restore.

In the following discussion, the term *items* refers to Web applications, content databases, SSPs, or content indexes and their associated search databases.

Performing a Farm-Level Backup from the GUI

1. Select the item you would like to back up. To back up the entire farm, check the box next to Farm, as shown in Figure 14-6.

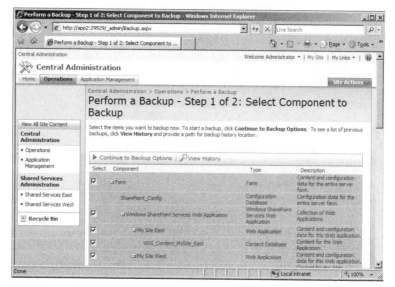

Figure 14-6 Select the component or set of components you want to back up.

2. After selecting the entire farm, all components should be highlighted.

3. Select Continue To Backup Operations.

4. If this is the first backup of the farm, check Full for the backup type.

> **Important** You cannot perform a differential backup of the farm until at least one full backup has occurred. You also cannot perform a differential backup after adding a content database or Web application. Whenever you add any of these components to the farm, you must run another full backup before a differential backup will be successful.

5. You must enter a location to back up to. You cannot back up to tape. The backup location should be in the same domain and shared. The following accounts should have write access to the NTFS directory and File Share:

   ❑ The account authenticated to Central Administration

   ❑ The Farm account (should be the Central Administration application pool identity)

   ❑ The SQL Server instance account, if you are using SQL authentication

❏   The SPTimer service account, which should be the farm account in most implementations

6. Select OK.

After selecting OK, the job is scheduled with Owstimer.exe (SPtimer). If your job should fail for any reason, you must *manually* delete the Timer Job Definition. Failing to do so prevents any further backup or restore from succeeding, whether the backup was initiated from the GUI or the command line.

Deleting a Failed Backup/Restore Job

1. Open Central Administration > Operations > Global Configuration > Timer Job Definitions.

2. Select Backup/Restore in the Title column.

3. Click on the Delete button.

Restoring Items from an Existing Backup

1. Open Central Administration > Operations > Backup And Restore > Restore From Backup.

2. Enter the location where the backup exists. There must be an Spbrtoc.xml file in the root of this backup location, or the restore will fail.

3. Select the backup that contains the item you wish to restore, and select Continue Restore Process. If you use multiple backup locations for disk management and do not see the correct backup listed, you may also change the directory from this interface from the menu.

4. From the Select Component To Restore screen, select the component to restore, such as an individual content database or an entire Web application that includes the IIS Virtual Server and associated content database(s).

5. Select Continue Restore Process.

6. Select the Type of restore you want to perform. You have two choices, as shown in Figure 14-7:

❏   Selecting New Configuration allows you to restore the Web application, content database, or both as a different name and thereby recover content. In addition, you can restore the content to a different SQL Server instance.

❏   The option Same Configuration actually means *Overwrite*. It completely overwrites any selected components, such as Web applications and content databases, with the backed-up content.

7. Select OK.

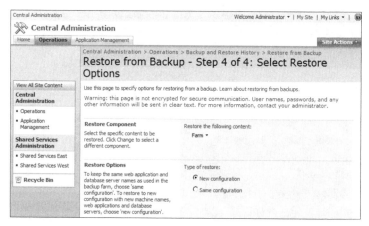

Figure 14-7   You must select New Configuration or Same Configuration to continue. Selecting Same Configuration overwrites your existing content.

If you choose to restore content to a different SQL Server instance or restore content databases with a different name to the same SQL Server instance, you must associate the content database with a Web application to retrieve the content. Never associate the restored content databases with Web applications that hosted the original content. Site collections, which are stored in those content databases, are assigned a unique identifier (UID) when created. UID conflicts are caused when associating restored content databases with a Web application with which the original content database is still associated. Therefore, always associate content databases that are restored, with the new option, to a different Web application from the one with which they were originally associated.

Important   The only time the configuration database is backed up is during a farm-level backup. The only way to restore the configuration database is by performing a farm-level restore.

Command-Line Farm-Level Backup and Restore

You can also back up your entire farm by using *stsadm.exe -o backup -directory*, also known as STSADM Catastrophic Mode. Using the *-directory* command-line option invokes additional options that you can use to back up the entire farm or individual items, such as Web applications or content databases. However, you cannot restore object-level items such as documents. Because you cannot schedule backup jobs from the Central Administration GUI, using the command line is the best way to reliably schedule backup jobs on your server farm. The following is an example of backing up an entire server farm using Stsadm.exe in Catastrophic Mode:

```
stsadm.exe -o backup -directory
\\backupservername\backups\ -backupmethod full
```

This example is the simplest form of backing up your entire server using the Full option. There are several optional parameters you can define when backing up, such as *-backupthreads,* that are useful and you may use them as well.

The parameters available using *stsadm.exe -o backup -directory* are as follows:

- **-item**   The *-item* option must be used in conjunction with the *-showtree* option. An item from the list generated by *showtree* must be specified and the command run again omitting the *showtree* parameter.

- **-percentage**   The *-percentage* parameter shows the progress increments on screen. For example, 10 would show the progress in 10% increments.

- **-backupthreads**   This value should be between 1 and 10. Be careful not to use high thread counts during content indexing or other system maintenance.

- **-showtree**   The *-showtree* parameter shows all items that can be backed up. This information can also be found in Central Administration Backup And Restore.

- **-quiet**   This option suppresses output and is used when scripting backups.

For example, the following command backs up a Web application named Portal and uses five CPU threads for the backup process:

```
stsadm -o backup -directory
\\backupservername\backups -backupmethod full
-item "Portal" -backupthreads 5 -quiet
```

Automating SharePoint Products and Technologies Backups

1. Create a batch file containing a tested command-line Catastrophic backup string, as shown previously.

2. Open Scheduled Tasks in Windows Server 2003 Control Panel.

3. Add a scheduled task, and click Next.

4. Select Browse and choose the batch file you created in step 1.

5. Name the Task; SharePoint Server backup, for example.

6. Select the frequency, usually Daily, and click Next.

7. Select the Start time. Be careful not to overlap with content indexing or other scheduled system maintenance.

8. Click Next.

9. Enter the username and password to execute the scheduled task. This user must have write access to the backup share destination and be a farm administrator.

10. Click Finish.

Restoring a Server Farm from a Farm-Level Backup

1. Find the backup ID either by running

```
stsadm.exe -o backuphistory -directory
\\backupserver\sharename -restore
```

   or by viewing the history in Central Administration > Operations > Backup And Restore > Backup And Restore History. Every backup or restore job is assigned a unique identifier.

2. From the 12 Hive\Bin directory, execute

```
stsadm.exe -o restore -directory
\\backupservername\sharename -restoremethod [ new | overwrite ]
-item <item>
```

   If you do not select the item, such as a Web application or content database, the entire farm is restored.

3. If prompted, you must enter the Web application pool identity and associated password for each component restored. Alternatively, you can define these in the script using the *-username* and *-password* command-line options.

4. After restoring components to a server farm, it is always a good idea to perform an IISReset on every server in the farm.

From the command line, you also have the option to select a new database server. For example, you would execute the following command to restore databases to a new SQL Server instance named DEV:

```
stsadm.exe -o restore -directory
\\backupservername\sharename -restoremethod new
-backupid <id> -newdatabaseserver DEV
```

Command-Line Site Collection Backup and Restore

If you used the previous versions of SharePoint Products, you may be familiar with the *stsadm.exe -o [backup | restore]* commands. Without the *-directory* option, Stsadm.exe backs up and restores site collections instead of farm-level components. Although using Stsadm.exe to back up and restore site collections does indeed do a complete backup of these site collections, it does not back up any configuration database information, content indexes, or search databases. It is possible to back up an SSP's site collection with Stsadm.exe, but the restoration will not be complete. For this reason, only use *stsadm.exe -o [backup | restore]* to back up and restore standard site collections.

To back up a site collection using Stsadm.exe, execute the following from the 12 Hive\Bin directory:

```
stsadm.exe -o backup -url <Site Collection URL>
-filename <backup file name>
```

The URL should include the site collection name—for example, *http://portal.contoso.msft/sites/accounting*—if accounting is a site collection. You can also include the *-overwrite* option if you wish to write to the same file repeatedly. This backup file can be restored to the same server farm or to another server farm.

To restore a site collection using Stsadm.exe, execute the following from the 12 Hive\Bin directory:

```
stsadm.exe -o restore -url <Site Collection URL>
-filename <backup file name>
```

Although it is possible to restore this site collection with a different URL, thus creating a cloned site collection in the original Web application, doing so introduces the possibility of a site collection ID conflict. When a site collection is created, it is assigned a Unique ID in the server farm. You should remove or overwrite the original site collection if you need to restore the backup to the same Web application.

Restoring Application Server Roles to the Farm

There may be times when you need to restore individual physical servers to a farm. Remember that most application server configuration data are stored in the configuration database. So, if the server farm is intact and you have only lost a single server, restoration is usually a simple matter. This section provides an overview of restoring a single physical application server to a farm.

Restoring Index Servers

Content indexes cannot be restored with an Window Server 2003 operating system backup and restore. The only way to restore content indexes is by using SharePoint Products Backup And Restore to restore the entire Shared Services Provider (SSP) that managed a single content index. Therefore, if multiple indexes existed on an Index server, you would have to restore each SSP that managed each of those individual content indexes. As part of this restore process, the associated Search database is restored as well. If either the content index or search database fails during restore, you must reset the index and re-crawl all content sources before search and indexing will resume successfully.

Resetting and Re-crawling All Content Sources After a Failure

1. Open Shared Services Provider Administration.

2. Open Search Settings.

3. Select Reset All Crawled Content, as shown at the bottom of Figure 14-8.

4. Open Content Sources And Crawl Schedules.

5. From the Quick Launch, select Start All Crawls.

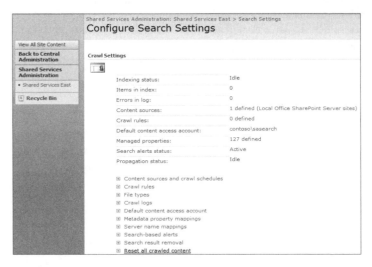

Figure 14-8 Resetting all crawled content does not automate the rebuilding of the content index.

If you use a third-party tool to back up your SharePoint Products implementation, it is still wise to use the native tools to back up your Shared Services Providers; doing so ensures the ability to restore your content indexes successfully. If your indexes are quite small, you can simply add a new index server to the farm, associate it with an SSP, and use the previous numbered list to re-crawl all content sources.

Restoring a Shared Services Provider and the Associated Content Index

1. Open Central Administration > Operations > Backup And Restore > Restore From Backup.

2. Select the backup location that contains the most recent backup of this SSP.

3. Select the desired existing backup, and choose Continue Restore Process from the menu.

4. Select the SSP that managed the content index you wish to restore.

5. Select Continue Restore Process from the menu.

6. Select either a New configuration or Same (overwrite) configuration. You will usually select the Same configuration.

   When selecting the Same configuration, you must enter the farm account's user-name and password and the SSP application pool identity username and pass-word when using SQL Server authentication. Otherwise, the restore process uses your currently logged-on account for authentication.

7. Click OK.

Restoring Query Servers

Query servers that are dedicated to the service are updated automatically after a server or server farm failure if the following are true:

- They connect to the server farm configuration database.

- The original index location exists.

- The file share for propagation is configured correctly.

If dedicated Query servers do not function after a failure, the simplest way to restore them is to remove the server from the farm, re-add the server to the farm, and follow the steps in Chapter 13, "Scaling Out to a SharePoint Technologies Server Farm," to add a Query server to a farm.

Generic Application Servers

The settings for Document Conversion Launcher Services, Document Conversions Load Balancer Service, and Excel Calculation Services server roles are stored in the configuration database. Therefore, simply adding any of these application servers back to a farm will re-enable them as application servers. Alternatively, you can rebuild these servers and run the SharePoint Products and Technologies Configuration Wizard to add them back to the server farm. Remember to enable the correct services in Central Administration > Operations > Topology And Services > Services On Server after running the wizard.

Likewise, the Windows SharePoint Services Help Search server can be restored in much the same manner. You can always select the Windows SharePoint Services Help content in a farm-level restore, but you may alternatively add a new server to the farm and enable it to service this role from the Farm Topology Web Part.

Backing Up Other Required Content

In addition to backing up all SharePoint Products content, you must also back up information that is not stored in the configuration or content databases. The following items must be backed up independently of your SharePoint Products and Technologies backups.

Operating System Files

Using the native Windows Server 2003 Backup or Restore tool, you can back up all files on the server including the system state. Verify in your complete operating system backup that you include the following:

- **System State**   Verify you are backing up the System State that includes the Certificate Store and system logs. These are required to restore a server to a functional state, should the server fail.

- **12 Hive** You must also verify you are backing up the 12 Hive at \Program Files\Common Files\Microsoft Shared\Web Server Extensions\12\. All customized site definitions and trace logs are located there.

- **SharePoint Server Binaries** Configuration items, such as your Search and Indexing noise word files and thesaurus files, are located in the \program files\Microsoft Office Servers\12.0\ directory.

- **Inetpub Folder(s)** By default, this folder is c:\inetpub\wwwroot. Wherever this folder resides, be sure to include it in your backups because the subdirectory \wss\VirtualDirectories includes all of your Web application specific information. For example, you may have modified the Web.config file in these directories to change authentication or allow a longer timeout for uploading large files.

IIS Metabase

You must back up the IIS Metabase on each Web front-end (WFE) server in the farm. The IIS Metabase includes such information as SSL certificates, assigned IP addresses, and multiple host headers. Because this information is not stored in the configuration database, it is not restored when using the native SharePoint Products backup and restore tools.

Backing Up the IIS Metabase

1. Open Internet Information Services (IIS) Manager from Start > All Programs, Administrative Tools.

2. Right-click on the server name and select All Tasks > Backup/Restore Configuration..., as shown in Figure 14-9.

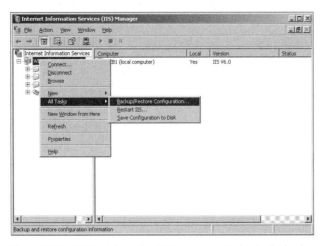

Figure 14-9 Right-click on the IIS Server name to begin the backup and restore process.

3. Select Create Backup.

4. Enter an easy-to-remember configuration backup name, such as the server name plus the backup date. For example, use WFE0106222007 for a server named WFE01 and a backup date of June 22, 2007.

5. Optionally, select Encrypt Backup Using Password. This allows the backup to become "portable," thus giving you the ability to restore the IIS Metabase to any server. Choose a simple password, such as PASSWORD, that is documented and all members of the IT staff know. This password is primarily for portability, not for security.

Note   If you wish to restore the IIS Metabase to another server, you must change or remove machine-specific information in the backup file. This process is explained in detail at *http://www.microsoft.com/technet/prodtechnol/windowsserver2003/library/ IIS/21972953-44d3-4177-b0d2-f8e2cdef2efd.mspx?mfr=true.*

Backing Up and Restoring the IIS Metabase from the Command Line

1. Either on *every* WFE server in the farm or on a centralized backup server, create a batch file with the command:

```
cscript.exe %systemroot%\system32\iisback.vbs
/backup /s Web1 /u administrator /p password
/b WeeklyBackup /v NEXT_VERSION /e backuppassword
```

2. In the previous command, *Web1* was the target server, *administrator* was the username, *password* was the username administrator's password, *WeeklyBackup* was the backup type, and *NEXT_VERSION* appended a version number, such as 2, to the backup name. Optionally, you may use the /*e* flag to include a backup password, thus making the backup portable.

3. Add as many lines to this batch file as necessary to back up all WFE servers in the farm. Each backup will reside in the respective WFE server's %systemroot%\system32\inetsrv\ directory.

4. Schedule this backup from the Windows Server 2003 Control Panel using Scheduled Tasks. Simply add a scheduled task by browsing to the batch file you just created and selecting the desired schedule. Verify that the username and password that will run the task have permissions both to back up the server farm and to have write access to each WFE server.

Chapter 15

Logging and Processing Analysis

Proper configuration of the native logging, auditing, reporting, and analysis tools allows you to maintain and continually improve your Windows SharePoint Services and SharePoint Server implementations. It is of particular importance to correctly configure logging and reporting in SharePoint Products, or you will have little data to troubleshoot in the event of a problem. Careful system monitoring can avert outages and is useful for quickly and accurately identifying and correcting problems should they arise. Note that, although it is important to maintain adequate system information, the amount of information can become overwhelming. Therefore, determine carefully and deliberately the levels of logging, auditing, reporting, and analysis you require because both too little and too much information can make interpretation difficult. Following is a list of the tools available to maintain and troubleshoot SharePoint Technologies:

- **System Monitor**   The System Monitor is useful for monitoring acute issues, such as memory utilization, CPU utilization, and disk I/O performance.

- **Counter Logs**   Counter Logs are ideal for long-term tracking of performance issues. They can be stored in an SQL database, which allows the data to be queried.

- **Alerts**   Alerts are triggered when critical values are met. They are useful for initiating monitoring or running other functions when a usage spike is encountered.

- **Trace Logs**   Trace Logs are useful when a server is severely affected or STOP errors are encountered.

- **Windows Event Logs**   Windows SharePoint Services and SharePoint Server are capable of sending events to the Windows Server Event Viewer, Eventvwr.exe. In fact, this is the most common method of routine monitoring and reporting of SharePoint Products.

Using Performance Monitor

All versions of Microsoft Windows Server include the basic set of tools required for successful performance monitoring. The most valuable native tool at your disposal is the Performance tool, which provides a core set of monitoring functions. The Performance tool can be found either by clicking on Start > All Programs > Administrative Tools > Performance, or from the Run prompt by typing **perfmon.exe** and ENTER. The default view of the Performance tool is System Monitor. When it opens you see the three default counters: Pages/Second, Average Disk Queue, and % of Processor Time.

System Monitor is the first view of the Performance tool and its most commonly used element. Figure 15-1 shows an example of the default view.

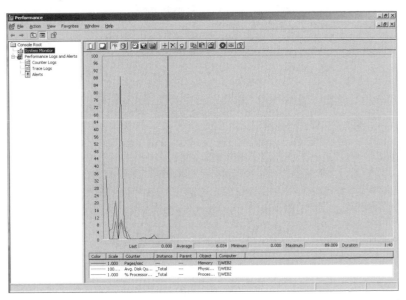

Figure 15-1   The default view of Windows System Monitor with Performance Logs And Alerts expanded.

Monitoring Performance Objects

1. To monitor a performance object, click on the "+" symbol on the tool bar and a new window will then open.

2. In the new window define the computer, object, counter, and instance properties for the performance counter. The instance property is not required. Many items do not have an instance or have only a default instance that will be chosen and grayed out.

3. Click Add to monitor the newly defined counter.

4. Repeat steps 1 and 2 to add multiple counters.

5. Click the Close button to return to the System Monitor window. There is no limit to the number of counters that can be added to System Monitor, but after six to eight counters the view becomes difficult to interpret.

Counter Logs

Counter Logs are located beneath the Performance Logs And Alerts heading of the Performance Monitor, as seen in Figure 15-2.

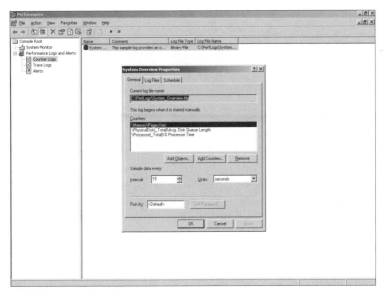

Figure 15-2   The Performance tool displayed with options for Counter Logs.

The Counter Logs are similar to the System Monitor, except that the output is sent to a file, rather than the screen. The same counters can be used, and it is possible to have multiple sets of counters monitoring at the same time. Monitoring Counter Logs adds several options, as explained in the following procedure.

Configuring Counter Logs

1. Click on Counter Logs in the left pane of the Perfmon.exe window.

2. Right-click on one of the items in the right pane and select New Log Settings.... Type in a name of your choice and click OK.

3. Click the Add Counters button.

4. Select the computer, object, counter, and instance properties for the counter. The instance property is not required.

5. Under the Log Files tab, specify the type of log file you want to use, such as text or binary. Binary is typically more size efficient, but can only be read by the Performance tool. Logging to a SQL Server can be very useful because it allows for queries on your log data and is the most space-efficient option.

6. Under the Schedule tab, you can set a schedule for the logging operation.

Trace Logs

Windows Server 2003 Trace Logs are not as configurable as counters and are therefore a less frequently used feature of the Performance tool. Trace Logs are meant to gather information from the system after the occurrence of a specific event. The events that trigger writing to a Trace Log are set by the system.

Trace Logs are typically used when there is a serious system problem that the Counter Logs are unable to record. Trace Logs use a lower level method of recording data that is less subject to system function interference. For example, if a certain type of network traffic is causing the system to crash, Counter Logs would not be able to gather data, but Trace Logs would.

SharePoint Products and Technologies provide rich trace logging, which is covered later in this chapter.

Alerts

Alerts help you know when servers are reaching high levels of utilization. Alerts can be set on any number of counter thresholds, and once those thresholds are met, Alerts can inform administrators in a variety of ways. If a counter or set of counters reaches a threshold, several actions can occur. Figure 15-3 shows the types of actions available to the systems administrator.

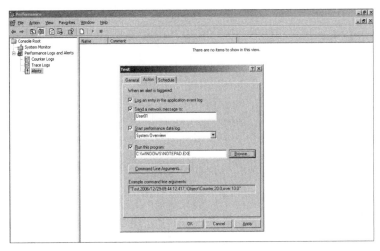

Figure 15-3   Alerts can send messages, start performance logging, and run programs.

Performance Monitoring Best Practices

As an administrator you are required to monitor performance issues with SharePoint Products and Technologies, SQL Server, Internet Information Services, Windows Server 2003, and the hardware on which they run. The complexity of the interaction between these systems can be daunting, but experience has shown that with careful, selective monitoring their actions can be understood and optimized. Use the following guidelines to help you identify the critical performance metrics for your installation.

Baselining Your Servers

Before you can analyze the performance of a system, you must develop its normal operational profile; before you can develop this profile, the system must be baselined. After you have a fully functional environment, you should start recording performance logs of your systems for at least 48 hours once a month. Many organizations already use Microsoft Operations Manager or a third-party tool that provides this functionality. It is imperative to record system performance in both peak and non-peak hours. Baseline information is indispensable when analyzing performance issues.

Windows Server 2003 Critical Counters

After determining the type of monitoring you require, you must define which elements need to be monitored. Several performance counters are invaluable in troubleshooting your environment. Select only those counters that are likely to be useful, because as the number of counters grows it becomes increasingly difficult to interpret their results.

Note   Counters are referred to in the following way: Object\Counter\Instance.

The types of counters that are salient to SharePoint Products and Technologies and the types of data that can be gathered from them are presented in this section.

- **Processor**   Monitors both individual and combined values for CPUs.

- **Memory**   Reports the details of the system's physical RAM.

- **Disk**   Returns details of both physical and logical disk information.

- **Network**   Returns details of the network hardware and protocol information.

- **WSS**   Gathers data on the core of the SharePoint Server.

- **OSS**   Reports on SharePoint Server functions, such as search and indexing.

- **SQL**   Monitors the database engine supporting SharePoint Products and Technologies.

Several specific counters are crucial when evaluating system performance issues. A description of the types of information they return and of the types of issues each can help resolve is presented next.

CPU

- **Processor\% Processor Time_Total**   Records current CPU utilization, which can be used to determine if a system is in need of additional processor capacity.

- **System\Processor Queue Length\(N/A)**   Logs the number of items waiting to be processed by the CPU(s). Values higher than 2 mean you should consider adding more or faster processors.

- **Processor\Interrupts\Sec**   Records the number of times that processing must stop to handle a hardware request for disk or memory I/O. Values in excess of 1,000 may indicate a hardware issue.

Memory

- **Memory\Pages/sec\(N\A)**   Monitors how much data are written to or read from memory. Values above 200 could mean the system is spending too much time writing out to disk or what is called a hard page fault. Consider increasing the amount of RAM.

- **Memory\Pages Faults/sec\(N\A)**   Records the number of times that a piece of data cannot be found in memory. Large numbers of page faults, defined as the number of drives multiplied by 4,096, mean that additional memory needs to be installed.

- **Memory\Available Mbytes\(N\A)**   Monitors the amount of memory available to the system in megabytes. If this number is consistently below 10% of your total physical memory, consider adding RAM.

- **Memory\Pool Nonpaged Bytes\(N\A)**   Logs the amount of data that cannot be paged to disk. In many cases, there is little you can do to change this behavior. Certain processes, such as Internet Information Services (Inetinfo.exe), SharePoint Services Timer (Owstimer.exe), and SharePoint Server Search (Mssearch.exe), use this type of memory. To ensure proper performance, confirm that there is sufficient available physical memory.

Tip   If there is less than 10% available of nonpaged bytes, IIS will stop serving pages. To resolve this problem, perform an IISReset.exe from the command line.

Disk

- **PhysicalDisk\% Disk Time\DriveLetter**   Logs the amount of time the disk is active during the previous monitoring period. Values higher than 80% should be investigated as they may indicate possible hard drive controller or insufficient memory problems.

- **PhysicalDisk\Current Disk Queue Length\DriveLetter**   Records the number of items waiting to be written or read from the disk. A value higher than 2 means either there is disk subsystem problem, such as a bad controller, or more likely that a disk upgrade is needed. There are three ways to upgrade the disk subsystem: add newer faster spinning drives, upgrade to a better controller, or add disks, such as a Redundant Array of Independent Disks (RAID) 5 or 10 set, which can improve read performance.

Tip   RAID 5 sets are made up of three or more disks, which provide protection from a single drive failure and give better read performance with a very slight impact on write performance. RAID 10 sets are made up of four or more disks and give better read performance with no impact on write performance. RAID 10 is also able to handle two drive failures without data loss. More RAID information can be found be found at *http://support.microsoft.com/kb/100110/en-us* and *http://support.microsoft.com/kb/170921/en-us*.

SharePoint Server Counters

Most counters involving SharePoint Products and Technologies are helper indicators. In other words, they help you understand how your environment is performing.

Without baselining it can be difficult and sometimes impossible to interpret the meaning of SharePoint Server specific counters. The following are commonly used counters when monitoring SharePoint Server:

- **SharePoint Search Gatherer\Document Entries**   Displays the number of documents being indexed at the current moment.

- **SharePoint Search Gatherer\Delayed Documents**   Logs the number of documents delayed from indexing. The value of this counter is dependent on the site hit frequency rules. This means that modifications to your site rules can affect this counter in real time.

- **SharePoint Search Gatherer\Documents Filtered**   Records the total number of documents that have been attempted to be filtered since the search service was last started. Another way to think of this value is the number of filter objects created. This value can help you assess the performance of your searches. When baselining your system, pay attention to this counter. Remember that the value of this counter is reset if the search service is restarted for any reason.

- **SharePoint Search Gatherer\Documents Filtered Rate**   Records the rate per second at which documents are filtered. This is another very useful counter in helping determine relative performance of your SharePoint Server.

- **SharePoint Search Gatherer\Documents Successfully Filtered**   Logs the number of documents that were indexed successfully since the search service was last started.

- **SharePoint Search Gatherer\Documents Success Fully Filtered Rate**   Records the rate at which documents are crawled completely. This is another very valuable counter for helping determine relative performance.

- **SharePoint Search Gatherer\Heartbeats**   Logs the number of heartbeats that have occurred since the search service was last started. After the search service is started, this counter is incremented every 10 minutes. To determine whether searching is occurring, confirm that this counter is incrementing.

- **SharePoint Search Gatherer Projects\Processed Documents Rate**   Records the rate at which documents were indexed during the current crawl.

Many other counters can also be used by the System Monitor or when configuring Performance Logs And Alerts. The following list is not meant to be complete, but it is indicative of the granularity available when monitoring SharePoint Server specific processes.

- Document Conversions Pending Conversions
- Excel Calculation Services Active Requests
- Excel Calculation Services Average Request Processing Time

- Excel Calculation Services Current Size Of Memory Cache
- Excel Calculation Services Sessions Per Second
- Excel Services Web Front End Requests Per Second
- Office Server Search Gatherer Accessing Robots.txt File
- Office Server Search Gatherer Active Queue Length
- Office Server Search Gatherer Processes Max
- Office Server Search Gatherer Heartbeats Rate
- Office Server Search Gatherer Performance Level
- Office Server Search Gatherer Reason To Back Off
- Office Server Search Gatherer Servers Currently Unavailable
- Office Server Search Gatherer Stemmers Cached
- Office Server Search Gatherer System IO Traffic Rate
- Office Server Search Gatherer Threads Accessing Network
- Office Server Search Indexer Catalogs Index Size
- Office Server Search Indexer Catalogs Queries Failed
- Office Server Search Indexer Catalogs Queries Succeeded
- Office Server Search Indexer Catalogs Shadow Merge Levels
- Shared Services Provider Number of Users Imported
- Shared Services Provider Personal Site Latency
- Shared Services Provider Personal Site Throughput
- Shared Services Provider Profile Sync Content Database Process Count
- Shared Services Provider Public Site Latency
- Shared Services Provider Public Site Throughput
- SharePoint Publishing Cache Publishing Hits/Sec
- SharePoint Publishing Cache Total Number Of Objects Added
- SharePoint Publishing Editing Mode Edit Sessions Opened/Second

Internet Information Services (IIS) Logging

IIS provides very detailed logging in the form of text files that are found at
C:\WINDOWS\system32\LogFiles by default. The location is configurable, and moving these to a different drive is a wise idea on busy WFE servers. To change the default
IIS log file directory, perform the following steps.

1. Open IIS Manager and expand Web Sites.

2. Right-click on the Web application you want to configure and select Properties.

3. Select the Web Site tab, as shown in Figure 15-4.

4. Click on the Properties button to view or change the log file directory.

Figure 15-4 Select Enable Logging and click the Properties tab to view or change the log file location.

If you do not move the default location, the system could be rendered unusable should the log files consume all available disk space. A full explanation of configuring IIS log files is beyond the scope of this book.

For more information on configuring IIS Logging, download and install the IIS 6.0 Resource kit. It can be found at http://www.microsoft.com/downloads *by searching for Iis60rkt.exe.*

Configuring Event Logs and Diagnostic Logging

Log files, although sometimes difficult and certainly tedious to read, are the best way to expose the kind of detailed information needed to resolve operational issues. There are two categories of logs:

■ **Event logs** These are the binary logs generated by Windows.

■ **Generic log** These log files are specific to the application or are part of the application.

Windows SharePoint Services and SharePoint Server use both types to log informa-
tional, warning, or error data. A very important and extremely useful new feature is the
ability to select the type of events you would like to log.

Selecting the Type of Events to Log

1. Browse to Diagnostic Logging by going to Central Administration > Operations
   > Diagnostic Logging, which is under Logging and Reporting. The options
   shown in Figure 15-5 allow you to configure event logging with an increased
   level of granularity.

2. The first option in the section deals with the Microsoft Customer Experience
   Improvement Program. Although the overhead of this feature is minimal, it still
   has an impact.

3. Next, you can choose to send your error reports automatically to Microsoft and
   their partners to help diagnose problems for future patches and service packs. If
   you choose to enable Error Reporting, you are given two options. The first
   option updates a file on the system to help diagnose problems. This is an automated version searching the Microsoft support site that brings possible solutions back without manual searches. The second option sends error reports to
   Microsoft without action required from an administrator.

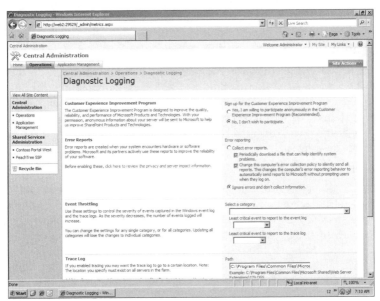

Figure 15-5   These are the default settings for Diagnostic Logging.

Event Throttling

Event Throttling allows you to determine the kinds events that you want to log in the Windows Server 2003 Event Log. You have the ability to choose a category and select the Least Critical Type Of Event To Report To The Event Log and the Least Critical Type Of Event To Report To The Trace Log.

Configuring Event Logging

1. Start by choosing the category of event you want to log. For example, choose MS Search Indexing.

2. Select the minimum level of event to write to the Event Log. Be aware that the lower the level of the event, the more items will be written to the event log. As an example, choose Warning under Least Critical Event To Report To The Event Log. After you understand how this works, go back and change the level to a setting that correlates to your organization's monitoring policy.

3. Choose the level of the Trace Log. You should set the Least Critical Event To Report To The Trace Log to Critical. There is no requirement that either log has to be selected for any category. Always set your event throttling to limit events and then scale when problems are suspected in your installation.

4. Click OK. Unfortunately, you must click OK after every category and level combination. You cannot make all of your choices and then select OK.

Configuring Logging and Reporting

Because you must click OK after every event level for every category, you probably want to document and script the process. In addition to the problem of clicking OK on every setting, accidentally selecting the category *All* will overwrite your previous settings. The most reliable and expedient manner to configure your Logging and Reporting settings is via the command-line tool Stsadm.exe. If you have an existing farm, you can run the command:

```
stsadm.exe -o listlogginglevels (-showhidden is optional)
```

This command lists all of your logging categories and the current trace level and logging level. If you use the *-showhidden* parameter, the categories such as Gatherer-Backup trace/logging level and IndexerPlugin trace/logging level can be seen and documented. Using the command line to set your Logging and Reporting levels has several advantages, but the two most noteworthy are setting hidden values not seen in Central Administration and creating a batch file that is easily redeployed. The following script is an example of setting the E-Mail Trace Log to Unexpected and the Event Log to Error:

```
stsadm.exe -o setlogginglevel -category e-mail
-tracelevel unexpected -windowslogginglevel error
```

Note that *-windowslogginglevel* refers to the Windows Server 2003 Event Log. If the category has spaces in the name, such as Forms Services Administration, then you must surround the service with quotation marks, like "Forms Services Administration." For example:

```
stsadm.exe -o setlogginglevel -category "Forms Services Administration"
-tracelevel unexpected -windowslogginglevel error
```

To configure all or part of the categories' event and trace logs, simply write a batch file to complete all of the settings. Although you can set the trace and event log settings simultaneously by using a semicolon between categories, it is generally better to put each command on a separate line. However, if you must set multiple categories simultaneously, follow this example that sets E-mail and Forms Services Administration in the same command:

```
stsadm.exe -o setlogginglevel
-category e-mail;"Forms Services Administration"
-tracelevel unexpected -windowslogginglevel error
```

Note that you must set all simultaneous categories to the *same* trace level and event log level.

> **Caution**   Choosing a low event value or the category All causes a very high number of items to be written to the Event Log. It is possible to completely fill a drive with superfluous Event Logs. In addition, it is possible to run the CPU usage to 100%. If a system is slowing beyond usefulness, check to see if Owstimer.exe is using the majority of the CPU. If it is, check any timer events, such as logging or backups, and delete or disable the timer job definition. You may re-enable the timer job when the problem is resolved.

Trace Logs

The Trace Log section allows you to determine details for the Trace Logs. It first allows you to specify a location for the Trace Log, which by default is C:\Program Files\ Common Files\Microsoft Shared\Web Server Extensions\12\LOGS\. Be careful with how many logs you choose and how long the system will write to that log. To help better manage your logs, consider changing the default location of the Trace Logs to the same parent directory as your IIS logs. This has the combined effect of relieving some of the workload on the system drive and helping maintain its organization. You also have the option of moving your existing log files. To ensure log integrity, disable Trace Logs before you move the existing files. If you have chosen a level of tracing that produces more logs, such as Verbose, it is important to set these limits. The default for Number Of Log Files is 96, and the Number of Minutes To Use A Log File is 30. The default numbers are good for a normal to critical level of logging, but not if the level is set to Unexpected or Monitorable. The numbers here are multiplied to find out how much data you are keeping. The default is 2 days (96 files × 30 minutes = 2,880 minutes).

There are cases in which one or more categories need an extended amount of time for Trace Logs.

Using Trace Logs also helps you resolve issues with configuration changes to your SharePoint environment. At times these logs can help resolve serious system issues. It recommended that you save these log files each time you make configuration changes to your test and production environments. These logs can be used to understand what changes were made and the impact of those changes, which is not always directly apparent.

Site Collection Auditing

Auditing specific actions for every document is critical to many different industries. Administrators now have the ability to audit items at the site collection level. Actions, such as opening, downloading, deleting, and moving, can be tracked throughout an item's entire life cycle. To audit events related to your site collection, follow these steps:

1. After you have reached the site, click on Site Actions > Site Settings.

2. Under Site Collection Administration, click Configure Audit Settings.

3. The Documents And Items section, as seen in Figure 15-6, controls auditing items and documents for the site collection. In addition to auditing changes to documents, you may also audit the opening of documents. This works much like a Web page hit counter by letting you know how many times documents have been read.

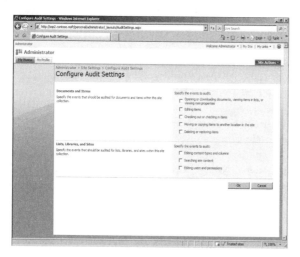

Figure 15-6   You can specify which events to audit for documents and items, as well as lists, libraries, and sites.

4. In the Lists, Libraries, And Sites section, you can choose to audit such actions as editing content types and columns, searching site content, and editing users and permissions.

By default, auditing log reports is not turned on. To enable the auditing of reports, do the following:

1. Go to Site Actions > Site Settings > Site Collection Features.

2. Click the Activate button in the Reporting Row.

3. Go back to Site Settings and under Site Collection Administration there is a link to Audit Log Reports. You can view standard reports or create your own custom reports.

If you do not wish to audit an entire site collection, you can define the Information Management Policies for a single Content Type. Refer to Chapter 6, "Using Workflows and Information Management Policies," for more information on configuring Content Type auditing.

Best Practices Analyzer for Windows SharePoint Services and SharePoint Server

If you need a general overview of the health and security of your farm, you can run the Best Practices Analyzer for Windows SharePoint Services and SharePoint Server. You must first download the tool at *http://www.microsoft.com/downloads/details.aspx?familyid=cb944b27-9d6b-4a1f-b3e1-778efda07df8&displaylang=en*.

Alternatively, you can browse to *http://www.microsoft.com/downloads* and search for *BestPracticeAnalyzer.exe*. When the executable is run, it extracts the contents to a folder, such as C:\BPA. After the contents are extracted, you run the tool from the Central Administration server in your farm. A sample command looks like this:

```
C:\bpa\sharepointbpa.exe -cmd analyze
-substitutions SERVER_NAME CentralAdministrationServer
```

In this example, *CentralAdministrationServer* should be replaced with your server name. At the time this book was published, there was very little information on extending the tool and writing custom rule sets. Visit *http://technet.microsoft.com* for updated details on the Best Practices Analyzer.

Appendix
Command-Line Options

Despite the advances in the Central Administration graphical user interface, there are times when the command-line tool Stsadm.exe is either the most appropriate or the only way to accomplish certain tasks. For example, you can set the Indexing service logging levels, automate farm-level backups, or set the maximum [import|export] limits only by using Stsadm.exe. In addition, you can write administrative scripts that include several Stsadm.exe commands to automate processes.

Stsadm.exe is located in the 12 Hive's Bin directory, C:\Program Files\Common Files\Microsoft Shared\web server extensions\12\Bin. A number of Stsadm.exe commands are included in this book. This appendix serves as a quick reference, presenting the commands in alphabetical order with short descriptions. Remember that all of the commands listed here must be prefaced with *stsadm.exe -o*.

stsadm.exe -o	Description	Page(s)
addsolution	Add a solution to the Solution Store	328
addtemplate	Add template to all site collections in farm	112
addwppack	Add Web Part from .cab file	124
addzoneurl	Associate zone with URL	33
authentication	Change authentication for Web application	33
backup	Back up sites and site collections	18, 343, 354–355, 356
backuphistory	Show history of backups and backup IDs	356
blockedfilelist	Block/unblock files with a given extension	90, 175
createadminvs	Return Central Administration URL	29
createsiteinnewdb	Create site in standalone content database	79
deletetemplate	Delete a template from the Central Gallery	112
deletezoneurl	Delete zone from URL	33
deletewppack	Delete Web Part package	125

stsadm.exe -o	Description	Page(s)
deploysolution	Deploy a solution stored in the Solution Store	328
deploywppack	Deploy Web Part package	125
email	Configure outbound e-mail settings	71
enumalternatedomains	List alternate domain mappings	68
enumservices	List all running Web and server services	57
enumsolutions	List all solutions in the Solution Store	328
enumtemplates	List all templates in the Central Gallery	112
enumusers	Enumerate all users for a site collection	86
enumwppacks	List all Web Part packages on server	124
export	Export using site migration tool	343, 348, 349
getadminport	Return Central Administration port	29
getproperty	Get configuration settings for sites	18
import	Import using site migration tool	343, 348, 350
installfeature	Deploy multiple page layouts as a feature	255
listlogginglevels	List current logging categories and trace levels	374
osearch	Modify SharePoint search settings; change index or propagation directories	42, 333
quiescefarm	Disallow new, keep existing connections	68
quiescefarmstatus	Show Quiesce Farm status	68
refreshdms	Synchronize Web application with Active Directory	59
refreshsitedms	Synchronize site with Active Directory	59
renameweb	Rename sites	18

stsadm.exe -o	Description	Page(s)
restore	Restore site collection or directory	343, 356, 357
retractsolution	Retract solution from virtual servers	328
retractwppack	Retract Web Part package	125
setadminport	Set port number for Central Administration	40, 182
setdefaultssp	Change the default Shared Services provider	193
set-ecsexternaldata	Set external data options for Excel Calculation Services	283
set-ecsloadbalancing	Set load balancing for Excel Calculation Services	282
set-ecsmemoryutilization	Set Excel Calculation Services memory utilization	283
set-ecssecurity	Set encryption for Excel Calculation Services	281
set-ecssessionmanagement	Configure Session Management for Excel Calculation Services	282
set-ecsworkbookcache	Set temporary storage for workbook elements	283
setlogginglevel	Set trace levels for individual logging categories	374–375
setproperty -pn max-template-document-size	Set the maximum size for site templates	349
setsitelock	Set access restrictions for site	79
setsspport	Change the Shared Services Provider port	189
unquiescefarm	Allow new connections to farm	68
updatefarmcredentials	Modify the server farm account	62

Index

Note: Page references in italics refer to figures; those followed by *t* refer to tables.

About the Author

Ben Curry (CISSP, MCP, CNE, CCNA) is an author and enterprise network architect specializing in knowledge management and collaboration technologies. Ben is a Senior Instructor and Consultant for Mindsharp, a company focused on the next generation of Microsoft products. Ben has been working with the Internet since 1991 and has been involved with the constant evolution of messaging, storage, and collaboration products. He enjoys designing enterprise solutions that appear simple to the end user. He has designed and implemented solutions for NASA, the Department of Defense, the Veterans Administration, and many of the Fortune 25. Ben is a PADI Master Scuba Diver Trainer and a certified Emergency First Responder instructor. In his spare time, he enjoys spending time with his family, taking trips to the ocean, collecting guns and participating in shooting sports, and lecturing at technology users' groups.

These industry experts contributed to this volume as well:

James Curry   A computer scientist with InfoPro Corporation of Huntsville, Alabama, James resides in Madison, Alabama, with the love of his life, his wife Joy.

Josh Meyer   A Senior Developer for Trident Systems in Birmingham, Alabama, Josh has been a contributing author for multiple SharePoint Products–related books and is often found on SharePoint Products newsgroups.

Milan Gross   A SharePoint architect and developer with more than 10 years of experience in designing and deploying Microsoft solutions, Milan (MCSD, MCSE, MCT, Solventis) also teaches SharePoint training classes as a Mindsharp contract instructor. You can reach him at www.synergyonline.com. He resides in Honolulu, Hawaii.

John Holliday   With more than 25 years of professional software development experience, John has been involved in a wide range of commercial software projects for the Fortune 100. He received a bachelor's degree in applied mathematics from Harvard and a J.D. from the University of Michigan. John is actively involved in humanitarian activities through Works of Wonder International, a nonprofit he co-founded with his wife Alice and the Art of Living Foundation.

Bill English   A founder and owner of Mindsharp (www.mindsharp.com), Bill (MCSE, MVP) is the author of 12 books on SharePoint Products, Exchange, and security topics. He resides in Minnesota, where summer is the six best days of the year.

William Jackson   A senior computer engineer at NASA, William focuses on Microsoft products and has 10 years of experience in the IT industry. He has a BS in Computer Science, with an MCSE in NT4.0, Windows 2000, and Windows 2003, as well as a CCNA. William lives in Huntsville, Alabama, with his beautiful wife, Dana.

2007 Microsoft® Office System Resources for Developers and Administrators

Microsoft Office SharePoint® Server 2007 Administrator's Companion

Bill English with the Microsoft SharePoint Community Experts
ISBN 9780735622821

Get your mission-critical collaboration and information management systems up and running. This comprehensive, single-volume reference details features and capabilities of SharePoint Server 2007. It delivers easy-to-follow procedures, practical workarounds, and key troubleshooting tactics—for on-the-job results.

Microsoft Windows® SharePoint Services Version 3.0 Inside Out

Jim Buyens
ISBN 9780735623231

Conquer Microsoft Windows SharePoint Services—from the inside out! This ultimate, in-depth reference packs hundreds of time-saving solutions, troubleshooting tips, and workarounds. You're beyond the basics, so now learn how the experts tackle information sharing and team collaboration—and challenge yourself to new levels of mastery!

Microsoft SharePoint Products and Tech-nologies Administrator's Pocket Consultant

Ben Curry
ISBN 9780735623828

Portable and precise, this pocket-sized guide delivers immediate answers for the day-to-day administration of Sharepoint Products and Technologies. Featuring easy-to-scan tables, step-by-step instructions, and handy lists, this book offers the straightforward information you need to get the job done—whether you're at your desk or in the field!

Inside Microsoft Windows SharePoint Services Version 3

Ted Pattison and Daniel Larson
ISBN 9780735623200

With this hands-on guide, you get a bottom-up view of the platform architecture, code samples, and task-oriented guidance for developing custom applications with Microsoft Visual Studio® 2005 and Collaborative Application Markup Language (CAML).

Inside Microsoft Office SharePoint Server 2007

Patrick Tisseghem
ISBN 9780735623682

Master the intricacies of Office SharePoint Server 2007. A bottom-up view of the platform architecture shows you how to manage and customize key components and how to integrate with Office programs.

Microsoft Office Communications Server 2007 Resource Kit

The Microsoft Office Communications Server Team
ISBN 9780735624061

Your definitive reference to Office Communications Server 2007. This comprehensive guide offers in-depth technical information and best practices for planning, designing, deploying, managing, and optimizing your systems. Includes a toolkit of valuable resources on CD.

Programming Applications for Microsoft Office Outlook® 2007

Randy Byrne and Ryan Greg
ISBN 9780735622494

Microsoft Office Visio® 2007 Programming Step by Step

David A. Edson
ISBN 9780735623798

See more resources at **microsoft.com/mspress** *and* **microsoft.com/learning**

Microsoft Press® products are available worldwide wherever quality computer books are sold. For more information, contact your bookseller, computer retailer, software reseller, or local Microsoft Sales Office, or visit our Web site at **microsoft. com/mspress**. To locate a source near you, or to order directly, call 1-800-MS-PRESS in the United States. (In Canada, call **1-800-268-2222**.)